# Getting started with
# MACAW

JOE CHELLMAN & REX RAINEY

## Getting Started with Macaw

Joe Chellman and Rex Rainey

Peachpit Press
Find us on the web at: www.peachpit.com

To report errors, please send a note to errata@peachpit.com
Peachpit Press is a division of Pearson Education

Copyright © 2015 Joe Chellman and Rex Rainey

Editor: Kim Wimpsett
Compositor: Danielle Foster
Indexer: Valerie Haynes Perry
Copyeditor: Liz Welch
Proofreader: Nancy Bell
Cover design: Aren Straiger
Interior design: Danielle Foster

## Notice of Rights

All rights reserved. No part of this book may be reproduced or transmitted in any form by any means, electronic, mechanical, photocopying, recording, or otherwise, without the prior written permission of the publisher. For information on getting permission for reprints and excerpts, contact permissions@peachpit.com.

## Notice of Liability

The information in this book is distributed on an "As Is" basis without warranty. While every precaution has been taken in the preparation of the book, neither the author nor Peachpit shall have any liability to any person or entity with respect to any loss or damage caused or alleged to be caused directly or indirectly by the instructions contained in this book or by the computer software and hardware products described in it.

## Trademarks

Macaw is a trademark of Macaw LLC. Many of the designations used by manufacturers and sellers to distinguish their products are claimed as trademarks. Where those designations appear in this book, and Peachpit was aware of a trademark claim, the designations appear as requested by the owner of the trademark. All other product names and services identified throughout this book are used in editorial fashion only and for the benefit of such companies with no intention of infringement of the trademark. No such use, or the use of any trade name, is intended to convey endorsement or other affiliation with this book.

ISBN 13:  978-0-133-99583-1
ISBN 10:      0-133-99583-6

10 9 8 7 6 5 4 3 2 1
Printed and bound in the United States of America

*For Kate and Monica*
*whose fault it is*
*we know each other*

# Acknowledgments

Joe wants to thank everyone on the book team: Kim for all her great work managing and editing, Cliff for his own work (and for bringing up the idea in the first place), and Rex for his excellent work as co-author and all-around fine fellow. Thanks to the Macaw team for making such cool and useful software and for fielding my questions and issues I've filed. Thanks to my friends and colleagues whose own books I've read and enjoyed, who inspired me to take the plunge myself. Thanks to my parents for (aside from everything) helping me enjoy learning and inspiring me to pass some along to others. Most of all, thanks to Kate for the love, the support, and the general cheering on.

Rex would like to thank Joe for bringing him on board the project and being so darn great to work with. A huge thanks to the rest of the book team: Kim, for cleaning up our writing and keeping us on task, as well as Cliff and the rest of the Pearson team for taking everything and putting it all together into the final publication. Thanks to the Macaw developers for creating such a handy new tool and constantly making it better. Thanks to my mom and dad for always being so incredibly encouraging. And an extra shout-out to my dad who always says, "Everyone should write a book." You're right, Dad, consider that one checked off the list. And a special thanks to Monica for her love and never-ending support.

# About the Authors

**Joe Chellman** is an old fart by Internet standards, having first used the web in text mode on a dial-up Unix system in the mid-1990s and learning HTML in the late 1990s. In any case, he got a little hooked and has been a web professional since 2000, currently operating the mostly-one-man web studio ShooFly Development and Design. He has also been a drummer for more than half his life, which is frankly alarming. He lives in Los Angeles with his wife and their frequently adorable, occasionally noisy cat.

PHOTO: JENN SPAIN PHOTOGRAPHY

**Rex Rainey** has loved making things on the computer since his family got their first one in the early 1990s, trying out any design applications he could get his hands on. After graduating with a degree in digital illustration, he got a job at an interactive agency in the early 2000s and quickly became a big fan of designing things for the web. He's currently an art director at a marketing and design agency in Grand Rapids, Michigan, where he lives with his wife and their two pets.

PHOTO: ADAM MIKRUT

# Contents

**CHAPTER 1** **Why Are You Here?**     **1**
    Who Are You?............................................... 2
    Who Are We?............................................... 2
    A Brief History of Everything ............................... 3
    Designing in the Browser Is Not Fun ........................ 4

**CHAPTER 2** **What Is Macaw?**     **7**
    Macaw, in Basic Terms ..................................... 8
    Don't Throw Away Your Other Tools! ....................... 8
    Built on a Web-Based Foundation ......................... 10
    Where to Get Macaw ..................................... 10

**CHAPTER 3** **Unique Tools**     **11**
    Breakpoints .............................................. 13
        Special importance of the default breakpoint ........... 15
        Setting breakpoints first ................................ 15
    Fluid Grids ............................................... 16
    Reusables: Global Styles and Components ................. 20
    Honorable Mentions ..................................... 24
        Outline .............................................. 24
        Pages ............................................... 25
        View Modes .......................................... 25
        Retina and HiDPI Images............................... 26

**CHAPTER 4** **The Rest of the Tools**     **27**
    The Interface ............................................. 28
        Top area............................................. 29
            Page Manager................................... 29
            Page tabs ...................................... 29

Options bar . . . . . . . . . . . . . . . . . . . . . . . . . . . . . . . . . . . . . . . . . . 30
 Breakpoint and DOM information . . . . . . . . . . . . . . . . . . . . . 30
 Left side . . . . . . . . . . . . . . . . . . . . . . . . . . . . . . . . . . . . . . . . . . . . . . 30
 Select tool . . . . . . . . . . . . . . . . . . . . . . . . . . . . . . . . . . . . . . . . . 30
 Direct Select tool . . . . . . . . . . . . . . . . . . . . . . . . . . . . . . . . . . 30
 Text tool . . . . . . . . . . . . . . . . . . . . . . . . . . . . . . . . . . . . . . . . . . 31
 Element tool . . . . . . . . . . . . . . . . . . . . . . . . . . . . . . . . . . . . . . 31
 Container tool . . . . . . . . . . . . . . . . . . . . . . . . . . . . . . . . . . . . . 31
 Button tool . . . . . . . . . . . . . . . . . . . . . . . . . . . . . . . . . . . . . . . 32
 Input tool(s) . . . . . . . . . . . . . . . . . . . . . . . . . . . . . . . . . . . . . . 32
 Embed tool . . . . . . . . . . . . . . . . . . . . . . . . . . . . . . . . . . . . . . . 32
 Hand tool . . . . . . . . . . . . . . . . . . . . . . . . . . . . . . . . . . . . . . . . 32
 Eyedropper tool . . . . . . . . . . . . . . . . . . . . . . . . . . . . . . . . . . . 32
 Global Styles . . . . . . . . . . . . . . . . . . . . . . . . . . . . . . . . . . . . . . 33
 Swatches . . . . . . . . . . . . . . . . . . . . . . . . . . . . . . . . . . . . . . . . 33
 Feedback . . . . . . . . . . . . . . . . . . . . . . . . . . . . . . . . . . . . . . . . 33
 The canvas . . . . . . . . . . . . . . . . . . . . . . . . . . . . . . . . . . . . . . . . . . 33
 The grid . . . . . . . . . . . . . . . . . . . . . . . . . . . . . . . . . . . . . . . . . 33
 Ruler and breakpoints . . . . . . . . . . . . . . . . . . . . . . . . . . . . . . 34
 Resize handle . . . . . . . . . . . . . . . . . . . . . . . . . . . . . . . . . . . . . 34
 The right side . . . . . . . . . . . . . . . . . . . . . . . . . . . . . . . . . . . . . . . 35
 Inspector . . . . . . . . . . . . . . . . . . . . . . . . . . . . . . . . . . . . . . . . 35
 Outline . . . . . . . . . . . . . . . . . . . . . . . . . . . . . . . . . . . . . . . . . . 36
 Library . . . . . . . . . . . . . . . . . . . . . . . . . . . . . . . . . . . . . . . . . . 36
 The menu bar . . . . . . . . . . . . . . . . . . . . . . . . . . . . . . . . . . . . . . . . 37

**CHAPTER 5** **Consider Your Workflow**      **39**

Make Some Sketches . . . . . . . . . . . . . . . . . . . . . . . . . . . . . . . . . . . 40
Think About Mobile First . . . . . . . . . . . . . . . . . . . . . . . . . . . . . . . 40
Set Some Breakpoints . . . . . . . . . . . . . . . . . . . . . . . . . . . . . . . . . 41
Don't Forget to Resize . . . . . . . . . . . . . . . . . . . . . . . . . . . . . . . . . 42
Care About Semantics . . . . . . . . . . . . . . . . . . . . . . . . . . . . . . . . . 42
Use Containers (Grouping) Liberally . . . . . . . . . . . . . . . . . . . . . . 43

Reuse Everything You Can . . . . . . . . . . . . . . . . . . . . . . . . . . . . . . . 43
Let Macaw Do the Work. . . . . . . . . . . . . . . . . . . . . . . . . . . . . . . . . 45

**CHAPTER 6** **Let's Build a Prototype**       **47**

Setting the Breakpoints. . . . . . . . . . . . . . . . . . . . . . . . . . . . . . . . .48
Setting Up the Grid . . . . . . . . . . . . . . . . . . . . . . . . . . . . . . . . . . . 51
Working with the Outline. . . . . . . . . . . . . . . . . . . . . . . . . . . . . . . 57
    An overview of the Outline . . . . . . . . . . . . . . . . . . . . . . . . 58
    The Outline in action. . . . . . . . . . . . . . . . . . . . . . . . . . . . . .60
Putting Elements into Place . . . . . . . . . . . . . . . . . . . . . . . . . . . . 61
    Static positioning and flow . . . . . . . . . . . . . . . . . . . . . . . . 61
    Position and breakpoints . . . . . . . . . . . . . . . . . . . . . . . . . . 65
    Fixed position and origins . . . . . . . . . . . . . . . . . . . . . . . . . 66
    Origins . . . . . . . . . . . . . . . . . . . . . . . . . . . . . . . . . . . . . . . . 70
    Absolute positioning. . . . . . . . . . . . . . . . . . . . . . . . . . . . . . 72
    Containers . . . . . . . . . . . . . . . . . . . . . . . . . . . . . . . . . . . . . 73
    Conclusion. . . . . . . . . . . . . . . . . . . . . . . . . . . . . . . . . . . . . .84

**CHAPTER 7** **Building a Website: Part 1**       **85**

Think First, Think Often. . . . . . . . . . . . . . . . . . . . . . . . . . . . . . . .86
Setting Up the Breakpoints, Grid, and Containers . . . . . . . . . . .89
    Page header and background image. . . . . . . . . . . . . . . . . . 91
    Menu bar and background gradient . . . . . . . . . . . . . . . . . 92
    Main and secondary content . . . . . . . . . . . . . . . . . . . . . . .94
    Footer and page background . . . . . . . . . . . . . . . . . . . . . . 95
    Initial review . . . . . . . . . . . . . . . . . . . . . . . . . . . . . . . . . . . 96
Building the Header . . . . . . . . . . . . . . . . . . . . . . . . . . . . . . . . . .98
    Medium breakpoint . . . . . . . . . . . . . . . . . . . . . . . . . . . . . 103
    Small breakpoint . . . . . . . . . . . . . . . . . . . . . . . . . . . . . . .104
Building the Navigation. . . . . . . . . . . . . . . . . . . . . . . . . . . . . . 107
    Medium breakpoint . . . . . . . . . . . . . . . . . . . . . . . . . . . . . 114
    Small breakpoint . . . . . . . . . . . . . . . . . . . . . . . . . . . . . . .117

The Importance of Preview . . . . . . . . . . . . . . . . . . . . . . . . . . . . . 120
Next Steps . . . . . . . . . . . . . . . . . . . . . . . . . . . . . . . . . . . . . . . . . . . 124

**CHAPTER 8** **Building a Website: Part 2**     **125**

Highlights . . . . . . . . . . . . . . . . . . . . . . . . . . . . . . . . . . . . . . . . . . . 126
    A brief intermission for global styles . . . . . . . . . . . . . . . . .131
    Back to highlights . . . . . . . . . . . . . . . . . . . . . . . . . . . . . . . 133
    Medium breakpoint. . . . . . . . . . . . . . . . . . . . . . . . . . . . . . 136
    Medium-small breakpoint: no mock-up. . . . . . . . . . . . . . 139
    Small breakpoint . . . . . . . . . . . . . . . . . . . . . . . . . . . . . . . . 139
    Medium-small breakpoint: all yours . . . . . . . . . . . . . . . . .141
Testimonials: A Challenge . . . . . . . . . . . . . . . . . . . . . . . . . . . . 142
    Current solution: mock it up . . . . . . . . . . . . . . . . . . . . . . 144
    Medium breakpoint. . . . . . . . . . . . . . . . . . . . . . . . . . . . . . 150
    Small breakpoint . . . . . . . . . . . . . . . . . . . . . . . . . . . . . . . . 150
Secondary content:
"Meet the Developers" . . . . . . . . . . . . . . . . . . . . . . . . . . . . . . . 152
    Medium breakpoint. . . . . . . . . . . . . . . . . . . . . . . . . . . . . . 155
    Small breakpoint . . . . . . . . . . . . . . . . . . . . . . . . . . . . . . . . 156
Footer: Pleasantly Easy . . . . . . . . . . . . . . . . . . . . . . . . . . . . . . 157
    Footer fixes for other breakpoints . . . . . . . . . . . . . . . . . . 159
A Full Page: Done! . . . . . . . . . . . . . . . . . . . . . . . . . . . . . . . . . . 160

**CHAPTER 9** **Building a Website: Part 3**     **161**

Review the Mock-ups . . . . . . . . . . . . . . . . . . . . . . . . . . . . . . . 162
Create a New Page. . . . . . . . . . . . . . . . . . . . . . . . . . . . . . . . . . 162
    Revise the header . . . . . . . . . . . . . . . . . . . . . . . . . . . . . . . 163
    Medium breakpoint . . . . . . . . . . . . . . . . . . . . . . . . . . . . . 165
    Medium-small breakpoint. . . . . . . . . . . . . . . . . . . . . . . . 166
    Small breakpoint . . . . . . . . . . . . . . . . . . . . . . . . . . . . . . . . 166
Revise the Navigation . . . . . . . . . . . . . . . . . . . . . . . . . . . . . . . 167
    Adding links . . . . . . . . . . . . . . . . . . . . . . . . . . . . . . . . . . . 168

Build the Content Area . . . . . . . . . . . . . . . . . . . . . . . . . . . . . . . . . . . 169
    Big text box . . . . . . . . . . . . . . . . . . . . . . . . . . . . . . . . . . . . . . . . . . 170
    The image grid: first image . . . . . . . . . . . . . . . . . . . . . . . . . . . .171
    Image grid: the other three . . . . . . . . . . . . . . . . . . . . . . . . . . . 174
Take a Break: More on Images . . . . . . . . . . . . . . . . . . . . . . . . . . . . 176
    In-App cropping . . . . . . . . . . . . . . . . . . . . . . . . . . . . . . . . . . . . . 176
    CSS transforms and filters . . . . . . . . . . . . . . . . . . . . . . . . . . . 177
    Device-specific images . . . . . . . . . . . . . . . . . . . . . . . . . . . . . . 178
Back to Work . . . . . . . . . . . . . . . . . . . . . . . . . . . . . . . . . . . . . . . . . . 179
    Medium breakpoint . . . . . . . . . . . . . . . . . . . . . . . . . . . . . . . . .181
    Small breakpoint . . . . . . . . . . . . . . . . . . . . . . . . . . . . . . . . . . . 182
    A small bug, and a solution . . . . . . . . . . . . . . . . . . . . . . . . . . . 184
Secondary Content: Embedded Map . . . . . . . . . . . . . . . . . . . . . . 185
Next Steps . . . . . . . . . . . . . . . . . . . . . . . . . . . . . . . . . . . . . . . . . . . . 188

## CHAPTER 10  Building a Website: Part 4    189

Review the Mock-ups . . . . . . . . . . . . . . . . . . . . . . . . . . . . . . . . . . .190
Create the Page . . . . . . . . . . . . . . . . . . . . . . . . . . . . . . . . . . . . . . . .190
Build the Form . . . . . . . . . . . . . . . . . . . . . . . . . . . . . . . . . . . . . . . .191
    Build and style the first field . . . . . . . . . . . . . . . . . . . . . . . . . . 192
    Create the other text fields . . . . . . . . . . . . . . . . . . . . . . . . . . . 196
    Add the radio buttons . . . . . . . . . . . . . . . . . . . . . . . . . . . . . . . 197
    Add the select box . . . . . . . . . . . . . . . . . . . . . . . . . . . . . . . . . . 198
    Add the last elements . . . . . . . . . . . . . . . . . . . . . . . . . . . . . . . 200
    Positioning cleanup . . . . . . . . . . . . . . . . . . . . . . . . . . . . . . . . .204
    Medium breakpoint . . . . . . . . . . . . . . . . . . . . . . . . . . . . . . . . .204
    Small breakpoint . . . . . . . . . . . . . . . . . . . . . . . . . . . . . . . . . . .206
That's It! . . . . . . . . . . . . . . . . . . . . . . . . . . . . . . . . . . . . . . . . . . . . .207

## CHAPTER 11  Preview and Publish                                209

Resulting Files ........................................... 210
Project Settings .......................................... 212
    Pages ............................................... 212
    Head & Tail ......................................... 213
General Settings ......................................... 214
    Styles ............................................... 214
    Units................................................ 215
    Grids................................................ 216
    Images .............................................. 216
    Remote Preview...................................... 216
Published and Done! ..................................... 217

## CHAPTER 12  The Possible Future of Macaw                       219

Big Things................................................220
    Mobile-first workflow.................................220
    Integration of popular frameworks or preset
    components libraries ................................ 221
    Linked image assets ................................. 221
    Custom fonts, especially icons........................222
    Template files.......................................222
    Better component editing ............................222
    Export/import/share components
    and global styles ....................................223
    Add custom states to elements........................223
    Enhanced SVG styling ...............................224
Little Things .............................................224
    Multiple open projects...............................224
    Swap an image from the library.......................224
    More global styles options ...........................224
    Custom library folders ...............................224
    Workspace customization ...........................225

Enhanced swatches . . . . . . . . . . . . . . . . . . . . . . . . . . . . . . . . . . . . . 225
Use different background images at
different breakpoints . . . . . . . . . . . . . . . . . . . . . . . . . . . . . . . . . 225
A Bright Future . . . . . . . . . . . . . . . . . . . . . . . . . . . . . . . . . . . . . . . . . . 225

**APPENDIX A** **Helpful Shortcuts**     **227**

**APPENDIX B** **Further Reading**     **233**

More on Macaw . . . . . . . . . . . . . . . . . . . . . . . . . . . . . . . . . . . . . . . . .234
    Macaw Forums . . . . . . . . . . . . . . . . . . . . . . . . . . . . . . . . . . . . . . 234
    Macaw Documentation. . . . . . . . . . . . . . . . . . . . . . . . . . . . . . 234
    Macaw Videos . . . . . . . . . . . . . . . . . . . . . . . . . . . . . . . . . . . . . . .234
    *Designing and Building Websites with Macaw,*
    by Adi Purdila . . . . . . . . . . . . . . . . . . . . . . . . . . . . . . . . . . . . . . . 234
Responsive Web Design . . . . . . . . . . . . . . . . . . . . . . . . . . . . . . . . .235
    *Responsive Web Design,* by Ethan Marcotte. . . . . . . . . . . . . 235
    *Responsive Web Design: Learn by Video,* by Tim Kadlec. . . . 235
    Articles on responsive design from A List Apart . . . . . . . . .*235*
    *Mobile First,* by Luke Wroblewski. . . . . . . . . . . . . . . . . . . . . . . 235
Making Good Mock-ups . . . . . . . . . . . . . . . . . . . . . . . . . . . . . . . . .236
    Adobe Photoshop . . . . . . . . . . . . . . . . . . . . . . . . . . . . . . . . . . . 236
    Sketch. . . . . . . . . . . . . . . . . . . . . . . . . . . . . . . . . . . . . . . . . . . . . .236
    Pixelmator . . . . . . . . . . . . . . . . . . . . . . . . . . . . . . . . . . . . . . . . . . 236
    Adobe Fireworks . . . . . . . . . . . . . . . . . . . . . . . . . . . . . . . . . . . . 236
    Tuts+. . . . . . . . . . . . . . . . . . . . . . . . . . . . . . . . . . . . . . . . . . . . . . . 237
    Smashing Magazine . . . . . . . . . . . . . . . . . . . . . . . . . . . . . . . . . 237
    Photoshop Etiquette . . . . . . . . . . . . . . . . . . . . . . . . . . . . . . . . 237
Front-End Web Developer Tools . . . . . . . . . . . . . . . . . . . . . . . . . 238
Other Areas of Interest . . . . . . . . . . . . . . . . . . . . . . . . . . . . . . . . . . 239
    Accessibility . . . . . . . . . . . . . . . . . . . . . . . . . . . . . . . . . . . . . . . . 239
    CSS transforms, transforms, and filters . . . . . . . . . . . . . . . . 239
        *CSS Animations and Transitions for the Modern Web,*
        by Steven Bradley. . . . . . . . . . . . . . . . . . . . . . . . . . . . . . . . . .239

Contents **xiii**

    *CSS Transitions and Transforms*, by Joseph Lowery . . . . . 239
    *CSS Transforms and CSS Animations*,
    both by Vicky Murley . . . . . . . . . . . . . . . . . . . . . . . . . . . . . 239
  Retina-safe and responsive images. . . . . . . . . . . . . . . . . . . . . 240
    *Retinafy your Web Sites & Apps*,
    by Thomas Fuchs. . . . . . . . . . . . . . . . . . . . . . . . . . . . . . . . . 240
    Articles on responsive images from Opera . . . . . . . . . . . 240
  Better embedded maps . . . . . . . . . . . . . . . . . . . . . . . . . . . . . . .240
  Hosted front-end toolkits . . . . . . . . . . . . . . . . . . . . . . . . . . . . . 241
  Stationery files on OS X. . . . . . . . . . . . . . . . . . . . . . . . . . . . . . 241

## APPENDIX C  Troubleshooting    243
Save, Quit, and Restart . . . . . . . . . . . . . . . . . . . . . . . . . . . . . . . .244
Create a New Project, and Then Switch Back . . . . . . . . . . . . . .244
Send Feedback. . . . . . . . . . . . . . . . . . . . . . . . . . . . . . . . . . . . . .245
Post in the Forums . . . . . . . . . . . . . . . . . . . . . . . . . . . . . . . . . . .245

## APPENDIX D  Custom Integrations    247
Custom CSS. . . . . . . . . . . . . . . . . . . . . . . . . . . . . . . . . . . . . . . .248
Custom Web Fonts. . . . . . . . . . . . . . . . . . . . . . . . . . . . . . . . . . .250
  Making fonts available. . . . . . . . . . . . . . . . . . . . . . . . . . . . . . 251
  Adding the custom CSS. . . . . . . . . . . . . . . . . . . . . . . . . . . . .252
  Changes before uploading . . . . . . . . . . . . . . . . . . . . . . . . . .254
  Loading fonts from the Internet. . . . . . . . . . . . . . . . . . . . . . .254
Custom JavaScript . . . . . . . . . . . . . . . . . . . . . . . . . . . . . . . . . . .254
  Loading the plugin. . . . . . . . . . . . . . . . . . . . . . . . . . . . . . . . .255
  Activating the plugin . . . . . . . . . . . . . . . . . . . . . . . . . . . . . . .257
  Recommendation . . . . . . . . . . . . . . . . . . . . . . . . . . . . . . . . .259

## Index    261

# 1

# Why Are You Here?

The question asked in the title of this chapter could be philosophical, but let's go with a simple answer: You're here to learn about Macaw, a new web design and development tool. Welcome to *Getting Started with Macaw*!

## Who Are You?

Macaw is a tool created to help build websites using the latest and greatest techniques, or as close to them as possible. Because of this, it's good to have some familiarity with the current state of web design and development before you start using Macaw. Therefore, we're assuming that you have experience making web pages and websites, most likely as a professional, semiprofessional, or enthusiastic amateur. If you're a beginner in this field, you can still get a lot out of Macaw, and we hope a lot from this book, but undoubtedly some techniques and assumptions will come up here that may be unfamiliar to you.

The web-building techniques that Macaw is built to support are current best practices, and the workflows we recommend in this book are in keeping with those practices. To use any tool effectively, you should know how much work it saves you. If you've worked as a web professional, or at least played around with building the web a little yourself, you'll have a better idea of the kind of work Macaw saves you and how it gets you through some tedious chores to get to a more creative place.

We've made recommendations on books and other resources to help catch you up on many pieces of web building in Appendix B.

## Who Are We?

We are a pair of developer-designers, or designer-developers (depending on how you look at it), with more expertise on one side of the hyphen or the other. Rex comes from a background in graphic design and illustration but has also learned a bit of code while involved in many web projects. Joe's background leans more in the direction of code than design; although he has built dozens of websites from scratch, he has worked much more as a developer than a designer.

This is important to mention because Macaw has aspects that are appealing to each of these ways of looking at building the web. Our different perspectives helped us figure out the best ways to use this new tool in its current state, as well as reflect on its future.

## A Brief History of Everything

Let's take a brief trip down (for some of us) memory lane to see why tools that might seem similar to Macaw have proved insufficient and what's different now.

Web design has come a long way in the past couple of decades. In the beginning (all right, the mid-1990s), we learned HTML, which was just barely good enough to make pages that weren't completely horrible looking. Later there came Cascading Style Sheets (CSS), which made it easier to keep things from looking terrible but proved to be a compatibility nightmare. You couldn't be sure anything originally designed in Browser A would look good in Browser B, so the most reliable designs were minimalistic, barely functional, and very much about getting the content out into the world without much visual help.

Starting in the late 1990s, the Web Standards Project helped usher in an era of standards across web browsers, making it practical (and easy) to use the technologies available. Everyone got excited about the possibility of exerting control over every pixel and having some expectation that the designs would look right on any computer. Joy!

Even at this point, professionals were still building everything by hand, in markup. There were visual web editors, but if they worked at all, they had a bunch of workarounds built in to deal with older (read: crappy) web browsers, and the markup was a nightmare—bloated and hard to use in a professional context. They kept everything where you put it on the page for the most part, but it was hard to make a case for using them in a professional environment. But hey, at least everything looked like it was under control. The HTML might be bloated and unmaintainable, the CSS a tangled web of apparent nonsense, but it pretty much worked. Right?

As we so often say when working in technology, Things Are Different Now. The pendulum of web design has swung in the other direction. Where in the early days we couldn't concern ourselves with visual design very much because it just didn't work well everywhere, we're now in an era when the major complication is the explosion of different devices that can access the web. There are so many now, and so many yet to come, that making good web pages means something totally different. We need to be responsive—or die trying! We can't assume that the device looking at the page is a desktop computer anymore (we never should have, but in the heady days of standardization of CSS and JavaScript, we all kinda did). We also need to be efficient because many devices are low powered or accessing the Internet over slow connections (maybe not 300-baud modem slow, but slow).

> ### What is responsive web design?
>
> For our purposes, responsive web design is the process of developing websites that can change and adapt to different screen sizes. Text sizes may change, elements on the page may reorganize, and so on—all so the information hierarchy and the design can be as effective as possible, no matter what size device the user has. For more on the subject, see Appendix B.

So here we are, knowing that we need to work in a new way that casts aside assumptions of how someone is viewing our sites and apps. The crop of WYSIWYG tools from years gone by just won't cut it anymore; we need something new.

## Designing in the Browser Is Not Fun

One way of attempting to deal with this responsive world is "design in the browser." The thinking goes like this:

The web is an interactive medium. The object being designed is itself interactive.

A browser, or something like it, is the final destination, the final arbiter of how the designed page, site, or app will look.

Making the distance between the initial design and the browser as short as possible will not only shorten the work cycle but will encourage us as designers to use the medium to its best effect.

Unfortunately, designing in the browser kind of stinks. It's just not all that satisfying to design a highly visual artifact by typing out markup and CSS. Tools that auto-reload the browser, or otherwise show you what you're doing as you go, are a huge help, but it's not the same as using an image editor or illustration application. This is one of the reasons why Adobe Photoshop, wonderful for what it is, is continually a favorite among designers targeting the web. Being able to drop something onto a canvas directly and setting properties visually is satisfying creatively in a way that typing out markup and code is not (for most people anyway).

So, there's a gap between the popular visual tools and the interactive final object. Older WYSIWYG web editors tried to replicate the image editing–style experience but with their fixed canvases were ill equipped to deal with responsive design. Wouldn't it be nice if we had a tool that enhanced the visual building of web stuff using familiar tools, but was also built natively for the web, and had current best practices in mind?

That is Macaw.

It's coming to steal your Photoshop.[*]

## What Will We Be Doing?

The next several chapters will introduce Macaw and discuss workflow, including aspects that are unique and aspects that will probably be familiar. Starting in Chapter 6, you'll start really using Macaw. You'll work through a couple example projects: a prototyping/wireframing example and a full (small) site build from mockups that we provide. You can find everything you'll need to work through the examples, including the mockup, at http://macawbook.com/example-files/.

All right, let's dive in!

---

[*] Just kidding. It can be a substantial portion of your tool chain, but it cannot and will not displace your favorite image editor.

# 2

# What Is Macaw?

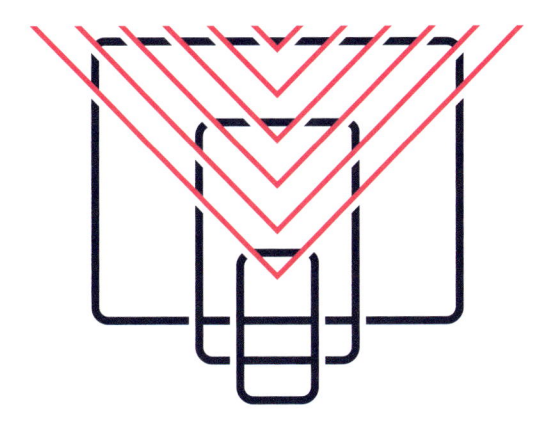

In this chapter, we'll go into a little more detail about what type of tool Macaw is, where it might fit into your workflow, and where you can get it.

## Macaw, in Basic Terms

Simply put, Macaw is a web development tool. But it's a web development tool like you've never seen before (see **Figure 2.1**)—it has the familiarity and flexibility of standard image editors, it includes unique and powerful tools for creating responsive designs/prototypes, and it generates semantic HTML and CSS for use as, or integration into, final production code. It was created for the sole purpose of being a more web-centric development tool, with a feature set more focused on creating high-quality, responsive web designs than what's possible in standard image editors. We'll go over Macaw's full interface in Chapters 3 and 4. If you've been looking for a better tool for creating or prototyping sites for the modern web, Macaw is what you've been waiting for.

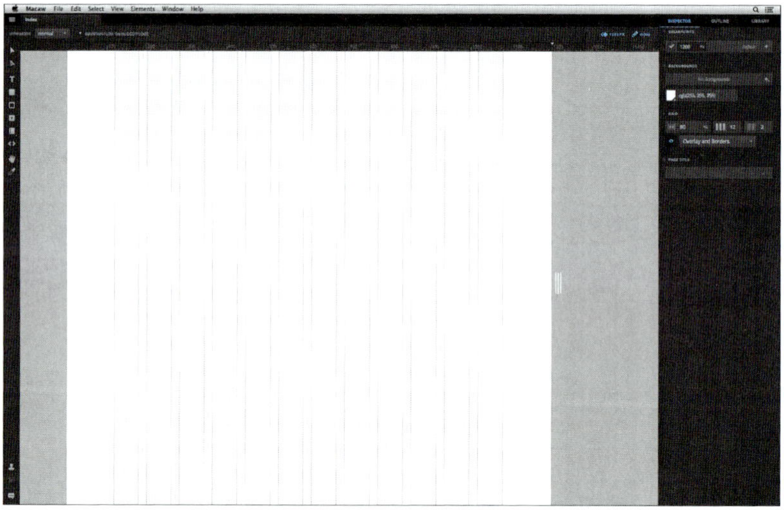

**Figure 2.1** Macaw's default interface

## Don't Throw Away Your Other Tools!

Macaw can be different things to different people. This is important to remember. It's a tool. And like any other tool, one person may not use it exactly like another. Some may see Macaw as a complete replacement for their design and development needs. Others may add it as another step in their process. And even others may use it only sparingly, when

**Chapter 2:** What Is Macaw?   9

they need a quick way to test an idea or to prototype a small portion of a larger project. Figure out how Macaw can best work for you and integrate it into your process appropriately. Keep in mind it may not be the best tool for every situation. (That's what your other tools are for!)

In its short existence, a couple of small trends in Macaw usage have started to form that may help you determine how Macaw can fit into your process:

- Web professionals tend to use Macaw more as a prototyping tool (after the static design has been created in a standard image editor), as shown in **Figure 2.2**. Prototyping an existing design in Macaw is a way to try different ideas with the design much quicker than starting with traditional code. Furthermore, from this prototype, code can be generated to act as a starting point for additional customization in the final development environment before launching the final site.

- On the other side of the spectrum, web design and development beginners tend to use Macaw as a more complete design and development solution, as shown in **Figure 2.3**. For many basic and even intermediate needs, Macaw's tools and features are robust enough to get the job done. For these users, the HTML and CSS generated by Macaw is more than suitable for use in their final site production.

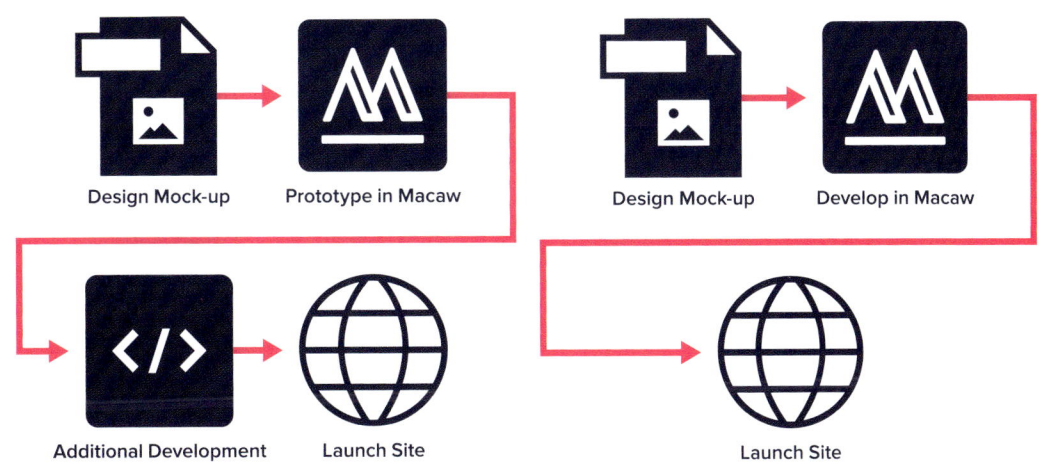

**Figure 2.2** Typical Macaw workflow among professionals

**Figure 2.3** Typical Macaw workflow among beginners

## Built on a Web-Based Foundation

Macaw is a tool that was built for the web, but more than that, it is a tool built *of* the web. It is built on foundational pieces like Chromium, the engine that runs the browser Google Chrome; Node.js, the JavaScript engine; CodeMirror, a browser-based text editor written in JavaScript; and the languages that all websites are made with: HTML and CSS. This partial list of ingredients indicates one of the reasons that Macaw can "speak web design" more fluently—its main engine is a web browser. Previous WYSIWYG web design packages embedded browser frames for the purpose of previewing your work, but you couldn't directly manipulate what was in that preview window visually.

The way Macaw is put together seems to us to point to a future in which the web plays a much bigger role in the creation of the software we use every day, a fusion between native applications for desktop computers and the web. It's not just useful—it's nifty!

## Where to Get Macaw

Macaw is available for download directly from the developer at Macaw.co. It's compatible with both Windows and Mac. You can download a full version of Macaw and try it free for 30 days before you decide to buy. After you download the app, be sure to install it on your computer following the normal installation procedures native to your operating system. In addition, purchasers of this book can get $80 off the price of the app by by using the discount code PEACHPIT when checking out. There's no reason not to download the app. Go get it!

# 3

# Unique Tools

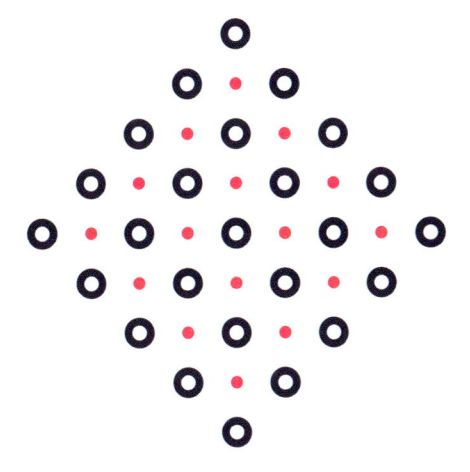

If you've used any graphics application before, many of the tools you'll use in Macaw will look familiar. We'll cover those standard tools in Chapter 4, but first we want to introduce some of the tools and features that make Macaw unique and well suited to responsive web design. In other words, these are the parts we find exciting. Don't judge.

You can find breakpoints in the Inspector in the sidebar on the right (see **Figure 3.2**).

**Figure 3.2** The breakpoint palette with the single, default breakpoint

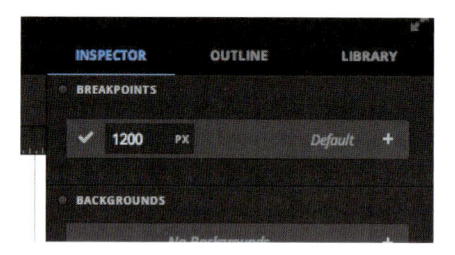

They appear with the largest on top to smallest on the bottom, and they sort themselves to stay that way. Remember, the default breakpoint is the largest one; designing in Macaw currently starts on the largest possible canvas. This may change in a future version to support the "mobile first" way of working (basically small to large), but for now you'll need to work with the largest size first.

Click the plus button to create a new breakpoint; to delete a breakpoint, move your cursor over the breakpoint and click the trash can (see **Figure 3.3**). In the current version of Macaw, breakpoints are always set in pixels.

**Figure 3.3** The breakpoint palette, now with two breakpoints

> **NOTE** Macaw uses custom check boxes throughout its user interface (UI)—that is, there are no boxes! If a check box is selected, you'll just see a check mark. If it is clear, there is a plain dot. There are many, many places in the Macaw UI that might not look clickable at first, so don't be shy with your input device! As another example, try clicking the little circle next to the Breakpoints label now—it's not a check box, but it is clickable, letting you collapse the palette. Click it again to expand that it.

Breakpoints and other canvas-level properties are always shown when nothing is selected, so if you want to change them, click the canvas background. If your canvas is covered in goodies, scroll over to the side and click there.

## Special importance of the default breakpoint

Note that in the header, just above the right edge of the ruler, there is an indicator showing the active breakpoint. This will update itself as you change breakpoints. There is also a DOM label, with either a pencil or a lock. Macaw will let you create elements (that is, add elements to the project's Document Object Model, a browser's way of interacting with the objects you've created) only when you're working with the default breakpoint. When the lock is shown, you're not allowed to create elements, and all tools that might let you add things are disabled. In nondefault breakpoints, you can change things, but you can't add anything new until you switch back to the default breakpoint and see that pencil next to DOM.

### [Break]point of reference

Because everything can change with different breakpoints, while working in Macaw you can almost think of breakpoints the way you might have thought about frames in Fireworks or layer comps in Photoshop: They store a state of the canvas.

## Setting breakpoints first

We recommend you make any breakpoints you know you'll need first, before you add any elements or make any pages. This is helpful because it gives you some structure to design toward. Generally speaking, four major breakpoints are commonly used when designing for the responsive web: Small (phones), Medium (tablets), Large (laptops/smaller desktops), and Extra Large (large desktops). What actual pixel values are used to define these breakpoints can vary from developer to developer, and best practices may change in the future as newer and newer devices are released.

In later chapters, when we get into actually creating a project, we'll cover our recommended breakpoints in more detail.

Also of note, once you've worked on your project for a while and have more elements or pages made, you can add more breakpoints for more subtle shifts in content (where it feels appropriate for the design). You may add a breakpoint here and there just to adjust font sizes on a couple elements, or change an element's alignment to fit better in a smaller space... that's perfectly fine! Just be careful not to get too carried away. Too many breakpoints can be a hassle to maintain and keep organized, even using Macaw. You can think of your breakpoints kind of like dash marks on a ruler—the initial breakpoints (Small, Medium, Large, and Extra Large) are like the whole number increments (where major shifts or changes in the design happen). Any additional breakpoints (if needed) between the initial breakpoints are like the tiny dash marks on a ruler, where no major changes occur, but subtle things may shift slightly to better fit and flow with the design.

One more quick note about breakpoints: You don't necessarily have to use more than one. If you have occasion to build a project with a static width for some reason, you can just change the default breakpoint, consider it your canvas width, and go crazy. Breakpoints are a big part of modern web design, but if you have a reason not to use them, you don't have to.

# Fluid Grids

Pretty much every design tool features a grid and the ability to snap elements to that grid. In most design tools, however, that grid is static—you might have grid lines every 30 pixels, across the entire canvas, and that's it. This works well if the canvas is static, but the web is not a static medium, and in responsive design, you want to be able to use a grid that can adapt to varying device sizes. To support this, Macaw features a fluid grid system that responds to breakpoints.

Fluid grid in this case means a grid that maintains the number of columns, and the spacing relationships between them, at different widths. A bit below the breakpoints in the Inspector, you'll see where you can set up a grid (see **Figure 3.4**).

**Figure 3.4** The default grid settings: 80% width, 12 columns, 2% width gutters.

From left to right, top to bottom, these elements are the width of the grid system relative to the page, how many columns are in the grid, how much space is between the columns, and visibility settings for the grid. The first three all respond to breakpoints, so you can have a 12-column grid that takes up 90 percent of a 1200px wide canvas, and switch to a 4-column grid taking up 100 percent of a 320px wide canvas.

> **NOTE** If you want to work statically, the grid may also be set to pixels. Click the percent sign to change the units. We generally recommend sticking with percentage widths, though.

Of course, we said that these grids are fluid and can use the same number of columns at different widths. This is true, but being able to change the grid system at different breakpoints is also very helpful. Here's an example:

1. If you haven't already done so, add a second breakpoint of 600px (see **Figure 3.5**).

2. The default 12-column grid system is still in place at this width, but note that the columns are very narrow indeed. They maintain their relationships to one another, but having so many columns in so small a space isn't necessarily all that great.

3. Change the grid settings to 100% wide, 6 columns, leaving spacing at 2%. That's much better (see **Figure 3.6**).

**Figure 3.5** When creating a new breakpoint, Macaw switches to it right away. The default grid is still used but looks a little squished.

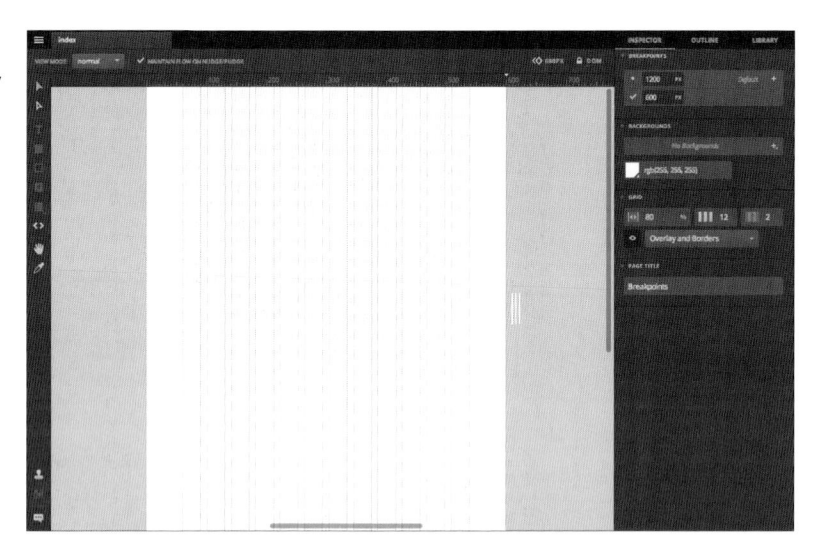

**Figure 3.6** How the grid appears after changing the settings.

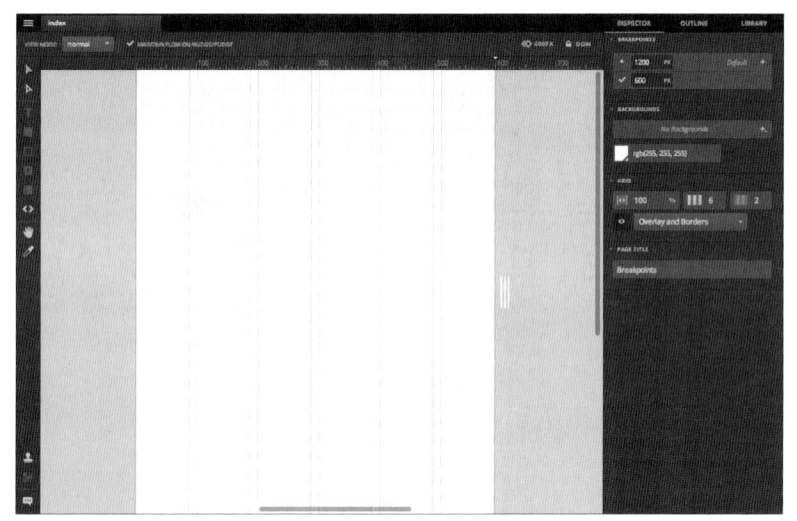

Just off the right edge of the canvas are three white vertical lines. This is a resize handle that lets you see how your canvas responds to real-time width changes. Click and drag it to the left to squish your four-column grid a bit; then let go to watch it snap back to the 600px breakpoint. If you drag it to the right, past 600 pixels, you'll see the 12-column grid return, and if you let go, the canvas will snap to the next largest size, in this case the default breakpoint.

**Chapter 3:** Unique Tools    19

**NOTE**  You can also create breakpoints with the resize handle. While dragging, you can press ⌘(Mac) or Ctrl (Windows) to set a breakpoint at the current size you've dragged to.

You may want to see what you're working on without seeing the grid on top. The grid visibility settings are global, independent of breakpoints. The eye icon toggles the grid's visibility (⌘-; or Ctrl-; will also do this), and the popup menu lets you choose to show the grid's shaded overlay, the border lines, or both.

Objects that you place on the page will try to snap to the grid lines, as you would expect. You can still see the grid but not let elements snap to it by turning off Toggle Snap in the View menu (when the grid is not visible, snapping is completely disabled). What's interesting about the fluid grid in Macaw is that objects will stay snapped to those grid lines even when the width of the window changes (see **Figure 3.7** and **Figure 3.8**). Responsive!

**Figure 3.7** We've added an element that's snapped to the grid—watch its left and right edges, which stick to the grid borders...

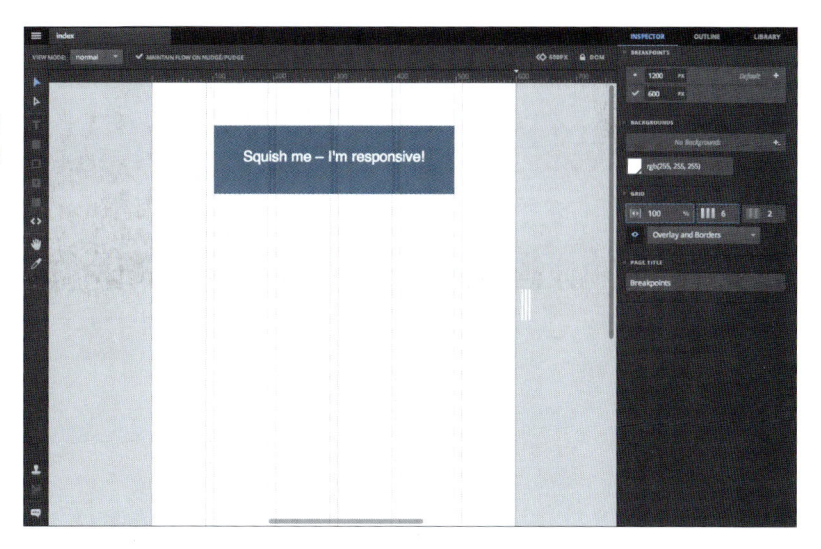

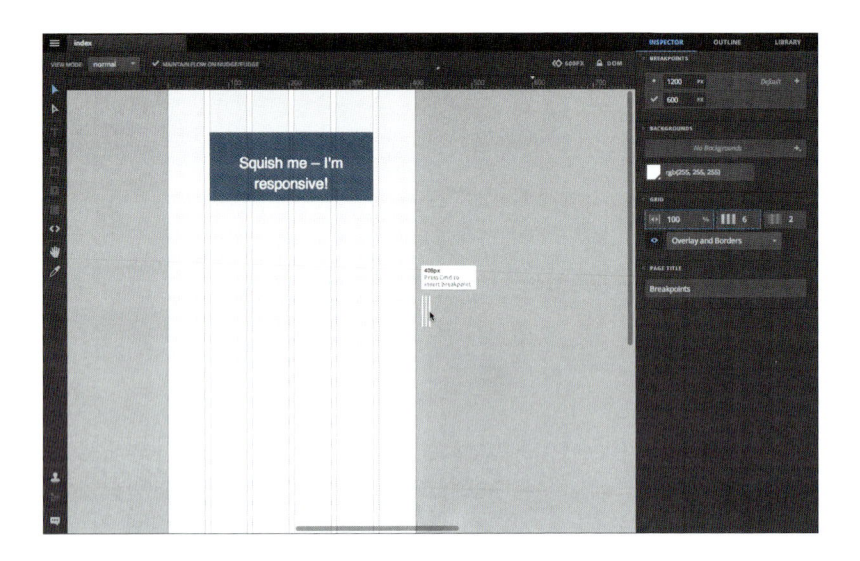

**Figure 3.8** ...even when you make the canvas narrower.

If the grid settings change at a certain breakpoint, Macaw doesn't try to guess where you wanted objects to be placed (it's clever, but there are limits), so you'll need to drag any objects into their new locations on the new grid. But within that grid system, they will stick.

# Reusables: Global Styles and Components

Being able to set up an element just the way you like it, and reuse it without having to do the same work over again, is really useful. Macaw has a couple of features that help you not repeat yourself: global styles and components.

Global styles let you collect a set of visual attributes and reuse them. This is the sort of task classes are used for when writing CSS by hand, and Macaw manages that for you.

## Control freak note

Please note that global styles will not be mapped one-to-one with CSS classes in the generated CSS. Macaw's developers want the CSS to be as succinct as possible while preserving your flexibility in the design process. Macaw generates nice CSS, but if you're a real control freak, you may find yourself wanting to make adjustments to it after publishing.

You can select any element you've created and styled, and extract many parts of it into a global style, including its size, background(s), color, borders, font, opacity, and CSS effects. You can apply multiple styles to a single element as well, so for example you can have a "buy it" style that's bright orange with a darker, rounded border, which could be applied to buttons or callout boxes. You could use a separate style for the page's default typography, which might be applied to any element on the page with type in it, including the same button. **Figure 3.9** and **Figure 3.10** show examples.

**Figure 3.9** These two buttons use a global style called "Big Button," which defines their colors, size, and border properties. They also use one called "Big Text," which covers only the typography. With one of the buttons selected here, you can see its applied styles.

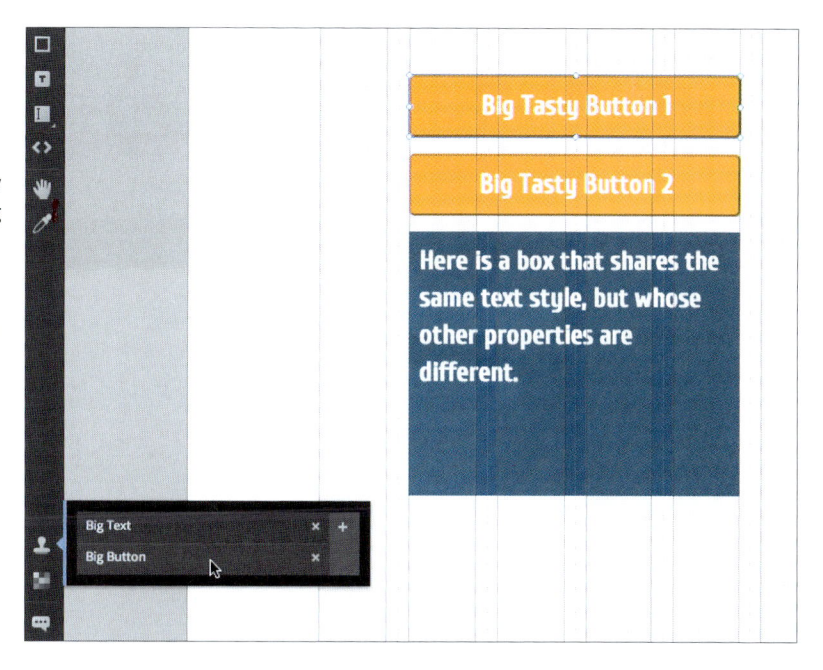

**Figure 3.10** The blue text box (selected in this screenshot) has only the "Big Text" style applied. The plus button next to "Big Button" means it may be added to this element if you want to.

Global styles are managed using the Stamp icon on the lower left (shown earlier in Figure 3.9). Clicking it once will reveal all global styles defined in the current project and which ones are used on the selected element. If an element is selected, you can define global styles based on however you've styled that element and add other styles that may not yet be applied. You can also just click the plus button with nothing selected and create styles from scratch (see **Figure 3.11**).

**Figure 3.11** When creating a global style, you give it a name and then page through the available properties to see which ones should be included.

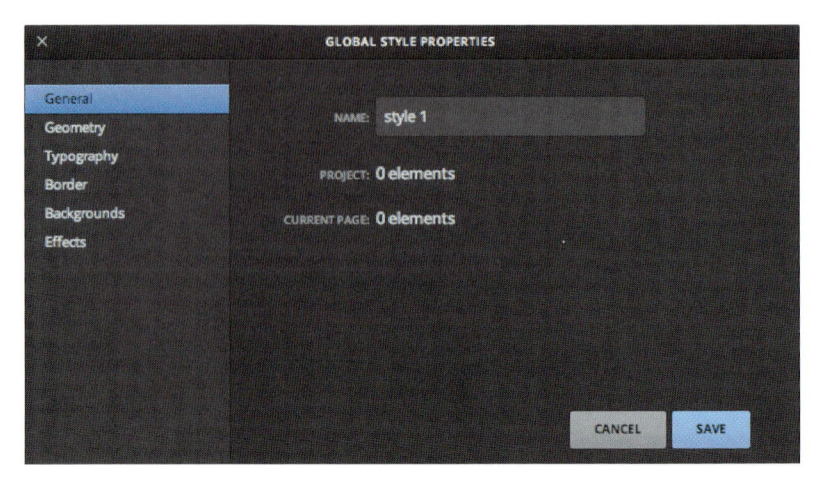

There is quite a bit more that can be done with global styles, which we'll cover when we get into some projects later in the book.

Components go a step beyond global styles in that they are reusable groups of elements. These could be UI widgets like custom-designed buttons (which could have global styles applied to them), headers and footers made up of banner images and navigation elements, forms with a bunch of fields included, or anything else that you might want to use more than once.

## Components templates

If you build many projects that are similar, but not similar enough to be pages within a single project, you can create a huge library of components in a single project and save it. Then when it's time to start a new project, you could make a duplicate of your template and start with that instead of a default, blank project.

To create a component from some elements, you select them all and choose Create Component from the Elements menu. You'll be prompted to give it a name, and then it becomes available in the Library pane in the right sidebar. The newest component you've made is always listed first. Click the component's name to see a preview of it (see **Figure 3.12**).

**Figure 3.12** Big Tasty Button 1 was added to the library as a component called Big Orange Button, and it is now available for reuse across this project.

To place a component on the canvas, just click and drag it from the Library. Once placed on the canvas, a component may be edited; it is not tied to other instances. Editing or updating all instances of a component at once is not currently possible —global styles allow you to change multiple items at once.

You cannot edit a component once it has been added to the Library. You can, however, create the new one with the same name as the old one and delete the old one—just watch the preview to make sure you delete the right one (see **Figure 3.13**)!

**Figure 3.13** Hover your cursor over a component's name to see its delete button. Note that the older component that you want to delete here has the same name but is on the bottom.

# Honorable Mentions

We've gone over some of the bigger unique features that you should know about before starting to build projects. There are several other unique features that deserve a brief mention so you know they're there; we'll discuss them in greater depth in the subsequent chapters when we're building actual prototypes and pages.

## Outline

The Outline shows you every element on the active page, letting you control the visual stacking order, the nesting of elements, and even the type of HTML element. It's very powerful. This pane is a sibling to the Inspector and has a permanent home in the right sidebar (see **Figure 3.14**). You can activate it with Opt/Alt-O (Mac) or Alt-O (Windows).

**Figure 3.14**
The Outline panel, with some elements of different types

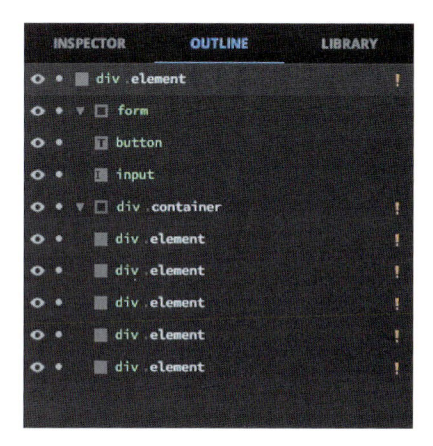

## Pages

This isn't earth-shattering on its face, but Macaw lets you create all the pages you need for your project in a single document. Every page shares the same asset library, global styles, color swatches, and components, so it's really helpful.

## View Modes

A lot of the work you'll do in Macaw will likely be visual design, live and will likely be high-fidelity visual design. It can also be used for wireframes and other kinds of lower-fidelity mockups. Macaw has three view modes that affect the way the entire page is displayed: normal, outline, and wireframe (see **Figure 3.15**). Outline in this case refers to the outlines of each element (in HTML and CSS terms, the outline of each element's box in the DOM), not the overall document outline that's displayed in the Outline panel. Wireframe mode basically desaturates everything on the page, resulting in wireframes that help keep attention on layout more than overall appearance.

**Figure 3.15** The view options popup menu, with its options displayed

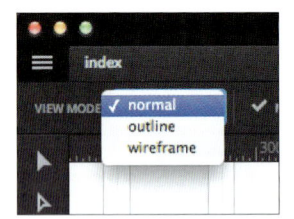

## Retina and HiDPI Images

Macaw supports SVG images for resolution independence. Of course, there will still be plenty of times where you need to use bitmaps (JPEGs, PNGs, and so on), and in those cases, you'll need to prepare high-resolution versions for Retina/HiDPI (high-resolution) displays. When bringing these images into Macaw, you'll have opportunities to tell it "this is a retina image, treat it accordingly." Macaw can generate lower-resolution derivative images automatically for lower-resolution displays and include the right image based on whether the browser is retina capable.

> **NOTE** This swapping is done using a custom jQuery plug-in. If and when the HTML5 working group finishes work on the `<picture>` element, and all browsers support it well, we can probably expect Macaw to support responsive images using that browser-native way.
>
> See more on the HTML5 picture element, and other aspects of responsive images, in Appendix B.

# 4

# The Rest of the Tools

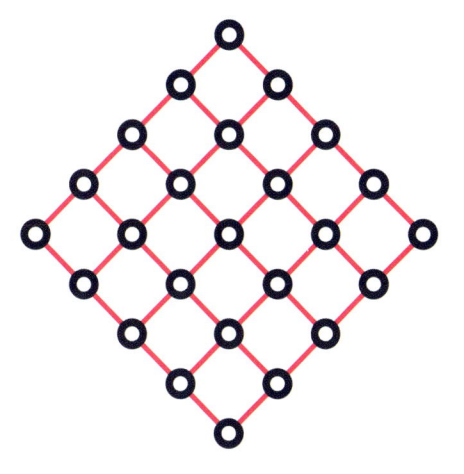

Here we'll introduce you to all of Macaw's other tools and show you where they're located throughout the application.

## The Interface

Macaw's interface is more akin to the interface of a graphics application than a web design text editor. This is part of its appeal because for many users the interface of a graphics application is much more familiar, and less intimidating, than a traditional text editor. These types of interfaces tend to be more approachable because users can draw shapes and text directly on a canvas or page, without having to create everything through lines of code. To make it easier to describe Macaw's interface as well as to help you get oriented to where everything is, we've divided it into five main areas (see **Figure 4.1**):

- The top area contains the Page Manager, page tabs, options bar, breakpoint and DOM information.
- The left side contains the toolbar and links for global styles, swatches, and feedback.
- The large area in the middle is the canvas (where you'll create your site).

**Figure 4.1** Macaw's full interface.

- The right side contains the Inspector, Outline, and Library panes. Each shows different information, based on which element(s) are selected on the canvas.

- Lastly, at the very top of the screen (or window if you're on Windows) is the standard operating system menu bar. All sorts of actions can be accessed here. The various drop-down menus work just like other applications you have on your computer.

## Top area

The top area contains a handful of helpful items.

### *Page Manager*

**Figure 4.2** Page Manager icon.

In the upper-left corner is a small, three-line list icon that accesses the Page Manager (see **Figure 4.2**). Clicking this icon shows a list of all of your pages. There you can add, rename, or copy pages.

> **NOTE** When you create a new page, Macaw automatically adds a tab for that page to the right of the Page Manager icon. If you close the tab for a particular page, it does not delete the page—it just closes the window/tab view of that page. If you do intend to delete a particular page, you need to click the trash icon next to that page in the Page Manager.

### *Page tabs*

The tabs next to the Page Manager icon are open windows for any of your site's pages (see **Figure 4.3**). Each new project you create starts with a blank page with the title "index" (feel free to keep or rename this page as desired).

**Figure 4.3** Page tab.

### Options bar

The information shown in the options bar changes depending on what is currently selected, whether it be a tool from the toolbar or an element on the page (see **Figure 4.4**). It consists of information and settings that can be adjusted to alter the next action you'll make with your currently selected tool or to modify attributes of any currently selected element.

**Figure 4.4** Options bar.

**Figure 4.5** View Mode toggle.

One common item that shows up in the options bar is the View Mode toggle (see **Figure 4.5**).

This toggle allows you to switch between normal, outline, and wireframe view modes. Keep in mind that the options bar is visible only when certain tools are selected.

### Breakpoint and DOM information

**Figure 4.6** Breakpoint and DOM information.

To the right of the options bar is the breakpoint and Document Object Model (DOM) information (see **Figure 4.6**). This area simply tells you which breakpoint you're currently looking at and whether you can edit the DOM. The "DOM" text turns blue, and a little pencil icon appears when you can edit the DOM. When you cannot edit the DOM, the "DOM" text turns gray, and the pencil icon changes to a lock icon.

## Left side

The left side contains the toolbar and a few other commonly used items.

### Select tool

You use the Select tool (keyboard shortcut: V) to select whole elements or groups on the canvas.

### Direct Select tool

You use the Direct Select tool (keyboard shortcut: A) to select a single element within a group or component.

### Text tool

You use the Text tool (keyboard shortcut: T) to create or edit text elements. Macaw has two types of text elements: point text and paragraph text. Clicking once on the canvas with the Text tool will make a point text field that has auto width and behaves like an inline element. Clicking and dragging on the canvas with the Text tool will create paragraph text, which has set dimensions and behaves like a block element (which means it can also be made scrollable if desired—more on that later). The actual text within text elements can have various tags applied to them: spans, links, regular and strong emphasis. Each of those tags may be styled as well.

### Element tool

You use the Element tool (keyboard shortcut: R) to create or edit basic elements. With this tool, you can create empty elements that don't have any content in them. This tool comes in handy when you're prototyping or creating initial styles. Keep in mind, though, these elements should eventually be converted to containers for better structure and semantics when you publish the final project (more on that later).

### Container tool

You use the Container tool (keyboard shortcut: G) for grouping multiple elements. Containers have their own dimensions and can be styled like any other element.

To create a container with the Container tool, first select the tool from the toolbar and then click and drag on the canvas. Drag over the elements you want to group in a container and those elements will highlight as you drag. All of the highlighted elements will then be placed inside the new container.

Containers can also be created by selecting a bunch of elements and then selecting the Elements > Group command from the menu bar, or by pressing ⌘-G (Mac) or Ctrl-G (Windows).

### Button tool

You use the Button tool (keyboard shortcut: B) to create or edit button elements. The text in buttons is centered by default. The button type (submit for forms, button for general use, and reset to clear a form) can be set in the Advanced palette in the Inspector.

### Input tool(s)

You use the Input tool (keyboard shortcut: N) to create or edit various form input elements: single-line text fields, multiline text areas, select (that is, popup or drop-down) menus, check boxes, and radio buttons. To access the various input elements, click and hold on the current Input Tool icon, or use the keyboard shortcut Shift-N. Keep in mind that input fields are editable. Any text you type inside the element will be used as placeholder text when you publish your project.

### Embed tool

You use the Embed tool (keyboard shortcut: M) to create or edit embedded elements such as HTML, iframes, maps, and videos. Unfortunately, Macaw doesn't always display every kind of embedded content while in the editor or while previewing in the browser. But the embedded content will display correctly when you publish your project.

### Hand tool

You use the Hand tool (keyboard shortcut: H or spacebar) to pan (click and drag) around your page. When this tool is active, a thumbnail of the whole canvas is displayed in the upper right, and can be clicked to pan quickly to anywhere on the canvas.

### Eyedropper tool

You use the Eyedropper tool (keyboard shortcut: I) to select and match colors from existing elements. This tool works very much like eyedropper tools in other standard graphics applications.

*Global Styles*

You use this tool to access any global styles you've created for the current project and create new ones.

*Swatches*

You use this tool to open the Swatches palette (Keyboard shortcut: S), which includes any swatches you saved for the current project. This icon is only clickable when an element that can have a swatch applied to it is selected on the canvas. Click a swatch to make it the background color of the selected element.

*Feedback*

You use the Feedback tool to send feedback directly to the developers of Macaw, right from within the app. As we mentioned earlier, Macaw is a pretty new tool and is constantly being refined and improved upon. If you run into a bug, or you have any feature requests, please let the developers know!

## The canvas

The large area in the middle is known as the canvas. This is where you'll do the bulk of your creating. Let's explore a few key portions of the canvas.

*The grid*

The grid—keyboard shortcut: ⌘ (Mac) or Ctrl (Windows)—is the invisible structure of your site (see **Figure 4.7**). Any quality site is designed using a grid. It gives you guidelines for separating and organizing your content. The default breakpoint is set with a 12-column grid, but this grid can be edited to your liking using the Inspector on the right. Various other attributes of the grid can be modified in the Inspector as well, but we'll get into those later in this book when we start making a site. You can turn the visibility of the grid on or off from the menu bar by selecting View > Toggle Grid.

**Figure 4.7** The grid (in light gray) over a blank page.

### Ruler and breakpoints

At the top of the canvas is your ruler (see **Figure 4.8**). The ruler shows you the width of your site. You can use the ruler to quickly jump between your various breakpoints (once you've created more than one).

**Figure 4.8** The ruler features arrow markers for each breakpoint (only one breakpoint is shown).

### Resize handle

To the right of the grid (but still within the canvas) you'll see the resize handle (see **Figure 4.9**). You can click and drag this handle to see how your site responds to various screen widths. If you have only one breakpoint, any elements on your page will just squish or stretch based on the adjusted width. Once you have more breakpoints and set various

**Figure 4.9** Resize handle.

properties for each element on your page (at each breakpoint), the various elements on your page will respond as you've defined in real time as you drag the resize handle.

## The right side

The right side is where the Inspector, Outline, and Library panes are located.

### *Inspector*

All the various properties, such as dimensions, color, font, border styles, and effects, that can be edited for the currently selected element show up here (see **Figure 4.10**). The properties that appear change depending on what element on the canvas is selected (not all properties are applicable to all elements). The Inspector will be used constantly to modify and tweak the various elements in your design. The various features of the Inspector will be covered in more detail when we create a project in later chapters. Even when you have nothing selected, properties appear in the Inspector that you can edit. These properties apply to your overall project: breakpoints (add, rename, delete), background images/color, grid properties, and page title.

**Figure 4.10**
The Inspector.

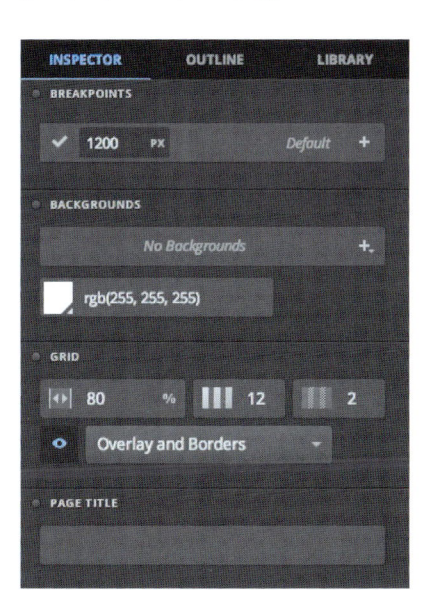

### Outline

The Outline pane shows you the structure of your site (see **Figure 4.11**). You can control how items are ordered visually, change their tag types, add or remove HTML classes, and nest elements within others. The outline gives you a lot of control over structure of your pages, so if you're a control freak, you're going to love it!

**Figure 4.11**
The Outline pane.

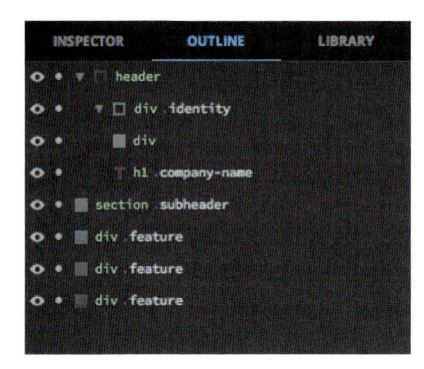

### Library

The Library lets you import images of all kinds (including SVG) for use on the canvas (see **Figure 4.12**). Any components you create will appear here as well. These items are shared among all pages in your project.

**Figure 4.12**
The Library pane.

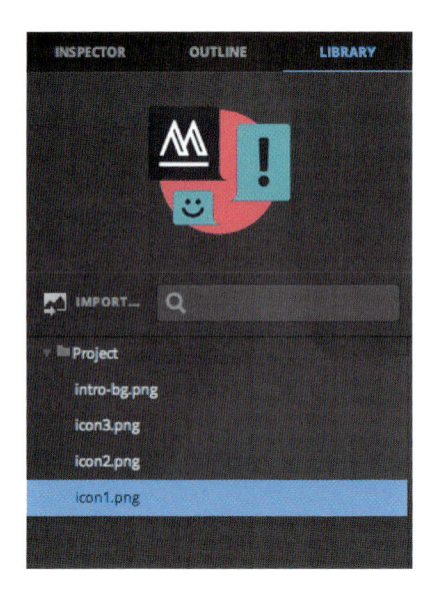

## The menu bar

The Macaw menu bar is located at the top of your screen. It functions like other menu bars in other applications on your computer (see **Figure 4.13**). You can access common actions associated with working with files and projects on your computer, actions such as setting preferences, saving, printing, copying/pasting, and grouping.

**Figure 4.13** Menu bar.

**NOTE** If you need further help getting to know Macaw's interface, please check out the in-depth documentation at http://docs.macaw.co.

# 5

## Consider Your Workflow

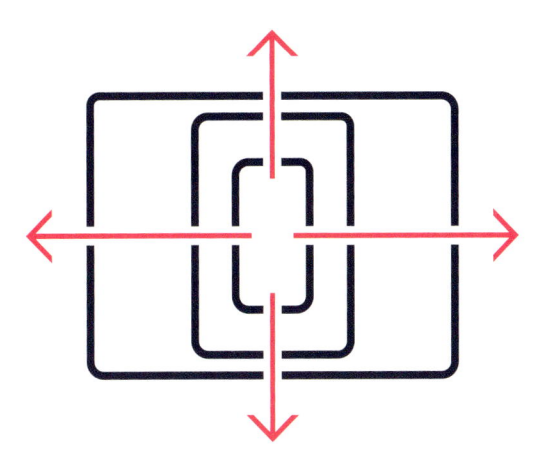

As with any tool, you can use Macaw however you like. And just like most tools, some ways of working with Macaw are more efficient than others.

In this chapter, we're going to step back a little bit from the particulars of Macaw's user interface elements and talk about process. These recommendations can work during prototyping or in making fully realized projects. We're not going to dictate a design process to you so much as recommend some workflow practices you can employ in your own process that will let you use Macaw in a way that is most helpful to you.

## Make Some Sketches

If you're coming to Macaw as a graphic or other visual designer, this is probably a no-brainer, but for those of you who are coming more from a developer's background, don't be afraid to do some sketches first, on paper or other medium, to start getting ideas down. Macaw can be great for working through ideas as well (you can draw boxes all over the place, add text, and generally do visual brainstorming), and we encourage you to try it that way, but sometimes there's nothing like going analog (see **Figure 5.1**).

**Figure 5.1** A preview of coming attractions.

## Think About Mobile First

Macaw doesn't directly support a mobile-first method of working right now; the default breakpoint, and the only one where you can add or remove elements from the canvas, is always the largest. That doesn't mean you necessarily have to plan your project that way, though. Just thinking about mobile devices first can give you editorial and design focus, determining what is most important (in this case mobile means smaller and/or simpler). If you consider the smaller widths first, those can be the first aspects of your design that you concentrate on, and then you can build up into the other areas that would either not be seen on a smaller device or be placed in such a way that they're of less importance in the larger canvas sizes. One of our favorite examples for this kind of thinking is for restaurant websites. On a mobile site, the most important things to show are probably the address, hours, phone number, and menus. Alas, so many restaurants do not present this information easily on their separate mobile, or smaller-viewport responsive sites. Thinking about mobile first will remind you to take care of these important elements—you can add in the animated pizza ovens and new age soundtracks afterward. That's not to say that establishing a mood through the use of rich media isn't a totally legitimate design decision, but making sure that the most important content on the site is treated as the most important is... well, it's important! Concentrating on mobile first is an effective way to make those decisions, if not easier, clearer.

Of course, as mentioned, when building up your project in Macaw, you will need to work from the largest breakpoint down, but having thought about the smaller sizes first can be especially helpful for content decisions; if it's important enough to be prominent on devices with very small screens, that probably means it's quite important indeed!

## Set Some Breakpoints

As covered in Chapter 2, breakpoints are a condition under which your design can react, changing things in various ways. If you're coming to a project with mock-ups in hand, this might just be a matter of setting the breakpoints to match what you (or the designer you're working with) have already created. If you're originating a project in Macaw, setting at least two breakpoints at the beginning will help give focus to your work. In the same way that thinking mobile first helps your editorial process, framing your responsive site via a couple of breakpoints establishes the boundaries of your canvas, promoting more focus in your visual decision making.

As the project progresses, you might find that you need to change the breakpoints, and that is just fine. Setting up breakpoints early also makes sure that you don't forget you're working on something responsive, which can be a real challenge at times for those of us who have been building websites for years before responsive design became so important.

## Don't Forget to Resize

Just because you've set breakpoints doesn't mean you've covered all your bases. Macaw's default values are set in percentages, so if you have elements that need to be exact widths, they might behave erratically as the browser window changes between breakpoints. Sometimes you'll want to add intermediate breakpoints; other times you'll just want to change the size or positioning of different elements so they don't flex even as items around them do. Whatever it is, just make sure you resize and see what happens.

## Care About Semantics

Use HTML tags that map onto the function they serve on the page (such as header, footer, aside, section… all that good HTML5 stuff). Using the right tag for the job will help keep your pages compatible with new browsers and devices and can be useful for keeping your pages sensible to the search engines, screen readers, and other machines that read them (as well as the humans). Macaw's Outline will warn you if you're using obviously generic tags, but in general it's up to you to make sure you do the right thing.

The same recommendation goes for classes as well. Instead of using class names like `red-box`, something indicative of function like `sidebar-widget` or `story-container` is much better. That way, anyone trying to make sense of your project (including you!) will have a better idea of what those elements in the Outline are for. If your project isn't going to live in Macaw long-term (that is, you're developing a template for a content management system or otherwise handing over the published assets to a web developer), this is especially helpful for other people working on the same stuff.

In practice with Macaw, keeping track of your semantics means keeping an eye on the Outline as you work, watching for warnings, and setting appropriate tag and class names on your elements. In the Inspector, you can also set unique IDs for each element (see **Figure 5.2**) and, if you're going to interact with an element with JavaScript later, a variable name (although JavaScript-savvy developers are probably fine using only the ID).

**Figure 5.2**
The inspector palette showing a generic element (a div tag) with an ID of "logo".

## Use Containers (Grouping) Liberally

You don't have to go crazy with nesting elements inside elements just for fun, but try to group related elements into containers. This not only helps your outline make semantic sense (you should be grouping elements that are sensibly related) and be easier to read, but it helps Macaw maintain positioning for elements in a way that's most likely to work in every browser. If your Outline has a lot of warnings about negative margins, you could be in for unexpected results in certain browsers (especially older ones).

When grouping items, when you see the "transfer presentation attributes?" question, the answer is most likely going to be yes every time. The new container will use the same styles from the element at the back of the grouped items, which will preserve how things look but also keep the HTML and CSS nice and lean.

## Reuse Everything You Can

The fact that Macaw lets you create global styles and components (even in components' relatively basic state) is really helpful. If you're working from a mock-up, you can look for elements of the design that have features that should be the same every time and turn them into global styles. You can do this to capture the full set of styles applied to a given element, allowing reuse of those styles throughout a project. Looking for opportunities to save future effort is one of the essential tasks of lazy web developers everywhere—lazy in the sense that we don't like doing the same work repeatedly.

It might not be as obvious, but global styles can be created for smaller "units of appearance" as well (see **Figure 5.3**). Grids are just one way that designers impose their will on a given task; frequently there are other elements that are made consistent to tie the whole work together. Any property that is shared in different areas of a design could be an opportunity for global styles. This could be as simple and small as the radius of the corners on rounded rectangles (see **Figure 5.4**). If that same value is used all over the design but the elements look otherwise different, you can create a global style with nothing in it but that single value (in Macaw and CSS, this would be the border radius), and you can apply it to any item with rounded corners.

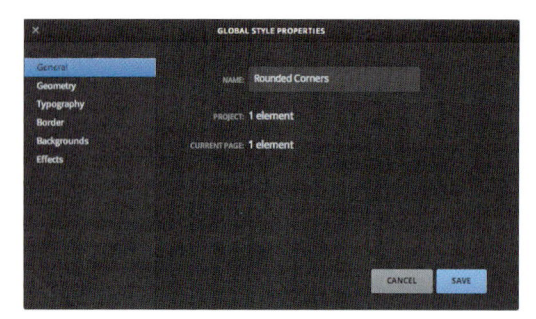

**Figure 5.3** Here a global style called Rounded Corners is defined. It is applied to one element in the project, which appears on the current page.

**Figure 5.4** The only piece of the global style that is defined here is the border radius of 15px. Now this global style can be applied to any element, and it will only affect that property.

You can create very granular global styles and apply them to different types of elements that might not share a lot in common otherwise. Don't worry about getting super clever with this; like with any strategy for productivity, chasing down "a better way" can get in the way of doing the actual work. Investing some time and effort into using global styles this way can save setting the same styles over again, and having to remember what those settings were supposed to be. Global styles effectively bring your site's style guide right into Macaw.

Components are not quite as powerful in their current state, but if you're going to use the same type of item repeatedly, it makes a lot of sense to make a component out of it. Components can have global styles applied to them as well, so if you're working on a page with a sidebar full of similar-looking widgets, you can make one, creating or applying global styles as needed and, when finished, create a component from it. Then you'll be able to drag as many copies as you need, wherever you need them.

Just as you can experiment with the level of granularity in which you create global styles, you can do the same with components. For certain projects with a lot of pages, you might finish up a whole section of the page (a sidebar, header, footer, whatever it is) and make a component from that, letting you drag a whole section. You could also duplicate the page you're working on; however, if only one section is going to be the same everywhere, creating the component could be faster than duplicating a page and deleting all the parts that aren't the same. There's more than one way to do it, so see what works best for you.

## Let Macaw Do the Work

If you're coming to Macaw as a skilled web developer, you may find yourself getting frustrated that Macaw doesn't work the same way you do. And of course, it's entirely possible that after publishing, you might find that you need to make some tweaks to the generated HTML, CSS, or JavaScript for the requirements of the project you're working on. That said, give Macaw a chance to impress you. The software is young, and really, at a few years old, so is the discipline of responsive web design. Allowing yourself the chance to work in a more visual way, instead of having to type everything out, can be liberating and can allow you to approach your work from a different perspective.

On a more nitty-gritty level, letting Macaw do the work means also using its features as much as possible. So if there's something you can do in Macaw to make an element look the way you want to, such as using its Effects palette to create shadows instead of using background images, consider using those features. All current browsers support (or at least mostly support) the CSS features that Macaw generates. If you need to add polyfills to support older browsers, do it later (you can add CSS workarounds in the Head & Tail area of Macaw's Publish Settings if needed). While you're in Macaw, you might as well let it do what it does so you can concentrate on being creative and clever in your own right.

### Polyfill? Is that some sort of parrot pun, you bird nerd?

Polyfill is a term for the workarounds web developers use, via CSS or JavaScript hacks, or whatever means, to fill the gaps in functionality that older browsers are missing.

# 6

# Let's Build a Prototype

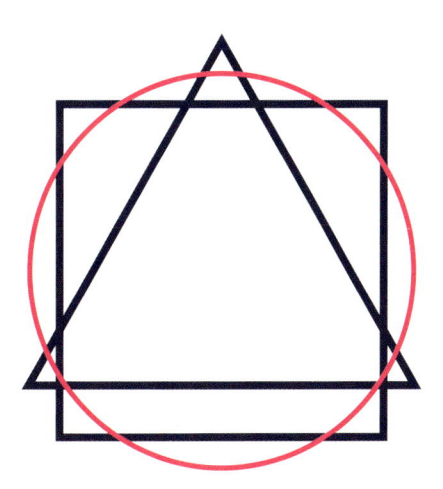

You've seen an overview of the user interface of Macaw, including where all the tools are and what they're generally for. Now we'll walk you through a basic prototyping/wireframing process to get a feel for how these things work in practice. A big part of putting together a website is making boxes, putting them in the right places on a page, and then filling them with content and decorating them. In this chapter, you'll work with many boxes. You're not going to build a complete page in this chapter (we'll do that later), but you'll start using Macaw and developing an understanding of how the tools work.

## Setting the Breakpoints

As we've mentioned, setting at least a couple of breakpoints at the beginning, even if you're going to change them, focuses your design, forcing you to keep in mind that everything changes with the size of the viewport. Remember, the default, largest breakpoint is not synonymous with the largest that your design could be. Let's look at an example.

**NOTE** The term *viewport*, for our purposes, means the part of the canvas (the HTML document) that's currently visible.

Create a new project, and set the initial breakpoint to 900px, or however large or small it needs to be so you can fit your entire canvas on the screen with all panels and tools visible. Leave the grid at its default. Make sure that Toggle Snap (⌘-U/Ctrl-U) is checked in the View menu.

Now create two elements. Select the Element tool (or press R on the keyboard), and drag a box from the leftmost edge of the canvas (not the grid) to the rightmost edge. It should look something like **Figure 6.1** (note that the Dimensions palette shows its width as 100%).

**Figure 6.1**
This element extends from one edge of the canvas to the other, and its width is set to 100%.

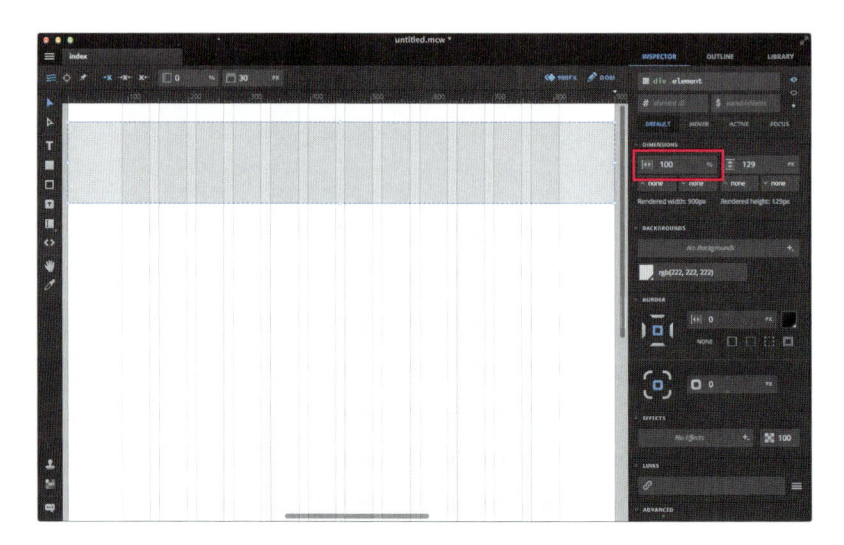

**Chapter 6:** Let's Build a Prototype  49

Now press R to select the Element tool again, and create a second element below the first one, this time creating it from the leftmost grid line to the rightmost. You'll see the grid lines turning green as you mouse over them before you start drawing (and while you're drawing). This lets you know the element will snap to those lines. When you're done, you should have something like **Figure 6.2**.

**Figure 6.2** You should have a full-canvas element and a full-grid element.

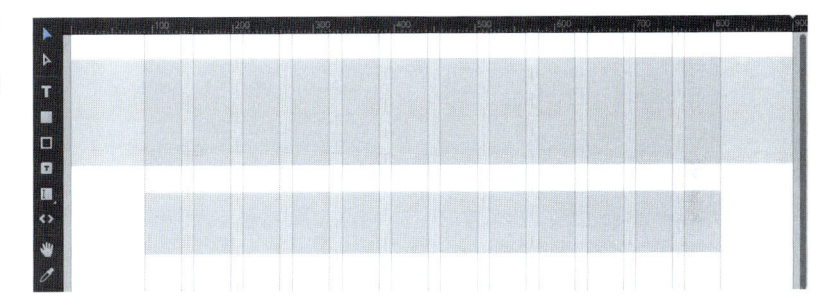

If you drag the resize handle to the left, you'll see everything "squeeze down." The elements stick with the lines they snapped to when you drew them (on either the canvas or the grid).

> **NOTE** As you'll see later, the elements don't technically snap to these lines. They're sized and positioned in such a way that they appear to—which is almost as good.

Now choose Publish from the File menu to open Macaw's preview window. You'll be prompted to save your project if you haven't already done so, and the Preview window will open. This causes Macaw to generate your project's HTML, CSS, and JavaScript (if applicable) in a folder with the same name as your project, but for now we just care about the Preview window. If you make the Preview window as big as you can, you'll see that the design doesn't keep a fixed width; the full-width element takes up 100 percent of the preview window's width, and the grid-snapped element takes up a smaller portion (80 percent in the case of the current, default grid). A small version of this appears in **Figure 6.3**.

**Figure 6.3** Here's the preview in the small version. Resize it and you'll see the top element stick to the window edges no matter how big it gets.

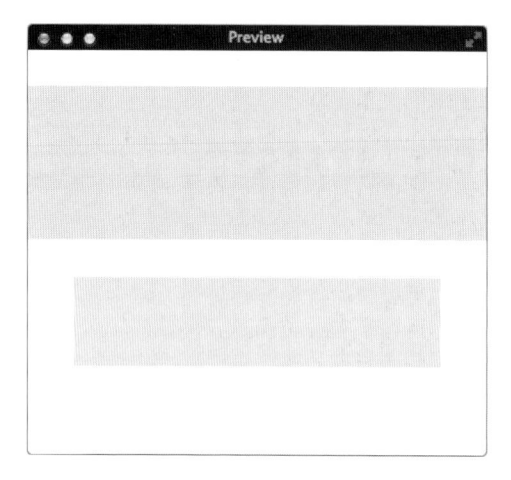

So, that initial breakpoint doesn't set the maximum width of your design, but it gives you (ideally) a sensible largest dimension to design to.

What breakpoints you use will depend on the project, but setting at least one reasonably large one that fits on your display, along with one or two smaller ones, is a good starting point. For now, let's add a second breakpoint at 480px. Make sure no element is selected (you can click the canvas to do this); then click the plus sign in the Breakpoints palette (see **Figure 6.4**) to add the new one.

**Figure 6.4** The Breakpoints palette is available when nothing is selected on the canvas. Click the plus to add breakpoints.

Macaw immediately switches to the new breakpoint, and you can see in **Figure 6.5** that the elements behave the same way they did at the default breakpoint, snapped to the canvas and the same grid lines they were before. When you create a new breakpoint, Macaw treats everything on the canvas the same as it does at the next-largest breakpoint. In this case, that's the default breakpoint.

With some breakpoints set, let's look at the grid.

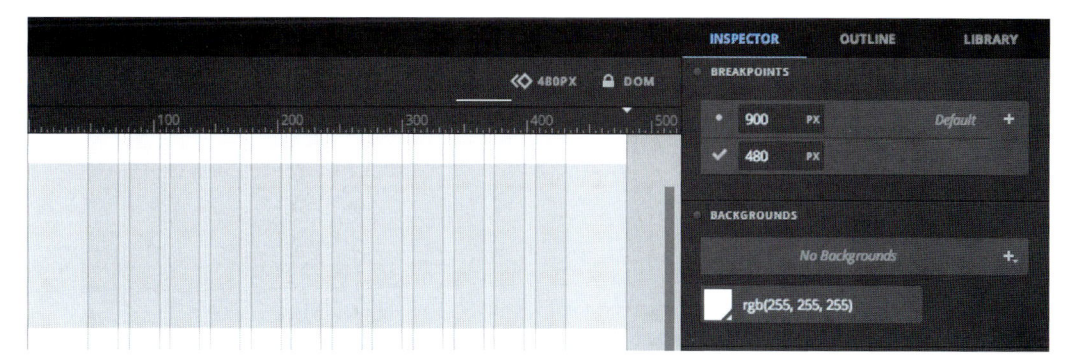

**Figure 6.5** Macaw switches to newly created breakpoints immediately.

# Setting Up the Grid

The grid goes hand in hand with your breakpoints for establishing your design's framework, but it also has a huge influence on how the elements on your canvas behave. Once again, the precise settings you want are going to vary from project to project, but let's look at how changing the grid, and your elements' relationship to the grid, makes a page behave. We're going to set up the grid at the default breakpoint, see how to set up a fixed-width grid, and observe how the grid interacts with breakpoints.

Switch to the default breakpoint and use the View > Center Canvas command (⌘-Opt-O on Mac/Ctrl-Alt-0), which centers the canvas.

With the grid, you can set the number and width of columns and the spacing between them. You can keep it flexible (that is, its width is set as a percentage of the canvas width), as it is by default, or you can make the grid a fixed size in pixels. Also, remember that you can change grid settings at each breakpoint.

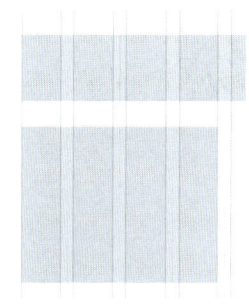

**Figure 6.6** The first element spans four grid columns.

To start, let's add three more elements to the canvas, each spanning four columns of the grid. Select the Element tool and create the first one, as shown in **Figure 6.6**.

To create the others, use the Duplicate command in the Edit menu (⌘-D/Ctrl-D). Note that when you duplicate an element in Macaw, the duplicate is immediately attached to your cursor, so you can drag it into place and click to drop it where it belongs. Use this command again to create another copy, and put it in place. The end result should look like **Figure 6.7**.

**Figure 6.7**
Three elements, top-aligned, spanning four columns each.

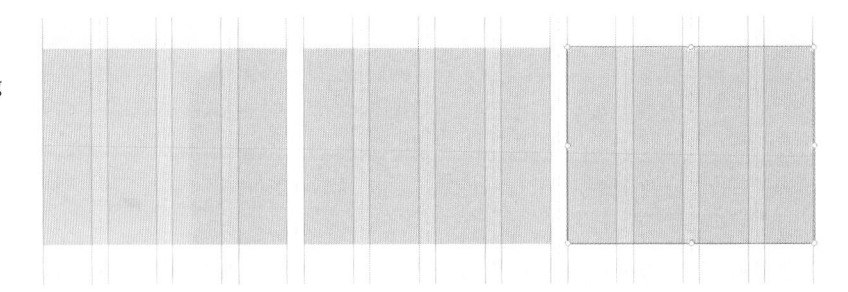

Let's give each of these its own color to help see what we're doing. Because we're working in web terms, we're setting a background color for the element (as opposed to a fill color you'd use in a graphics app). You'll find Backgrounds about halfway down the Inspector on the right side (see **Figure 6.8**). This element has two parts: images and gradients on top, with a flat color below.

**Figure 6.8**
The Backgrounds palette, with images and gradients above and color below.

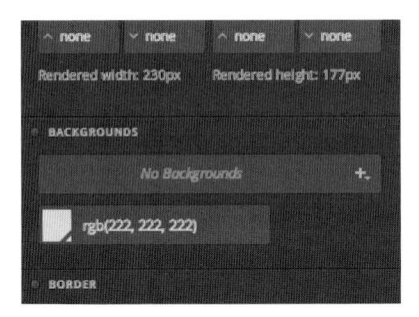

Macaw supports CSS3, which means you can have multiple background images (or gradients) on a single element—hence the plus button on the right side of the first box. For now, you'll use flat color. You can type a CSS-compatible color specification (for example, a hex code like #336699, or an `rgb()`, `rgba()`, `hsl()`, or `hsla()` spec) directly into the text field, or you can click the color swatch and choose one visually using the Color Picker (see **Figure 6.9**).

**Chapter 6:** Let's Build a Prototype 53

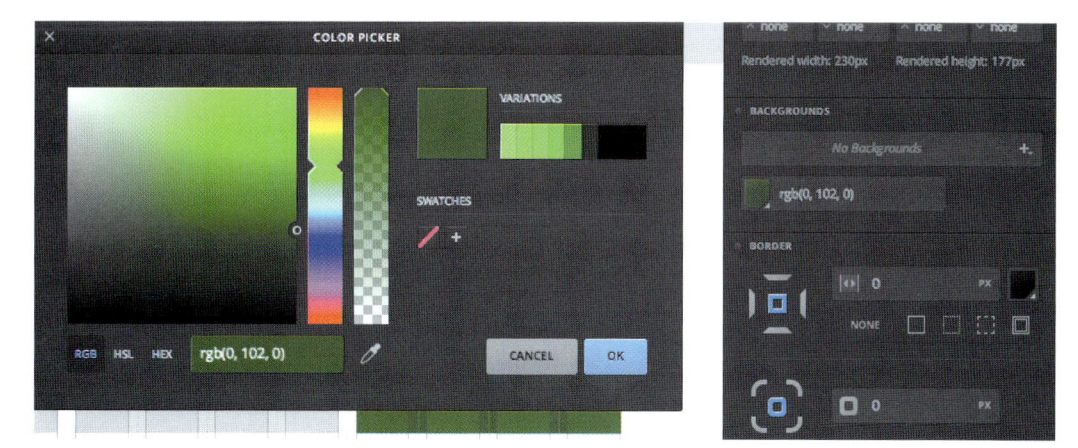

**Figure 6.9** As the background color is changed, the swatch in the palette, and the element on the canvas, both update.

The Color Picker lets you choose a color visually and has a few extra flourishes as well. You can see the RGB, HSL, and Hex color codes by clicking those labels and watching the text field update. The Eyedropper tool (below the Opacity slider) lets you sample the color of anything in Macaw by clicking the eyedropper icon and then the item you want to sample from (you can sample from anything in the Macaw window, not just the canvas). You can save colors as swatches that can be used throughout your project (click the plus button to add a new one). The Variations tiles let you choose a similar color with a darker or lighter value; keep in mind that clicking one of those tiles instantly updates the active color (and therefore creates a new set of variations).

After choosing a color, click OK. Give the other two elements in this row different colors, resulting in something like **Figure 6.10**.

**Figure 6.10**
When experimenting with layout, or just prototyping, having different colors helps make it clear which element is which, in case something gets out of place.

Now that you have some elements to play with, let's change the grid. First, you'll change it so the grid extends pretty much the whole way, with gutters. By default, the gutters are set to 2% (although there's no unit displayed, the gutter is always a percentage), so if you want 2% gutters on each side, that leaves 96% for the grid width. The settings are shown in **Figure 6.11**.

**Figure 6.11** The grid settings needed to make the grid extend the full page width (with gutters on both sides). Note the lack of units on the gutter setting—it is always a percentage.

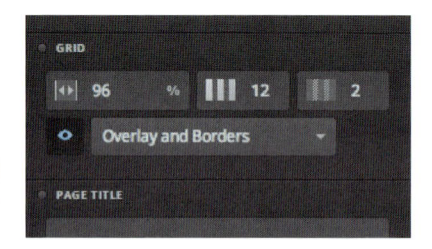

Notice that the elements on the canvas don't resize to the new grid lines when you change the grid settings. Grid snapping is used to help set element widths, but if you change the grid, it's up to you to reset the elements. Do that now, and preview the results to make sure everything works (that is, the three colored boxes maintain their spatial relationship). If it looks like **Figure 6.12**, you're in good shape so far.

**Figure 6.12** Everything in the preview window looks as it should.

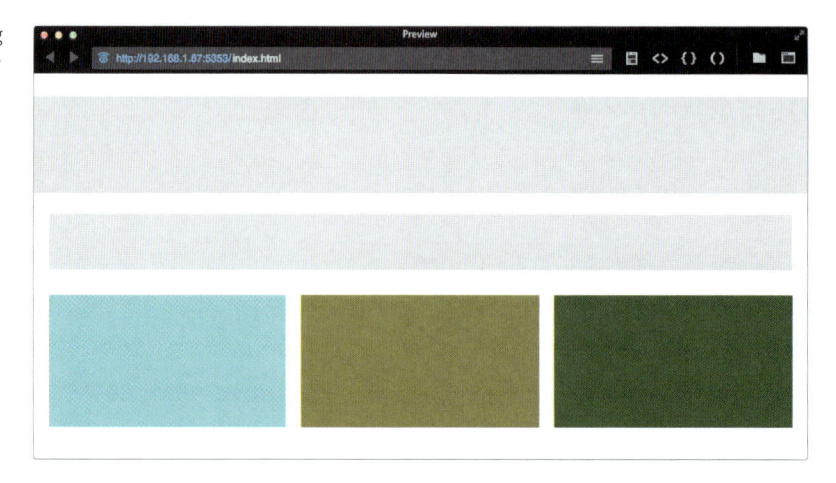

It's often desirable to limit the maximum width of the main content area on a site while still allowing background elements to span the full width of the window. In its current state, this prototype is close, but if you

**Chapter 6:** Let's Build a Prototype  55

really want to do this, it will take some adjusting and you'll have to use the grid to enforce that maximum fixed width.

To make a fixed-width grid, change the units to pixels by clicking the percent sign in the Grid palette and changing it to px. The width percentage is replaced with its equivalent in pixels, which you can change to whatever you like. Note that you can't currently change the number and units at the same time; if you try, you'll likely see some wacky results. Fortunately, it's not hard to recover. For now, let's use a grid width of 800px. Reset the four grid-contained blocks so they're snapped to the new grid line positions.

If you resize the canvas at this point, you'll see that the blocks don't snap to the grid borders but the grid stays at 800px wide (and runs off the canvas if the canvas is narrower than 800px), as shown in **Figure 6.13**.

**Figure 6.13** The first element is still 100 percent wide, but the other elements aren't aligned with the grid lines in the fixed grid.

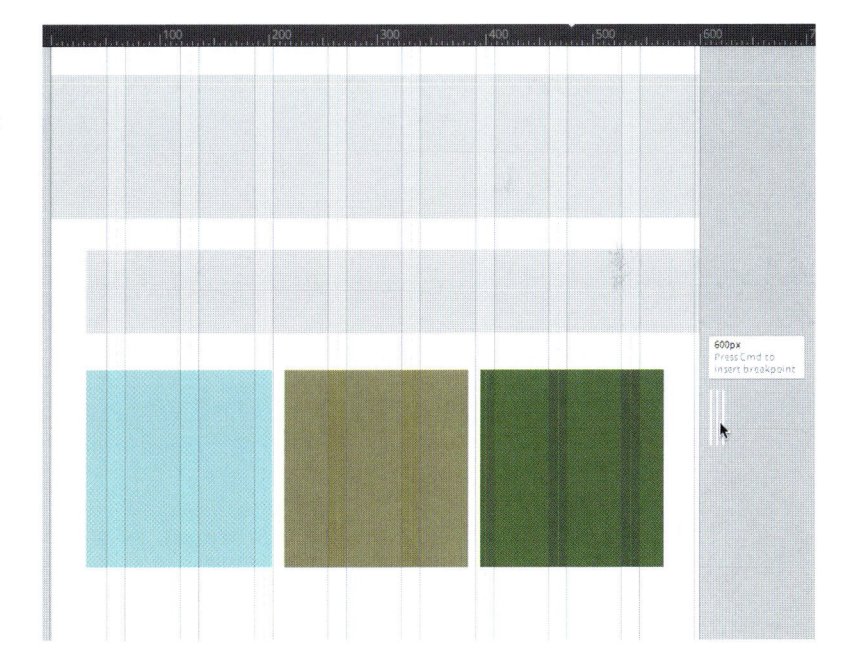

The grid is used only for snapping elements into place; what happens to elements on the page is a separate concern. We're going to look at positioning in more detail in "Putting Elements into Place" later in this chapter, so for now just note that the grid is always 800px wide at this point.

Now let's see how the grid and breakpoints interact. Reset the grid width unit to %, and switch to the smaller breakpoint. It's possible (from all the messing around with the grid we've been doing) that the boxes will jump around when you do this; if they do, just drag them back into alignment. Green guidelines (as shown in **Figure 6.14**) will appear when you get the edges close to alignment with those of other boxes.

**Figure 6.14** Green guidelines show when an element is lined up with grid lines or other elements on the canvas.

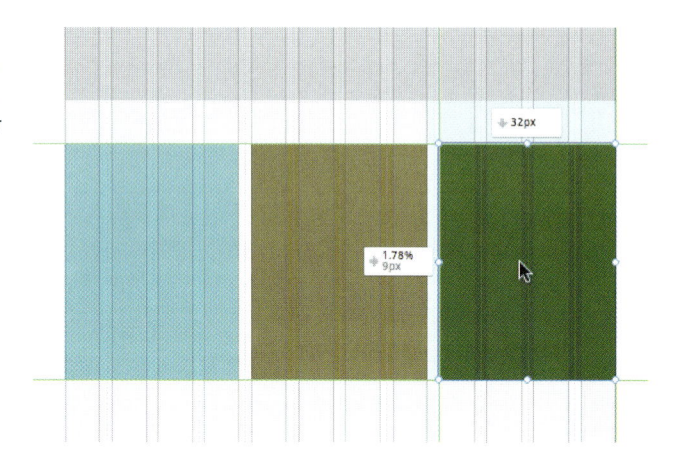

At this smaller width, having 12 columns might be overdoing it. Change the number of columns (the middle of the three grid settings) to 6. It might also be appropriate to use more of the canvas, so reset the width to 96%. The boxes will need to be resized and snapped to this new grid; **Figure 6.15** shows the result.

Click the canvas so you can see the Breakpoint palette again, and switch between the two breakpoints. The canvas will resize to that width, and the grid will change with it.

With these overall parameters in place, you can move on.

**Chapter 6:** Let's Build a Prototype    57

**Figure 6.15**
Six columns is much roomier at this smaller size but still useful.

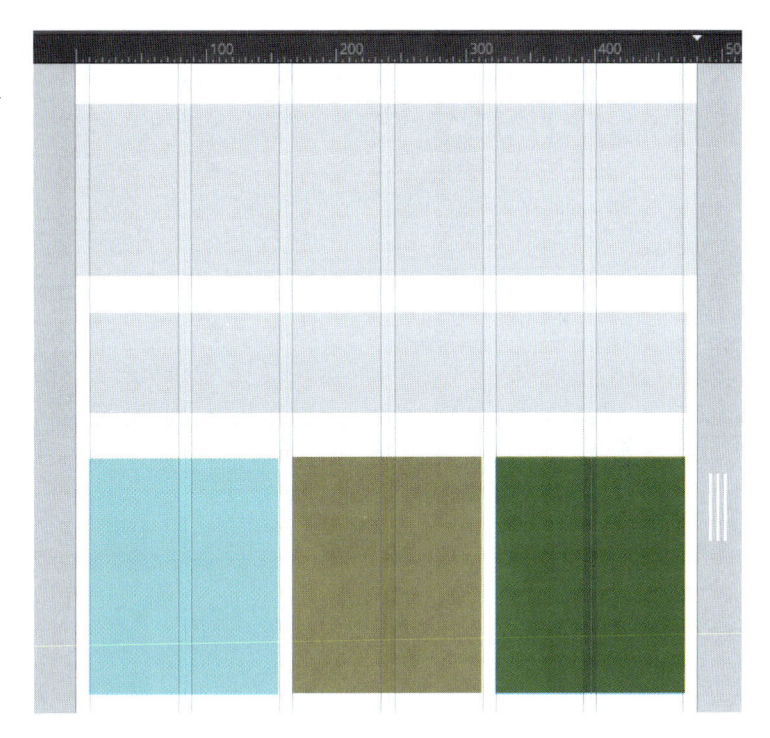

## Working with the Outline

The Outline is a unique and useful feature of Macaw. It has an almost alarming amount of functionality in a modest amount of space, letting you see and change the order in which objects appear on the canvas, specify what elements have others inside them, specify whether elements are displayed at all, identify what HTML tags Macaw will use for each of your elements, and more. In many respects, it's like the Layers palette in a graphics application on performance-enhancing drugs (the good kind, if there is such a thing).

> **TIP** You can switch the right sidebar to the Outline using Opt-O/Alt-O. Opt-I/Alt-I will switch to the Inspector, and Opt-L/Alt-L will switch to the Library.

### An overview of the Outline

Each line of the Outline represents an element on the canvas (see **Figure 6.16**). At this point, you just have five boxes, with no nesting, so it's pretty straightforward. Hovering your mouse over each line will cause the canvas to show an outline surrounding the element you're hovering over (and if you select an item on the canvas, it will be selected in the Outline).

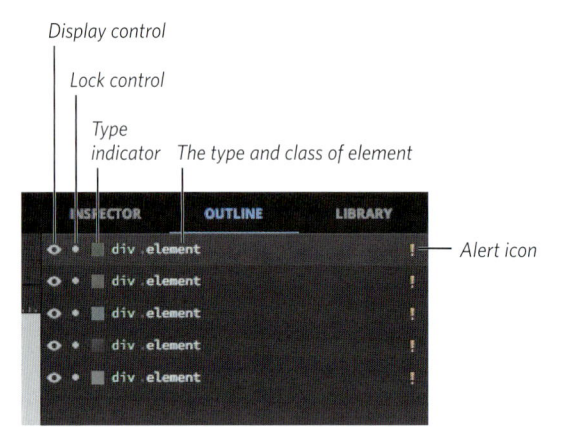

**Figure 6.16** The outline, with its major components annotated.

From left to right, you have the following:

1. **Display control.** By default, elements are visible, indicated by the eye icon (see **Figure 6.17**). Click this once to make the element invisible (in CSS terms, visibility: hidden), turning the eye icon into an outline of an eye. An invisible element is still in the flow of the document, affecting those around it, even if it can't be seen. ⌘-click/Ctrl-click the eye icon to set an element's Display to none, turning the eye icon into the bullet Macaw uses to indicate something is inactive. This hides the element completely and removes it from the flow of the document. Static elements won't move around it, but they will recalculate their positions to account for it not being there anymore. Display settings can vary by breakpoint. These same visibility controls are available in the Inspector at the top right.

**Figure 6.17** The visibility controls available on the Inspector include easy access to all three states.

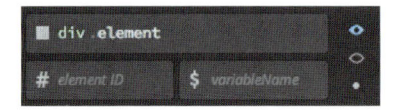

2. **Lock control**. This lets you lock an element to prevent it from being selected but doesn't change what happens during publishing. Click once to lock and again to unlock. Locking is also available via the Lock Selected command in the Elements menu, but the Outline is the only place where you can unlock just one element.

3. **Type indicator**. This indicates the type of element, with an icon similar to the corresponding tool icon in the toolbar. We just have generic boxes, so the icon is a little solid box that is tinted, just slightly, with the background color of that element. Clicking this preview icon will scroll the canvas so that element is as visible as possible.

4. **The type and class of element**. Both of these will be used in the HTML generated by Macaw. Different element types will have different default classes, but you can set your own (including no class) by double-clicking the element type or class (they become editable as one). These use CSS syntax, so you can add multiple classes by separating each one with periods like this:

    `div.menu.horizontal`

    `blockquote.testimonial.border-box.one-class-too-many`

    Being able to set your own classes is handy for working with JavaScript or if you need to do more sophisticated CSS work after publishing. If you plan to use a framework like Bootstrap, Foundation, or the next hot thing that comes down the line, you can use the class names those frameworks offer on elements to get their styles for free later (though not on the Macaw canvas—you can't directly import external CSS or JavaScript libraries).

**NOTE** Classes are optional, but the element type is not. If you try to remove the element type, Macaw will restore whatever was there before.

**NOTE** The classes in the outline aren't the only ones that will appear on your elements. Macaw's CSS-generating engine will add whatever other classes it needs to in order to make everything work. You can't stop it unless you open up the published HTML and CSS after the fact.

> **TIP** When you're in tag and class editing mode, you can press Tab and Shift-Tab to move up and down the elements and set the tag and class(es) of each in turn. When you're done, press Return/Enter.

5. **Alert icon**. You might see an orange exclamation mark on the far right of a line (as this project currently stands, you probably have one on each line). Such a mark indicates a warning, whose full text you can see by hovering your cursor over the exclamation mark. In our experience, the most common warnings are for "generic semantics" and using negative margins.

### *The Outline in action*

Let's get rid of the semantics warnings by setting some names for each of these elements. Double-click the one listed first (it might not be the topmost box), and give it a sensible class name. Using good semantics means giving elements tags and classes that reflect their purpose on the page—Macaw will try to autocomplete anything you type with a list of HTML5 tags to help you make a sensible choice, but what you use is up to you. Don't sweat it too much in this generic project, but in your real projects that will go on the Internet, good semantics are helpful for search engine optimization (SEO) and accessibility and are worth the small investment of time they'll take to establish.

As you work through renaming these elements, you can also drag them into a sensible top-to-bottom order, with the header first, followed by the other elements. As you're dragging, note that you can nest elements within others by dragging one line of the outline on top of another, showing a drag target that's a border around the containing element (see **Figure 6.18**). Right now, you just want to place items in a certain order, which means making sure the drag target is a line where you want the element to go (see **Figure 6.19**).

If you're working in a nondefault breakpoint while attempting to drag elements around in the Outline, you'll be prompted to switch to the default breakpoint. The order elements appear in the Outline affects all breakpoints; we'll talk more about that when we discuss positioning in the next section.

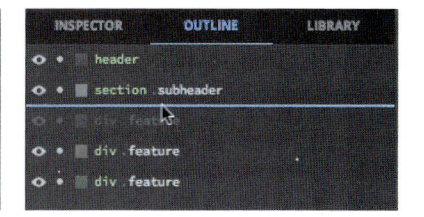

**Figure 6.18** When an item is outlined, the dragged item will become a child of the outlined element (which changes that element into a container if necessary).

**Figure 6.1** When you see a line, that means the item dragged will be moved between two items.

Each element now uses custom tags we've selected, so there are no more warnings about generic semantics, and we can move on to exploring how laying out elements works.

## Putting Elements into Place

Macaw can save a lot of hassle, but it can't read minds (at least, not yet). When elements are added to the canvas, Macaw sets up some initial positioning to make them stay where you placed them, but you'll need to understand how it works more deeply to make sure that they behave how they should as things change (unexpected behaviors when resizing or previewing can happen all the time on the web and in Macaw). As the saying goes, the only constant is change (especially on the web). We might go "into the weeds" a little bit here, so if there's too much talking about moving boxes around, you can always come back to this section.

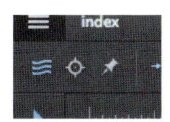

**Figure 6.20** Static positioning is the one indicated by the wave icon (static positioning means elements flow one after another).

### Static positioning and flow

Macaw gives you three methods for controlling element positioning: static, absolute, and fixed. These map quite closely to their CSS equivalents (so knowing CSS is generally helpful, but not necessary, in employing them effectively). These methods are indicated by the three icons shown in the options bar when an element is selected, as you can see in **Figure 6.20**. Static is the default in Macaw (as it is in your typical web browser).

When an element is selected, Macaw shows indicators for that element's position on the page. These appear along the edges of the element used to set that element's location and disappear after a brief delay. Every element can have distinct positioning, but elements can also affect one another. This is especially true for static positioning, so let's look at an example.

Click the topmost box, the one that spans the whole canvas, and you'll see one indicator on top, showing how far it is from the top of the canvas (as shown in **Figure 6.21**). This will translate to a top margin in the generated CSS.

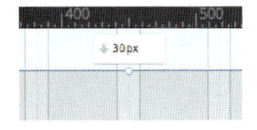

**Figure 6.21** This element is 30px from the top of the canvas.

Click the second box, and you'll see one indicator on the left side and one on the top, as shown in **Figure 6.22**. The left one shows how far that box is from the left edge of the canvas, and it's shown both as a percentage and what that percentage computes to as pixels for the current canvas size.

These indicators disappear after a short delay, but their values are always visible in the options bar when an element is selected (see **Figure 6.23**). The left box shows the horizontal offset; the right box shows the vertical. The vertical offset is always set in pixels; the horizontal offset can be changed from the default of percentage by clicking the unit label (see **Figure 6.24**).

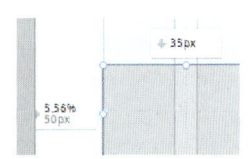

**Figure 6.22** Indicators here show the left and top margins of the selected element.

**Figure 6.23** The margins settings for a selected element.

**Figure 6.24** The margins settings for a selected element. The unit is changeable for the horizontal value, as they are in many fields throughout Macaw.

> **NOTE** These offsets translate into CSS margins, so we'll use the terms interchangeably.

We don't want to go down the rabbit hole of explaining every detail of CSS positioning here, but this simple explanation should work for now. In static positioning, every static element gets its position based on where previous elements on the page are (from top to bottom, left to right). Things get more complicated when you have nested elements, but that's a start. The topmost box only needs an offset from the top edge of the canvas to be placed where drawn, so that's all it gets, whereas the second box needs an offset from the first box's bottom edge and from the left edge of the canvas.

If you click each of the three colored boxes in turn, you'll see a top offset from the bottom edge of the previous box and left offsets from the left edge of the canvas or the previous box. The horizontal offsets are expressed as percentages, so they flex as the page is resized.

One more thing: If you have Maintain Flow checked and select multiple items to move, each item will nudge or pudge the amount you specify, which can cascade into items after them in the document flow. This is probably best observed in action, so give it a try and get a feel for it.

## Maintain Flow on Nudge/Pudge

While we're on the static positioning subject, if you click the canvas, you'll see the Maintain Flow On Nudge/Pudge check box in the options bar, as shown in **Figure 6.25**.

**Figure 6.25** The Maintain Flow On Nudge/Pudge check box, which is enabled by default.

This check box controls how Macaw reacts when you move (nudge) or resize (pudge) elements with the arrow keys. Click the top box and press the down arrow (if you don't see much difference, hold the Shift key to move in 10-pixel increments). With the box checked, every other item on the page moves down with it, maintaining their relationships in the document flow. They're all statically positioned, so they all move as shown in **Figure 6.26**.

*sidebar continues on next page*

## Maintain Flow on Nudge/Pudge *continued*

**Figure 6.26** With Maintain Flow enabled, moving the top element with the arrow keys, or via the text fields, will shift other statically positioned elements.

Likewise, if you hold the Option/Alt key while using the arrow keys, the item will resize/pudge (the bottom or right edges, as appropriate, will shift in the direction of the arrow), as shown in **Figure 6.27**. You can use the Shift key to change the increment from 1 to 10px here as well. Maintain Flow has the same effect here: If the resizing happens in a direction where other statically positioned elements exist, they will move.

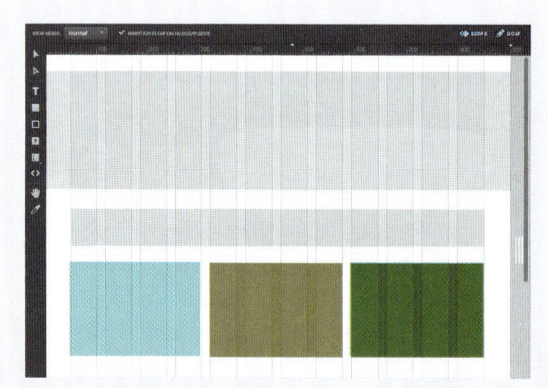

**Figure 6.27** With Maintain Flow enabled, resizing the top element with the arrow keys or via text fields will shift other statically positioned elements.

Now click the canvas, deselect the Maintain Flow check box, and try using the arrow keys to move and resize the top box. This time, only that selected box moves. Essentially, this makes the arrow keys behave the same as the mouse for moving and resizing purposes.

## Position and breakpoints

You can resize and move elements at different breakpoints. Let's make the page smaller and try this. Drag the resize handle to the left to shrink the canvas down to 480 or fewer pixels, and let go. The canvas will snap up to the 480px breakpoint.

Let's say it makes sense for the three colored boxes to go from three across to a single column at this size. Reposition them accordingly. Because there's no other content yet, you can make them strips of color, or make them bigger if you like, but the result should be arranged like **Figure 6.28**.

**Figure 6.28**
One possible arrangement of the elements in this new breakpoint.

Drag the resize handle to the right, and you'll see the elements jump back to their default positions and sizes. Just like that, you're making a responsive page! Change back to the smaller breakpoint by dragging the resize handle or clicking the 480px breakpoint in the Inspector. Click one of the colored boxes, and notice that the offsets in the options bar, and the element's height and width in the Dimensions palette, are all outlined in blue, as shown in **Figure 6.29**.

**Figure 6.29**
Two examples of options with blue borders showing, indicating that there are different settings on that element at different breakpoints.

Hover your mouse over the width field, and a popover will appear (see **Figure 6.30**). With this popover, you can switch to different breakpoints by clicking the top portion (with the numbers and arrows), or click the values to change the current value used in this breakpoint to the value used in that other one.

**Figure 6.30**
This popover shows the values for an element's width at different breakpoints.

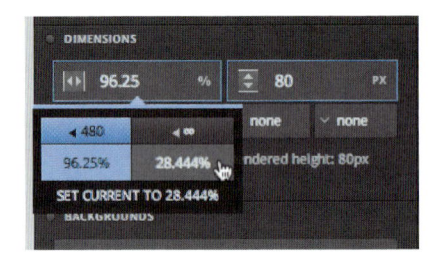

Popovers make it easy to fix mistakes, or just start over and try something else. Macaw lets you change most attributes at different breakpoints, not just size and position, so you'll see these popovers all over Macaw as you start building projects.

### *Fixed position and origins*

Static positioning is flexible, and nice if you're prototyping a theme for a content management system, or another situation where you have elements that could vary in size after publishing. But there are plenty of times when having elements stay in an exact place makes sense, and for that, we have Macaw's other two positioning types: fixed and absolute.

**Chapter 6:** Let's Build a Prototype    **67**

Of the two, absolute positioning is used more often in real work, but fixed is the easier one to see, so we'll start there. Change to the default breakpoint; then select the topmost box, make it black, and drag it to the top of the canvas. This will be the start of a sticky header for sitewide navigation or other elements you want to be visible at all times. In the options bar, click the pushpin icon, which will set this box's positioning to fixed. Several things happen: The outline of the box turns bright green, as does the pushpin button, and the positioning options change, as shown in **Figure 6.31**.

**Figure 6.31** Fixed positioning, indicated by the pushpin, turns all the positioning options bright green.

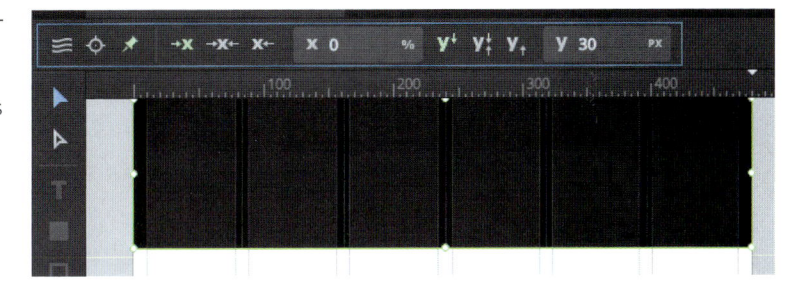

With fixed and absolute positioning, you choose the exact placement of an element, using X and Y coordinates (with the top-left corner as the 0 point). In the case of a fixed-positioned element, it will stay there regardless of how the window scrolls. Try scrolling down and watch the other elements move below the menu.

Sometimes, you might end up in a situation with elements appearing out of their expected order, resulting in something similar to **Figure 6.32**.

**Figure 6.32** The fixed element is meant to be fixed on top of everything else, not below!

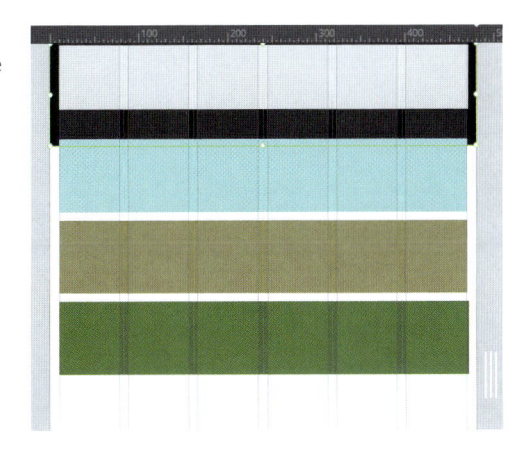

Issues like that can be fixed with the Outline, but you can also use the Send To Front command in the Edit menu. Changing the stacking order of elements (also called the Z index; if the page is flat, with X and Y for horizontal and vertical, Z is the "through the page" axis) in this way is a change to the DOM, so you'll be asked to switch to the default breakpoint. In so doing, the color and positioning changes you've made to that top block are reset, but you can fix that right quick.

## What is this thing called DOM?

The DOM is the Document Object Model, which is what your HTML source code gets turned into by a web browser for the purpose of rendering it, applying CSS styles, attaching JavaScript behaviors, and so forth. Anything that would change your HTML source code will change the DOM, and Macaw restricts such edits to the default breakpoint.

**Figure 6.33** The popover for viewing and copying background color settings.

Use the popovers to copy the settings for the background color and positioning from the 480px breakpoint. Mouse over the background color in the Backgrounds palette and click the black swatch that appears in the popover as shown in **Figure 6.33**.

Do the same for the positioning settings in the options bar, which must be copied all at once like this when the positioning type is different across breakpoints (that is, static now, changing to fixed). The other elements will likely shift when you make this change; they are statically positioned, and changing the first element to fixed will cause them to reflow. Depending on the order in which you've made your moves, Macaw can react differently, not just across pages or projects, but across breakpoints. Don't be alarmed if this happens—you'll just need to move some things around to account for the changes in the flow of the document.

You can now copy the offsets for the second box from the smaller breakpoint as shown in **Figure 6.34**, or move things into place with the mouse.

**Figure 6.34** When the positioning type is different at different breakpoints, the popovers show everything, not just the margins, and if any one piece is to be copied from one to another, all must be copied.

With all this done, you could select the top, black box again and use the Edit > Send To Front command to place it above everything else or instead drag it into place in the Outline. Scroll the window to confirm it works; then switch to the smaller breakpoint again to confirm it works there as well.

> **TIP** Here's another breakpoint-switching trick. In the ruler, you'll see little triangles indicating where the breakpoints are. Mouse over the ruler and the breakpoints will be highlighted—the default, largest one in blue and the smaller ones in gray—with a number labeling which one it is, as shown in **Figure 6.35**. Click the highlighted area to switch to that breakpoint. You can also switch breakpoints using the key commands Shift-[ (next smaller), Shift-] (next larger), and Shift-\ (default, largest).
>
> **Figure 6.35** A breakpoint at 480px. Its gray color shows it's not the default breakpoint.

> **NOTE** Breakpoints can also be resized using the three-line resize handle on the right side of the highlighted area, but to be precise, it's probably better to type the sizes out in the Breakpoints palette.

### Origins

You've seen that a header can be fixed-position, but what about a footer? To make this change, you need to look at the Origin settings for the element. By default, all elements have their positioning origin set to the left and top, which are indicated by the three X icons (X being the horizontal axis), and the Y icons for the vertical axis of fixed- and absolute-positioned elements, as shown in **Figure 6.36** (because they're tied to the document flow, static elements always get their vertical position from other elements, so they don't get a vertical origin setting).

**Figure 6.36** Fixed- and absolute-positioned elements have origin settings for both the X and Y axes, indicated by the sets of X and Y icons.

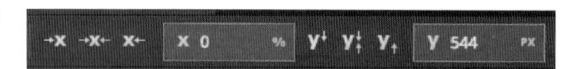

If you simply drag the header down to the bottom of the window and scroll, everything might seem to work at first—the footer stays in place while the other elements move. But if you resize the window vertically, you'll see that the footer doesn't stick to the bottom of the window—it stays a constant distance from the top of the window instead. That's because its positioning origin is the top of the viewport, and the number in the Y box tells Macaw how far from the top of the window to place the element. To get a sticky footer, you need to change the origin to the bottom, so Macaw will know to base the footer's position on the bottom of the viewport. This is the rightmost icon, with the arrow pointing up (see **Figure 6.37**). Click that, and set the offset to 0 by typing it in the Y box and pressing Return/Enter.

**Figure 6.37** A bottom origin, with a Y position of 0, makes an element stick to the bottom of the viewport.

Now you can resize the window vertically and scroll to your heart's content, and the footer will stay right where you want it to be.

The origin can also be set to the middle, which will make your fixed element stay vertically centered. Obscuring the middle of the canvas with a fixed element isn't something you'll probably do a lot, but it could be useful for special effects, hiding and revealing other things on the page as the user scrolls, or for notices that appear at certain times.

**Chapter 6:** Let's Build a Prototype   71

There are also horizontal origin settings. With a full-width element, they don't do anything, so let's change that sticky footer into a sticky square. This could be used for a logo badge or a small navigation element. Change the dimensions of the black rectangle to 100 pixels on each side (you might need to change the units first), and set its X and Y offsets to 0. This will result in a square, shown in **Figure 6.38**, pinned to the upper-left corner of the window and which stays there as you scroll.

**Figure 6.38** Some standard sticky square settings, sonny.

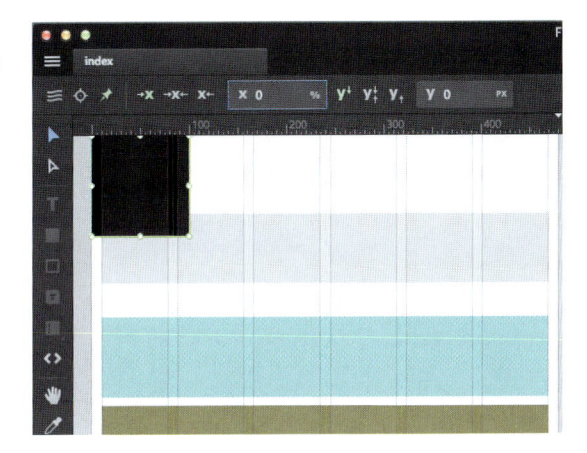

If you want this square to stick to the right edge, as with the sticky footer, just dragging it over there without changing the origin wouldn't work. So first change the origin to the right side (the rightmost X icon), and then drag it over to the right edge, or set the X value back to zero (percent or pixels—either works when it's zero!). If the box should stay centered, click the middle X icon with the two arrows, and there it will stay. Notice that when an item has a centered origin, you can't move it along that axis, but you can resize it, and it will stay centered along that axis even while resizing.

> **NOTE** When you use a centered origin, the offset value for that axis is removed, so you can't center the item horizontally or vertically and then shift it from that position by a certain percentage or number of pixels. You can, however, center a container this way, make it invisible, place elements inside the container, and shift those. Take a look at the upcoming section "Containers," and then try it as a little exercise.

### Absolute positioning

Absolute positioning is set using the crosshair icon in the options bar. When chosen, the positioning options turn light orange, as do the selection borders around the positioned element (see **Figure 6.39**). Set the black square to absolute and watch the changes.

**Figure 6.39** Absolute-positioned elements have an orange border matching their icons in the options bar.

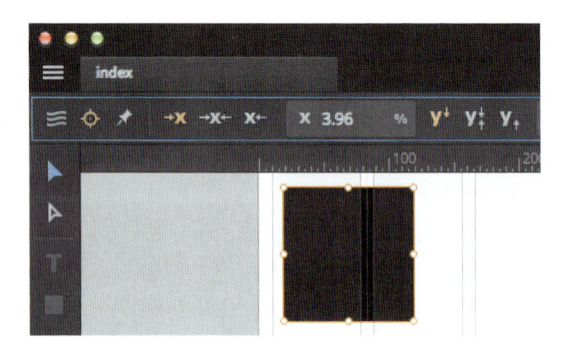

As with fixed, an absolute-positioned element is taken out of the flow of the document, so statically positioned elements will ignore it (and might jump above or below it—this is normal). Everything you know now about origins, positioning, and so forth applies here. The main difference for our purposes is that absolutely positioned elements don't scroll with the page; their offsets come from whatever element contains them, or the canvas if they're not inside a container. If you were writing CSS on your own, you'd find it's more complicated than this, but Macaw deals with all that nonsense for you.

When working with absolutely positioned elements, as with fixed elements, you'll need to think about their stacking order. You can manage this visually the way you might in other graphics apps using the Send To Back (⌘-Shift-[/Ctrl-Shift-[), Send To Front (⌘-Shift-]/Ctrl-Shift-]), Move Backward (⌘-]/Ctrl-]), and Move Forward (⌘-[/Ctrl-[) commands in the Edit menu. You can also use the Outline to drag elements into the correct order. Those arrangement commands still work while the Outline is visible, allowing you to see the elements move around in the DOM at the same time you watch them change on the canvas.

Absolute positioning allows you to make very precise, tightly controlled page layouts. Combined with breakpoints and the flexible grid, you end up with just about everything you'll need to create any layout you can imagine and make it responsive.

### Containers

So far, we've looked only at single elements interacting with one another on the canvas. Now we'll look at containers and how grouping elements together makes life easier. We're going to work with the ever-changing black box, which will become a new header. Start by switching to the default breakpoint, change its positioning back to static, and make sure it extends the full width of the canvas. You also want to make sure there's plenty of room inside, so make it at least 170px tall as shown in **Figure 6.40**.

**Figure 6.40** This black rectangle is 100% wide, 170px tall.

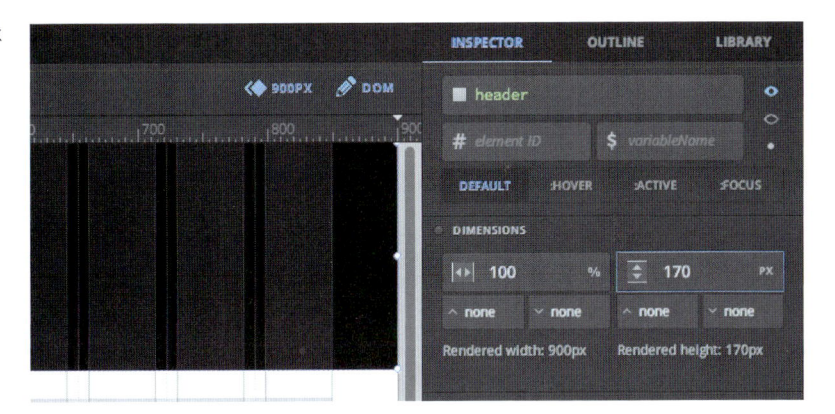

A typical site header will have at least a logo and name. You don't need a real logo for now, so you'll block one in using a generic element. Select the Element tool and create a 100px square—just draw it on the left side of the black box, and then set the width and height precisely by changing its units in the Dimensions palette to pixels and modifying the values. If you like, you can change its background color as well. Finally, you can remove the "element" class, which is no longer needed, and change its ID to #logo, since it's the main logo on the page. When you're done, you'll have the settings in **Figure 6.41**.

So far, this is nothing new, but to get slightly fancy, let's make it a circle. There's no circle tool, but you can make it happen using borders. The Border palette is just below Backgrounds in the Inspector (see **Figure 6.42**), and it lets you control the color, width, and style of all borders at once, or just certain sides.

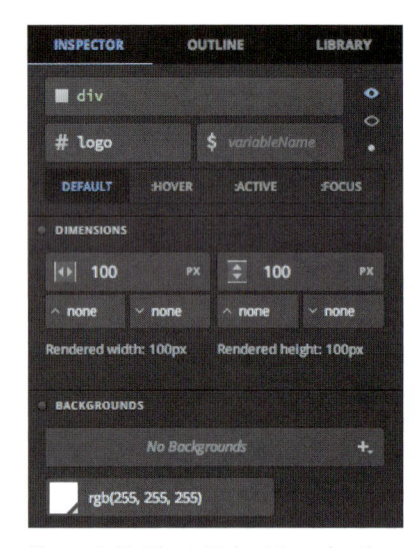

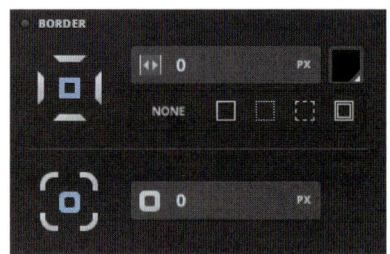

**Figure 6.41** The initial settings for the logo box.

**Figure 6.42** The Border palette.

The top section is for borders; the second section is for the border radius, or how rounded each corner is. Clicking the square in the middle will control all borders (or radii) at once, while clicking the surrounding shapes will control the border or corner as pictured.

To turn a square into a circle, set the border radius of the whole element to at least half the length of one of its sides. You have a 100px square, so setting the border radius to 50px should do it. **Figure 6.43** shows the settings and the result.

**Figure 6.43** The border radius section of the Border palette: setting all four corners to a radius of 50px, and the resulting circle.

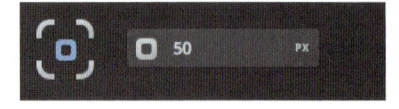

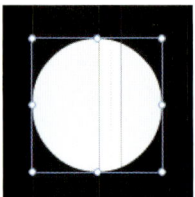

**Chapter 6:** Let's Build a Prototype

Now let's add a company name. Select the Text tool by pressing T on the keyboard or by clicking the T in the toolbar. You can add text to the canvas by clicking once, which is good for single lines (Macaw calls this Point Text), or by dragging out a box for longer runs of text (Macaw calls this Paragraph Text). One line is fine here, so just click to the right of the logo and type "WidgetCo" or whatever you like. Text defaults to black, so you won't see what you're doing at first! The Inspector will go almost blank while you're typing, which is one clue that you're in text editing mode.

When you're done, you have three choices: press ⌘-Return/Ctrl-Enter, click Done in the options bar (clicking Cancel will stop editing and remove the text), or double-click somewhere on the canvas. When you're done, you'll see a little outline surrounding your new text box, and a new Typography palette will show up in the Inspector, as in **Figure 6.44**.

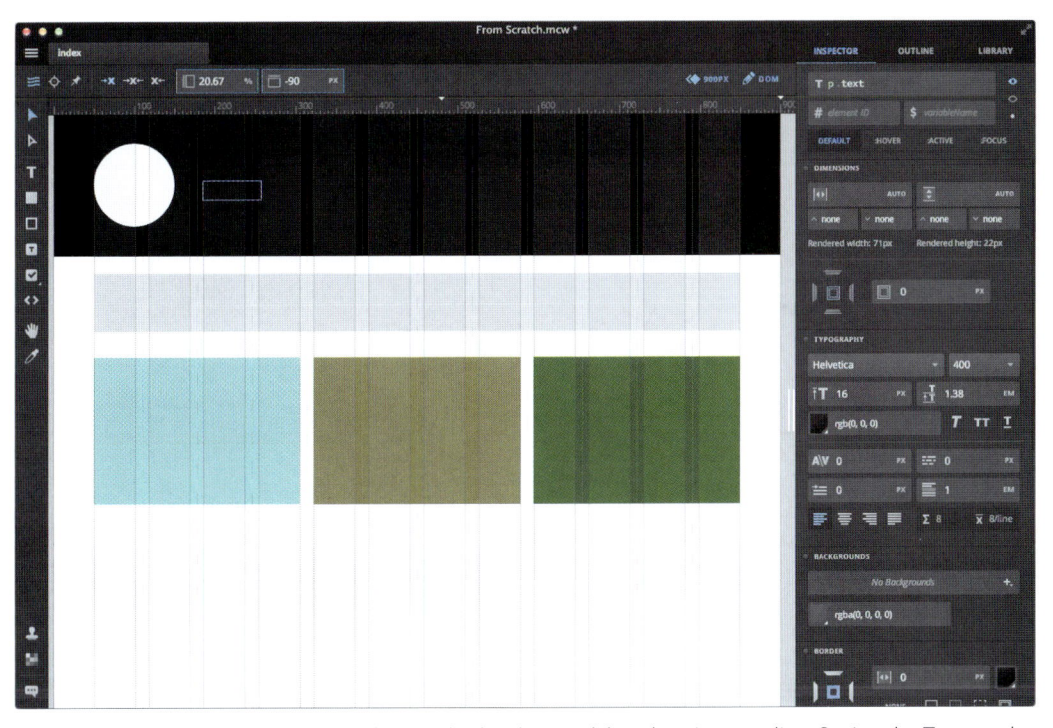

**Figure 6.44** Black text on a black background is hard to read, but there's an outline. Seeing the Typography palette in the Inspector also means a text element is selected.

The Typography palette has all the settings you'd expect: font family, weight, size, leading (aka line height in CSS), color, and the variations/styles of italic/oblique, uppercase, and underline.

> **NOTE** Macaw uses numeric values for the weights. If you're not accustomed to these, 400 is the same as normal, and 700 is bold. The full range in the CSS specification is 100–900; depending on the font you're using, others may be available, but you'll almost always have at least those two.

You'll first want to change the color of the text to anything other than black (so it's actually visible), and then change the font and other settings as needed so it looks good to you. Macaw comes bundled with a selection of free fonts from the Google Fonts library (www.google.com/fonts), and because they're built in, they work in Macaw even without an Internet connection (when published, your project will reference the online copies). These Google fonts are indicated with the red F icon, whereas standard web fonts are indicated with a sort of yin-yang icon, as shown in **Figure 6.45**.

**Figure 6.45**
The Macaw font panel, showing its custom selection of Google fonts and some standard web fonts.

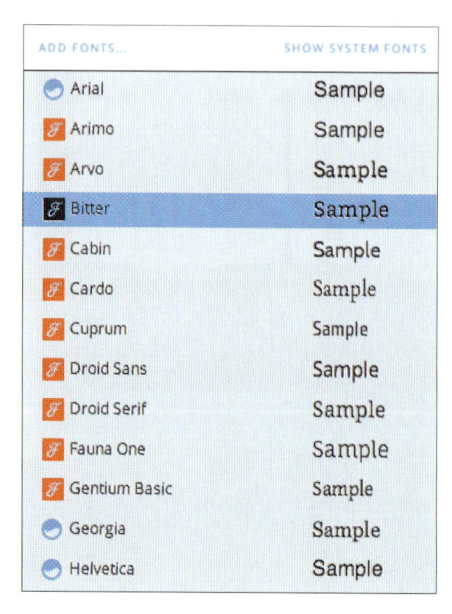

**Chapter 6:** Let's Build a Prototype 77

**NOTE** If you click Show System Fonts, you'll have access to other fonts you have on your system, though you'll probably need to edit the published CSS to make reference to web font versions. See Appendix X for more information on using custom web fonts. If you are a Typekit user, you can add your Typekit fonts to the project by clicking Add Fonts and following the brief instructions.

We're going to start grouping elements shortly, but first take a look at the Outline. There are warnings indicated by the Orange exclamation marks. The company name is the `p.text` element, which has a warning about generic semantics (because it's using the default tag and class), but there's also a warning about negative margins, which you'll see when hovering the mouse over the alert icons, as shown in **Figure 6.46**.

**Figure 6.46** Macaw provides warnings in the Outline about possible problems in the HTML and CSS it will generate.

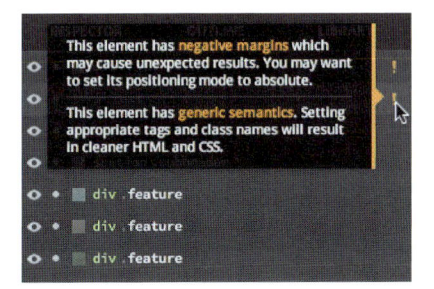

If you click the WidgetCo header, you'll see that its top margin has a negative value. Basically, Macaw is trying to place the item in the flow of the document based on what's nearby, which in this case is the black header bar—a negative top margin means it has been shifted up from its normal flow. Negative margins in CSS are notoriously problematic for older browsers, so avoiding them is a good idea. Changing from static positioning to absolute can help, but so can grouping elements, and since these elements go logically together, you can start with that and see if you need to make further adjustments afterward.

Select the logo circle and the company name by clicking one and Shift-clicking the other (you can also do this in the Outline by clicking one and ⌘-clicking/Ctrl-clicking the other). Now choose Tight Group from the Elements menu, or press ⌘-G/Ctrl-G. This will group the elements as one unit, but that's not the whole story. In a conventional graphics app, grouping lets you select many elements with one click, but in Macaw, creating a group results in another entry in the Outline: a container (grouping involves editing the DOM and is therefore something that can only be done in the default breakpoint). You can also create groups using the Container tool, which we'll look at later.

With the elements grouped like this, they can be positioned together. Look at the Outline again, and you'll see that the warning on the logo has gone away, and the one left on the company name concerned with its generic semantics. Change that to "h1.company-name," which is sensible semantically, and that warning will go away.

There's still a negative margin warning on the container, as well as a warning for generic semantics. First, give the container a sensible class name: "identity." This identity group goes with the black header bar, so you want to group them as well. Using a group command will create yet another element, though, but you don't need one—you just want to nest the identity group inside the header. You can do that in the Outline; drag div.identity onto the header so that the header is outlined, and drop it to change the header into a container. Its icon will change from a filled square to an outlined square, as shown in **Figure 6.47**.

**Figure 6.47** Both the header and div.identity have become containers, as indicated by their outlined icons.

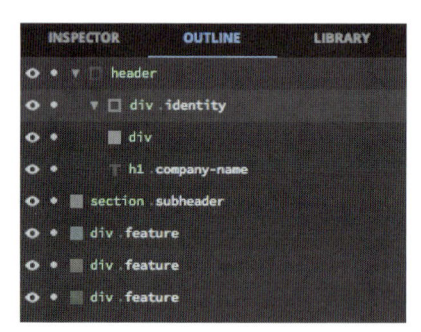

This arrangement makes sense, with all related elements grouped together in the Outline, and Macaw has recalculated the positioning of all the elements so there are no unsightly negative margins. Nice!

If the default selection tool is active (that's the top arrow in the toolbar), you'll find you can't select individual pieces of the header anymore, just the entire group at once. If you want to make changes to elements within a container, you can use the Direct Selection tool (type A to make it active), or switch to the Outline and click the item there.

You can also double-click a container to edit its contents (double-clicking to edit is a technique that works throughout Macaw). When you're editing "inside" an element this way, there are two ways to see what you're doing. The first is a footer that appears at the bottom of the window (see **Figure 6.48**), showing arrows indicating what group or element you're currently editing. You can click any of these items to go up to that level and edit what's inside (the Escape key will also take you up one level). Clicking "body" will take you back to the canvas (which is equivalent to the HTML body tag). It's possible to get a little lost and wonder why you can't edit something, so watch for this footer to help you stay oriented.

The Outline also updates as you descend into containers; it fades out other elements to focus on just the ones you're working with, as shown in **Figure 6.49**.

When you're done working inside a container, double-clicking anywhere on the canvas outside the container will get you out again.

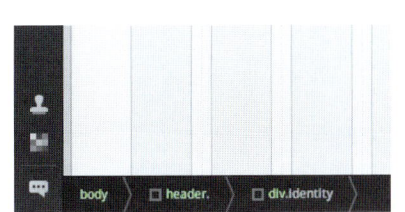

**Figure 6.48** This footer shows you which containers you're currently editing in and lets you go up one or more levels by clicking their names.

**Figure 6.49** The current editing context is div.identity, and everything outside that container is disabled in the Outline.

## Workflow recommendation for containers and content

When building up a page, you can start with content (such as text, images, form elements, and so on) or containers. If you start with content, you'll end up needing to group the elements into containers at some point, and if you start with containers, of course you'll need to add some content. Macaw supports either way of working just fine.

If you start with containers, it is generally a good idea to double-click them for editing before starting to add content, as opposed to creating elements on top of the container and moving them inside afterward. Creating elements inside the container prevents Macaw from using negative margins to position the new elements, helping avoid warnings and unexpected layout quirks on the canvas. Once again, however you want to work, Macaw can support it (indeed, you'll see both in this book), but avoiding negative margins is a good idea, and starting inside a container as early as possible can help avoid them.

If you create empty containers and later move them in the Outline, they might get turned into regular elements, which cannot be double-clicked for editing. To convert an element into a container, select it and use Elements > Tight Group (⌘/Ctrl-G).

Before you switch to the smaller breakpoint, let's try resizing the canvas to see how everything behaves. What you see appears in **Figure 6.50**.

To figure out what's wrong, you'll find it's helpful to set a temporary breakpoint. This is one you don't need long term; it lets you freeze the canvas at a particular size while you sort out a problem. Resize the canvas to the size where the issue appears, and tap ⌘/Ctrl. Macaw will ask if you want to set a breakpoint at that width, and you can click Yes.

In this case, the issue is the header's width. It's currently set to a percentage, about half the grid, which means it can't always fit what's inside. You can either make that container the full width of the grid to make sure it always (or mostly anyway) fits what's inside, or convert the percentage size to pixels. For now, with nothing else in the header, setting it to the full width of the grid is fine, so make that change by dragging or setting the value in Dimensions. Because you're working at a temporary, smaller breakpoint, you'll need to switch to the default and copy the same change there. You can also use the popover, as shown in **Figure 6.51**.

**Figure 6.50** This is not the desired effect when the window gets smaller.

**Figure 6.51** You can use the popover to copy the element's width to the default breakpoint.

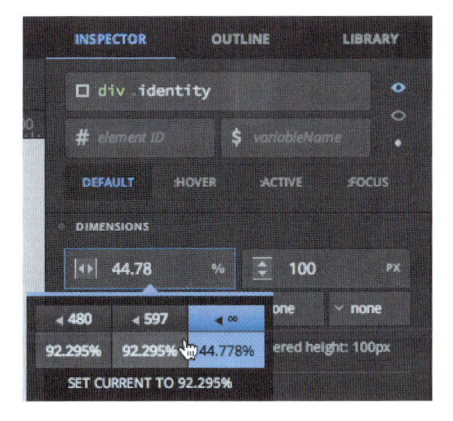

You may want to tweak the spacing some more, but for our purposes, this is working well. The logo doesn't get all weird while you resize the canvas anymore, and you don't see any more bad behavior, so we you delete the temporary breakpoint and take a look at the smaller breakpoint. Switch to that using the ruler or by choosing it in the Inspector. As you can see in **Figure 6.52**, it definitely needs work.

**Figure 6.52** This is kind of a mess.

Start by selecting the black header box and dragging it into place, extending the full width of the canvas. The other elements inside will move with it, which might look a little weird, but that's okay. Switch to the Outline, choose the identity container, and reset its dimensions and positioning so it fits (as in **Figure 6.53**)—we find that using the text fields for this is easier, since sometimes items have shifted off-canvas into weird places.

**Figure 6.53** The identity box after being restored to an at least partially sensible state.

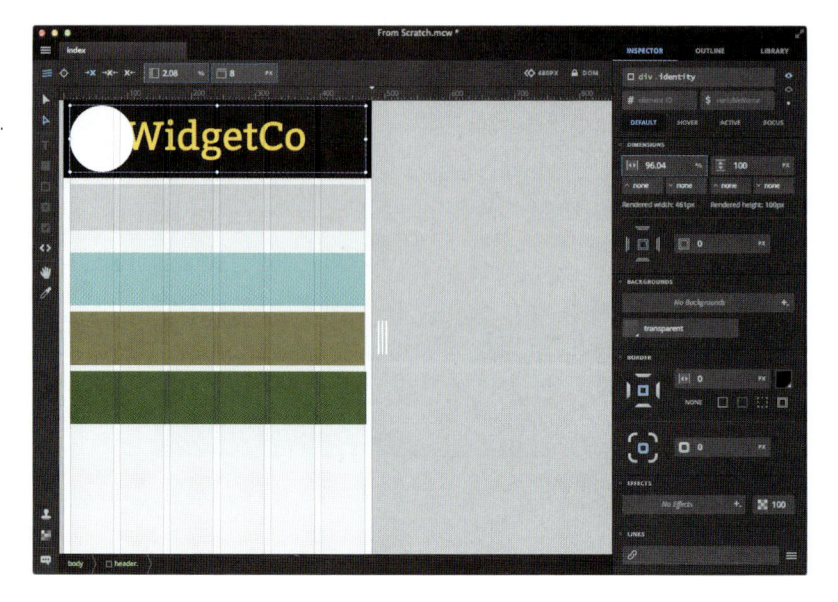

**Chapter 6:** Let's Build a Prototype  83

> **TIP** If containers have become too big for the canvas, you can use the Expand and Fit To Children commands in the Elements menu. Expand will cause a container to widen (or if it's larger than the canvas, contract) until it just fills the canvas, whereas Fit To Children will set the container's width and height exactly as big as they need to be to fit the elements contained within.

Now you can edit the elements in each group and move things into place. As you do so, Macaw will recompute everything it needs to, and as long as none of the elements overlap, you should see all warnings about negative margins disappear. **Figure 6.54** shows the result at this point.

**Figure 6.54** The identity header is readable, and everything is in place.

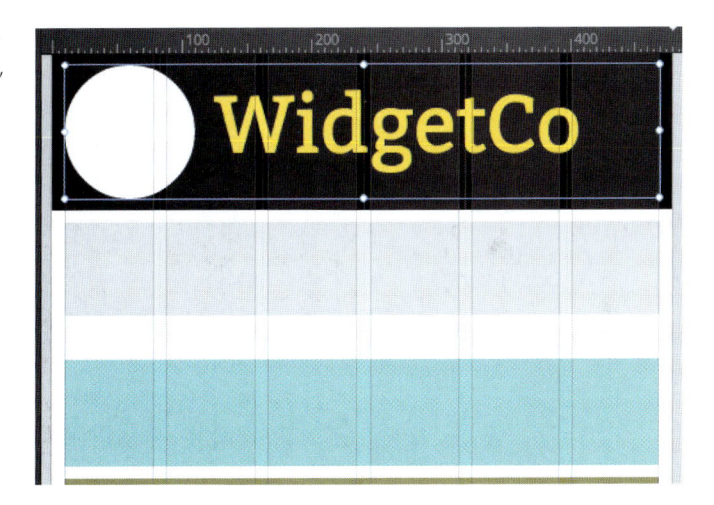

Let's make the identity group a little smaller and center it. Use the Direct Selection tool to select the logo circle, and drag it to a smaller size (hold Shift while dragging to keep it a circle instead of turning into a rounded rectangle). Select the company name and make it smaller using the font size control in the Typography palette. Drag them, or nudge them with the arrow keys, into a pleasing position.

| TIP | **Statically positioned elements can't be kept vertically centered the way absolute and fixed elements can. But you can switch to absolute positioning, click the centered origin Y button, and switch back to static positioning, to get that same alignment.** |

Finally, let's say you want to center the identity group. There's no center alignment button available for elements as there is for text blocks. Instead, switch to the Outline and click the identity group; then choose Fit To Children from the Elements menu (⌘-F/Ctrl-F). Doing so resizes the container to exactly fit its child elements. Click the centered origin button in the options bar, and you have a centered identity as shown in **Figure 6.55**.

**Figure 6.55**
The identity block, now centered.

## Conclusion

Now you've seen a lot of Macaw's layout and positioning capabilities, which should give you a solid start on building prototypes and wireframes. In the upcoming chapters, we'll work from a design to build up the real deal. You're welcome to save the project you've been working on to this point, but we'll be starting fresh on the next one.

# 7

# Building a Website: Part 1

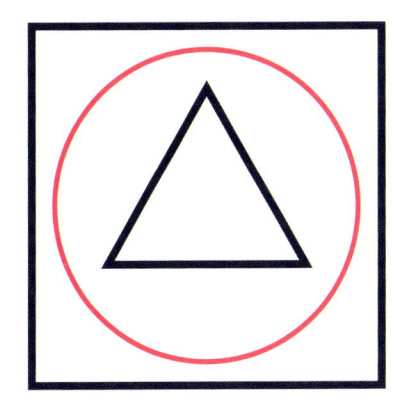

Over the next several chapters, you're going to build a real project: a small website for a conference about Macaw (let's call it "Macawfrence"). You can see the final version, published straight out of Macaw, at http://macawbook.com/macawfrence. You'll start with some mock-ups that were built in Adobe Photoshop, work through some decisions about how to take them apart (figuring out which images to export, what colors and type to capture, and so on), and reassemble it all into a working website in Macaw.

## Think First, Think Often

Before even opening Macaw, it's a good idea to do a little thinking first while reviewing the mock-ups. You can get the mock-up for this project from http://macawbook.com/assets/.

The starting point is three mock-ups of the home page for the conference. This will be a responsive website, so if you're starting with "paintings of web pages" (that is, static mockups from a graphics application), ideally you want the design process to have accounted for various device sizes that you can subsequently map onto breakpoints. This project has three mock-ups: small, medium, and large. Here are some things to consider right off the bat:

- The medium mock-up is wider, in pixels, than the large one because it's represents a 2x Retina device. This makes side-by-side comparisons at actual size a little funky but means you can pull out resources that are 2x-compatible.

- If the mock-up has custom fonts, as do the ones for the conference logo, they will need to be turned into images for Macaw, unless you have the fonts available via Typekit or Google Fonts. In this case, the fact that the type is in a custom font and tilted (doable with CSS3 transforms but perhaps not widely compatible enough in 2014) makes it a good candidate for conversion to an image. The other elements use fonts that are available in Macaw.

- The mock-up includes a testimonial quote carousel, which usually involves the integration of JavaScript via a jQuery plug-in. You can't import arbitrary JavaScript plug-ins into the Macaw canvas, so building something like this completely inside Macaw is not currently possible. You can, however, prototype it and integrate a plug-in after the fact. When looking over your mock-ups, note areas like this that call for the use of JavaScript events (clicks, taps, swipes, and so on).

Having noted some of these basic facts, it's time to start thinking. A big part of reviewing mock-ups is thinking about layers and movement. Layers can often translate into elements on a web page. A Photoshop mock-up always includes layers, sensibly organized into folders (we hope), with each layer consisting of a discrete element. There's an art to creating a good mock-up that's beyond the scope of this book, but ideally you, or other designers you work with, are good at this.

There are several nicely delineated regions on each page (see **Figure 7.1**): a clear header, a navigation menu, a main content area, a secondary content area, and a simple footer.

**Figure 7.1** The large mock-up, with the sections annotated.

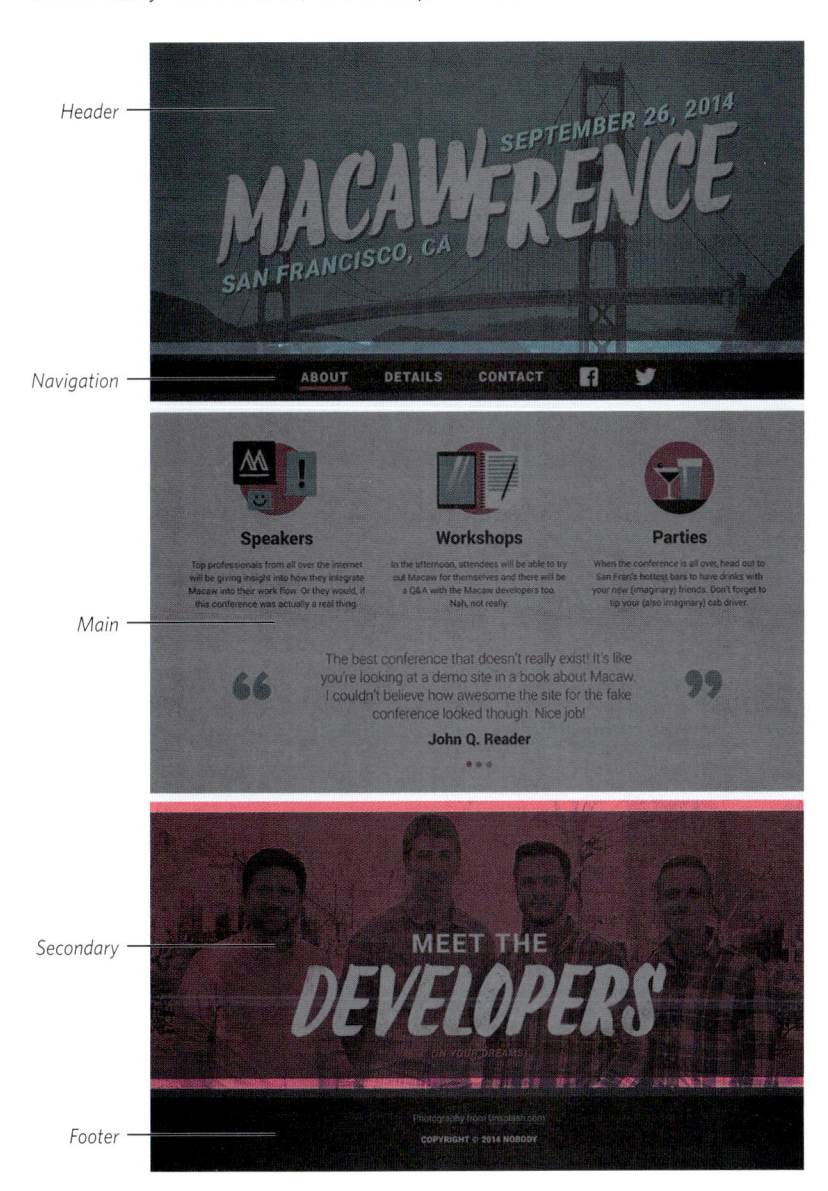

Within each section, you need to extract background and foreground images. For example, the header has a photo of the Golden Gate Bridge with the conference logotype (and the date and location) overlaid. These could be cut out as a single large image, but note that in the different sizes, the placement of the logotype is different, and in the small version, it's a totally different logotype! So the bridge photo should be its own image. You could also get clever and separate "Macawfrence" from the date and location, but we find that keeping those nicely lined up is too much trouble, so we export them as one image and include the location in the image's alt or title text.

The "Meet the Developers" secondary content region at the bottom of the page is similar, but you'll treat it a little differently. The photo will still be exported as a background image, but you're just going to make "Developers" an image (because of its custom font), keeping the other lines as actual text. With no tilted text and everything centered, this is an easier layout to control, and you should take every opportunity to use real text instead of pictures of text for readability, accessibility, and search engine optimization (SEO).

Back toward the top of the page, the navigation is straightforward. There's a brush stroke indicating the active page, also usable for the mouseover/hover state, and a couple of social network icons. These would be ideal candidates for icon fonts (which Macaw doesn't currently support directly) or SVG images (which Macaw does support). You'll stay old-school with these for now, exporting them as PNGs, but be sure to export them at twice the size they would be displayed in the browser, to make them Retina-safe and compatible with Macaw's treatment of high-DPI images (currently just 2x, but maybe more scaling factors will be offered in the future).

One thing to consider, for the navigation and elsewhere, is what happens in between the states illustrated in the mock-ups. The navigation items maintain a generally even spacing between the items, which can be tricky to keep looking nice at all sizes (type is generally rendered with a fixed pixel size, whereas the spacing is flexible—you may encounter situations where the elements run into one another). The menu also has a completely different layout in the small version, so the navigation will certainly be an area of special attention as you build.

Finally, let's look at the content area. The highlights of the conference are obviously going to be images (these are vector illustrations, so they could be exported as SVG files if the original vectors are available), and there's a subtle textured background to be exported. Note that the small mock-up uses a different treatment of the background for the testimonials: a subtle, translucent gradient. Macaw supports CSS gradients, so there's no need to export another image for this unless you're targeting an older browser that doesn't support gradients.

Lucky for you, we've already taken care of exporting all the images you'll need to put this site together. You can download them from http://macawbook.com/assets. Now you can proceed to the actual build.

## Setting Up the Breakpoints, Grid, and Containers

Let's start with a fresh project. Starting Macaw will do this on its own, or you can choose File > New Project (⌘-Shift-N/Ctrl-Shift-N) if you're working on something else.

Referring to the comps, you have a largest size of 1300px (which we'll call *large* from now on) and then two smaller sizes (when accounting for their 2x-ness) of 768px (medium) and 320px (small). Set up those three breakpoints, changing the default to 1300 and adding the others.

> **NOTE** **If you have a screen that doesn't fit the largest breakpoint of your mock-ups, you can still do the work. It will be a little tricky, and you'll probably want to make a lot of use of the Tab key, which hides all palettes, and possibly even full-screen mode so you can devote every last pixel you can to Macaw.**

Next up is the grid. The mock-ups have grid overlays notated with their values. The large one has twelve 60-pixel columns, with 40-pixel gutters, for 1160 total pixels of grid units. To be a flexible grid, this needs to be expressed as a percentage, but you can let Macaw do the math.

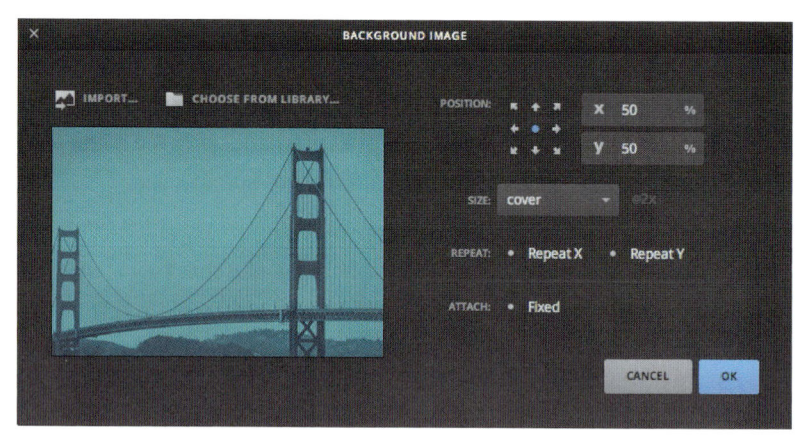

**Figure 7.3** The background settings for the project.

When you're finished with the background, click OK. Experiment with the resize handle to see how the background image behaves. Now wrap up the initial blocking of the header by giving it a sensible tag at the top of the Inspector. You'll go with the HTML5 `<header>` tag, but a `<div>` tag with an ID of #header or anything else with solid semantics would be fine.

## Menu bar and background gradient

The menu bar can be blocked out the same way as a 100 percent by 90px box. Make sure it butts right up against the header by setting its top and left margins to 0, just as you did for the header. Set its tag to the HTML5 `<nav>` tag. For its background, sample a color from the mock-up (#171e37) and apply that in the Backgrounds color field as you did before. This menu has a subtle vertical gradient toward the bottom, so add that by clicking the plus sign and choosing Gradient.

Set the left color to dark purple by double-clicking it to open the Color Picker, selecting the contents of the text field, typing in **#150e2c**, and pressing Return/Enter. Whatever you type in that field, Macaw will recognize and convert to the selected color system (RGB, HSL, or hex). RGB is selected by default, so if you have that selected, you'll see this conversion happen instantly. Neat!

## Gradients in Macaw

Gradients are generated by choosing color stops along a line, between which the browser interpolates the intermediate colors, like keyframes in animation. Each of these stops is represented by a diamond below the color band and can be dragged horizontally. Gradients can have as many color stops as you like but must have at least two. Macaw generates gradients in a way that's as broadly compatible as possible (especially if you enable "Add Browser Prefixes" in Publish Settings), but does not generate fallback images for much older browsers. Applying them over a sensible flat background color is an excellent example of progressive enhancement, where modern browsers get the best possible version of the design using the fast, image-free CSS gradient and older browsers still get something "good enough."

Set the right color to a not-quite-as-dark blue (#171e37) in the same way. Set its angle to 90 degrees, which makes the right color stop the color on top and the left color on the bottom. The gradient is applied only to the bottom edge of the menu in the mock-up, so you can drag the right color stop close to the left side; just eyeball it (see **Figure 7.4**). Macaw doesn't currently support all the same positioning settings for gradients that it does for regular background images, so you can't make the gradient smaller and attach it to the bottom of the menu directly. Fortunately, shifting the color stop works just fine.

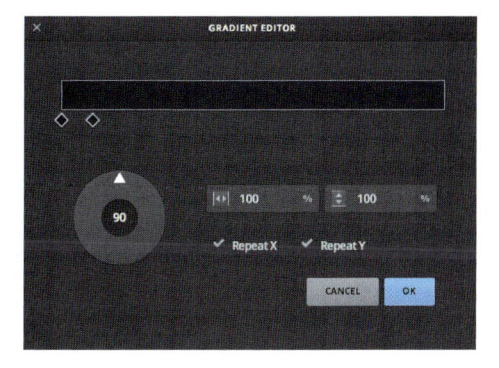

**Figure 7.4** The final gradient settings.

## Main and secondary content

Setting up the main and secondary content requires the same drill as the others: a full-width box butted right against the others (0 for the margins, 100 percent wide). The height will need to adjust to the size of the content, so set that to auto. But we want to be able to see what we're doing, so give it a minimum height of 800px. For the background color, use #e3e3e3 (sampled from the mock-up); there is also background image in the assets folder (bg-sand.png), which is a sandy texture. Import that image, and the default settings will cause it to tile without any more effort. Set the tag to `<section>` (the `<div>` tag's more semantically meaningful HTML5 cousin) and the class to `.main` (because this is used only once, we'd usually use an ID, but Macaw doesn't show IDs in the Outline at the moment, and a class is fine for our current purposes—you could even use both if you want to go really crazy). **Figure 7.5** shows the final settings.

**Figure 7.5** Settings for the main region.

Now for the secondary content area ("Meet the Developers"). This will be 100 percent wide, 550px tall, with a bright red background color (#e11b64). It can use a `<section>` tag, with a class of `secondary`. Import the background image bg-devs.jpg and set it to Cover, with its position set to top middle, disabling the repeats. **Figure 7.6** shows the resulting settings.

**Figure 7.6** Settings for the background of secondary content region.

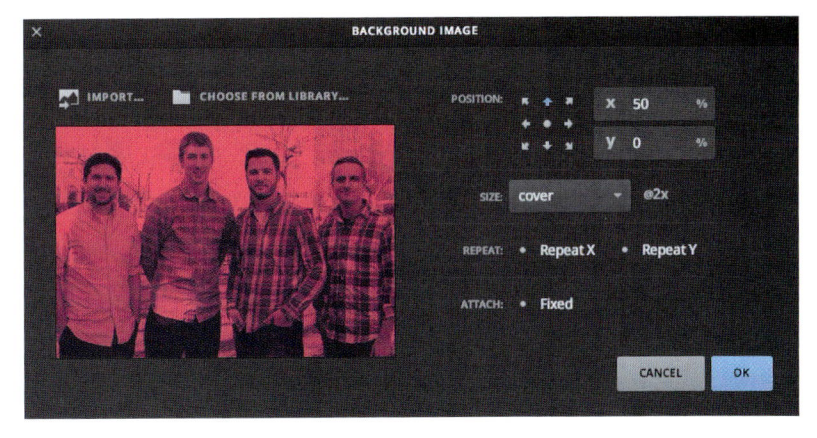

## Footer and page background

For the footer, create a final container as follows: 0 left and top margins, 100 percent width, 160px height, background color #171f37, tag `<footer>`. Now every major region of the home page is ready to go.

As you build this page, you'll notice that you never hit the bottom of the canvas. Macaw automatically expands the canvas vertically to ensure there's always room to add more stuff. When the project is previewed and published, the extra room is not included—Macaw exports only the content you've created. This also helps ensure you don't forget about the page's own background treatment, which you'll take care of now.

The footer is the last element on the page, and in the event that a visitor has a browser window long enough to display all of the page's content at once, you need to set a sensible background color. Because our regions all extend the full width of the window, the default background will never be shown on the sides, so you'll just use the same color as the footer (#171f37).

Having used this color a few times now, you should save it as a reusable swatch for easier reuse. Click the color swatch in the Backgrounds palette, or just press C to bring up the Color Picker from anywhere (shown in **Figure 7.7**). If the color you want isn't already selected, click the Eyedropper tool and click a spot that uses the color (the footer will do). If you have the grid overlays and borders enabled, they'll disappear while the Eyedropper tool is active, letting you see the actual colors in use. Then click the plus button under swatches to create one (if you accidentally create too many, right-click a swatch to bring up its context menu and delete it).

**Figure 7.7** Making a swatch in the Color Picker.

> **NOTE** The Eyedropper tool samples the final rendered color where you click, not how it was made. In other words, if you click a translucent area, the Color Picker will not sample the transparency.

Swatches can be used in the Color Picker and right on the canvas to directly change the background color of the selected element using the button shown in **Figure 7.8**.

## Initial review

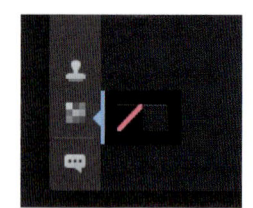

**Figure 7.8** Clicking a swatch in this pop-up menu will apply that background color to the selected element.

Let's take a quick quality assurance pass over the page to see whether everything is behaving well so far. First, check the Outline pane (Opt-O/Alt-O). There should be no warnings at this point, but elements are shown in the reverse order of their creation. The order in the Outline indicates the visual stacking order (the Z index in CSS), but these elements don't overlap. We like to see the order of the elements here match their placed order on the canvas, so you'll drag them into place, as shown in **Figure 7.9**.

**Figure 7.9** The Outline set in the right order. The classes help tell the two section tags apart.

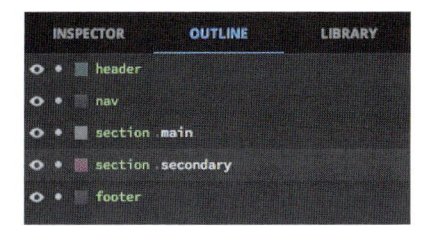

Note that when you do this, all the containers are reset to regular elements. That's not a problem: The only real difference between them is that elements do not contain any other elements. We like to stay in the habit of using the Container tool to create elements you know will be containers, but they're easily converted in the Outline or with the Elements > Tight Group (⌘/Ctrl-G) command.

## Dealing with warnings

If you do see warnings at this point and you've given all of the containers nondefault tags or classes, you're probably seeing negative margin warnings. Sometimes one or more breakpoints can have their settings messed up as a result of Macaw trying to do what it thinks you want. These issues are easily fixed with the Outline active. Click the element that shows warnings and then hover your mouse over its margin settings in the options bar. You can copy the settings from another breakpoint to the current one by hovering your mouse over the other breakpoint's settings in this popover. A simple click will copy the setting from that other breakpoint to the current one. If you hold ⌘/Ctrl when hovering, Set Current becomes Set All, which lets you copy the setting you click to all breakpoints at once (see **Figure 7.10**). Remember that shortcut—it is a saver of much time and many headaches! If the warnings don't disappear right away and you think they should, switch to the Inspector (Opt-I/Alt-I) and then back to the Outline to give Macaw a nudge.

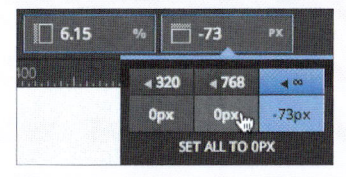

**Figure 7.10** When ⌘/Ctrl is held down, Set Current becomes Set All in settings popovers.

Now try hiding all tools and palettes by pressing the Tab key, and use the ruler to switch between your breakpoints and make sure everything is correctly placed so far. Of course you haven't made any adjustments to the small breakpoints yet; we just want you to form a habit of checking the other breakpoints regularly. You can also use the resize handle to see how things are working between breakpoints.

Press Tab again to bring back all the tools and palettes and then show the Outline. Before moving on, it's a good idea to lock all of these containers by clicking the dot to the right of each eye icon in the outline, which changes to a lock icon. This will prevent accidental selections of elements you didn't mean to touch (although it doesn't stop automatic reflows if surrounding elements move). Leave `<header>` unlocked, because that's first up for editing.

## Building the Header

The header content is a logotype in an attractive but nonstandard font. It has other custom treatments (tilting, shadow) that make it a good candidate for an image. In considering how to build this, you could get clever, splitting the header into its "Macawfrence" and date-and-location components, making them separate images and overlaying them. You're welcome to try this, but here you're going to go with the less complex version where the header image includes all its text but you'll use CSS image replacement to allow some real text into the document. Visually replacing text with images is (in web terms) an old technique that you don't have to use nearly as often with the advent of web fonts, but it still comes in handy at times like this. It has the virtue of making text look exactly how you want while staying compatible with older browsers, and it's easy to do in Macaw.

Start by double-clicking the header. If nothing happens, it's still an element and needs to be converted to a container, so use ⌘/Ctrl-G to do that. Macaw might ask you to transfer presentation elements to the new group, and you can click Yes. At this point, you can double-click the header container and start adding items to it.

Choose the Text tool (T), click anywhere in the header, and drag out a box that seems about big enough for the logo (you can fix it later). Type

**Chapter 7:** Building a Website: Part 1      99

the text you need (**Macawfrence - September 26, 2014 - San Francisco, CA**). When finished, press ⌘-Return/Ctrl-Enter or double-click outside the text box. Finally, change its tag to `h1.macawfrence`. When you're done, you'll have something like **Figure 7.11**.

**Figure 7.11** What the header and its settings should look at this point.

> **NOTE** Macaw includes a CSS reset style sheet, so you can use semantic tags like <h1> without worrying about default browser styles (extra margins, padding, and so on).

Now let's add the background image. You can see in the mock-ups that the medium and large versions use the same header image, but the small one is different. You'll deal with that later in this chapter. For now, just add MacawfrenceHeader-2x.png as the background image for the header. It's twice as big as it is displayed on the largest breakpoint, which should be plenty of pixels for most devices. Set its size to Contain and its position to Centered, and deselect the X and Y repeat settings so it will show only once in the box. At this point, you can see the real text and the background image, as shown in **Figure 7.12**.

**Figure 7.12** The header with text visible and its background image applied.

To finish it off, you need to position the heading correctly and hide the text, leaving just the image. In the large mock-up, the logo is centered horizontally and vertically. Set the origin of the heading to center in the options bar. To get vertical centering, change its positioning to Absolute and select the vertically centered origin. **Figure 7.13** shows the resulting settings.

**Figure 7.13** The origin settings in the toolbar, showing the horizontal and vertical centered.

**TIP** When working on items in containers, you might want to select something quickly without double-clicking the container. That's what the Direct Selection tool is for, but there's a shortcut to get to it even more quickly than using the A shortcut. With the default Select tool active, you can hold ⌘/Ctrl to switch to Direct Selection temporarily—the toolbar doesn't show this as active, but it will work. For lots of work inside groups, it's probably still better to switch tools, but for quick one-offs, this is a handy shortcut. Thanks to the Tips and Tricks post on http://forum.macaw.co for this one.

Next, drag its edges so they snap to the correct grid lines on each side, about where its edges are in the mock-up. The image is 2040 pixels wide by 760 pixels tall (at 2x resolution, that's 1020 by 380), so set the height to 380px and the image will fill the box, as you can see in **Figure 7.14**.

**Figure 7.14** The background image fills its container nicely.

**Chapter 7:** Building a Website: Part 1    **101**

To make sure it's never displayed larger than that, set the maximum width on the header to 1020px. Minimum and maximum element width and height are set in text fields in the Dimensions palette. The second one from the left (see **Figure 7.15**) is the maximum width. These are always set in pixels in Macaw, so just type **1020**.

There are a variety of techniques you could use to hide the text, and they all involve text indentation, which is available in Macaw's full Typography palette (meaning you can see all of its tools—it will look like **Figure 7.16** when the Advanced settings are visible).

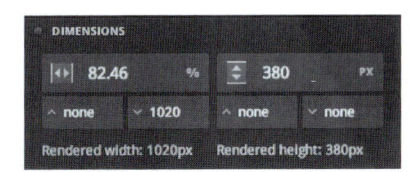

**Figure 7.15** The top two fields with units are width and height, with a minimum and maximum for each one below.

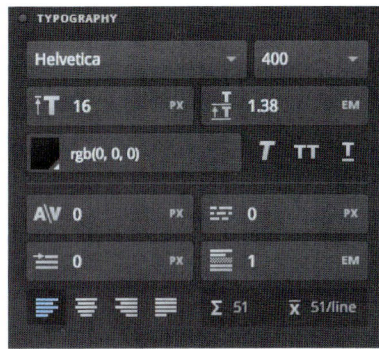

**Figure 7.16** The Typography palette with its advanced settings showing.

Try clicking the palette header a couple of times to cycle through the closed, open, and advanced states. If you're ever wondering why you can't center the text in a text block, it's probably because your Typography palette is merely open, not advanced.

The image replacement techniques you can use on the canvas (there are more advanced techniques that work only on a published site—see Appendix D for one example) all invoke the text indentation setting, and they all involve trade-offs. The oldest technique involves setting your text indentation to a large negative value, but this caused performance problems on Apple iPads and other unsightly artifacts in some browsers. So you'll use a more recent version that works a bit better.

Select the `<h1>`, and set the text indent to 1020px. It needs to be at least as large as the box will ever be—you have a maximum width set here, so you can be sure this will always work. Doing so will move the text to the right (because you're working in English, which reads left-to-right) but will cause it to wrap to the next line. Scroll down to the Advanced palette, which has several more CSS properties you can use for any element. Change white-space to Nowrap and overflow to Hidden. **Figure 7.17** shows where to find all these settings.

**Figure 7.17** All the settings you need for this image replacement technique.

With those changes, the text is gone from the canvas. What you've done is make sure the `<h1>` text stays on one line and indented so far to the right that it goes outside the box, using the Overflow setting to ensure that nothing outside the box's (currently invisible) border is shown.

The text is still accessible to search engines and screen readers, which is good. What's not as good is that it will still be hidden if images are turned off while CSS is still turned on. If that's not an acceptable trade-off, you could consider just using the image directly and placing the heading text in the `alt` attribute (which Macaw keeps in the Advanced settings for every placed image). In that case, you lose the semantic- and SEO-friendly `<h1>` tag. If it's not one thing, it's another.

Unfortunately, advanced CSS properties cannot currently be captured in global styles, so you can't reuse these settings easily. On the other hand, you won't need to use them that much in this project, so for now let's grit our teeth and bear it.

## Medium breakpoint

Switch to the medium breakpoint and you'll make some adjustments. First, let's shrink the header area from 600px to 338px in the mock-up (which is in 2x pixels, so it measures to 676px onscreen). Change the height value directly in the Dimensions palette, and the rest of the page will stay in flow, moving up to compensate.

The header image should be reset as well, which you can do visually. Select it (using Direct Select if you're not in the header tag) and then pull in its left edge to the right border of the first grid column, and the header image's right edge will move along with it. The result is shown in **Figure 7.18**.

**Figure 7.18**
The medium-sized header, resized to the correct columns.

Observe that the width and height values in the Dimensions palette are now outlined, showing that there are different values at different breakpoints. Check the page's resize behavior with the resize handle, check the Outline to make sure no warnings have appeared anywhere, and then move on to the small breakpoint.

## Small breakpoint

There is a different Macawfrence image here, and the location and date are shown on their own as a subheader, using a font you have in Macaw (Roboto). This subheader appears only at this size, so you need to add an element that's only shown here, which you'll include as part of the header area to preserve the relationships of the five major regions you created before. It will have the same background color as the navigation but will be its own separate element.

Measuring the mock-up, you need about 110px for the bridge area and another 40px for the subheader. Change the header height to that total of 150px. The `<h1>` will stay centered horizontally and vertically. You can't add the subheader while working on this breakpoint (the tools are all disabled, and the DOM indicator on the right side above the ruler is locked), so switch to the default breakpoint now (Shift-\). You'll add the element, set some initial styles on it, and then hide it where it's not needed.

Double-click the `<header>` to open it for editing if needed. Select the Text tool (T) and drag out a text box. Change its tag to **h2.date-location** and set its width to 100 percent and height to 40px. Make sure its minimum and maximum heights and widths are set to None.

Under Typography, set its font family to Roboto, weight to 900, size to 11px, color to #74f6ff (create a swatch for this while you're at it), and alignment to Center. Remember, if you don't see text alignment options, click the Typography palette label until they come back. If you didn't enter the text in uppercase, you can use the uppercase button to transform the text to uppercase—this button is shown enabled in **Figure 7.19**.

**Figure 7.19** Typography settings for the subheader.

## Are you really setting type in pixels?

If you've been working in web design for a while, you know that you don't usually set type sizes in pixels. If you're a designer without much web development experience, this has probably driven you up a wall. To try to make everyone happy, Macaw gives you direct control over your font sizes while designing but will generate CSS that uses relative units like ems, percents, or even the relatively recent rems. You can change the units Macaw uses in the Publish Settings (⌘-Shift-P/Ctrl-Shift-P) under Units. If you don't care about this, the defaults Macaw uses will be sensible and you need not worry.

You can vertically align the text by setting the line height. The containing box is 40px tall, and the text is 11px tall. If you set the line height to whatever 40/11 is, that will do it. Check it out—just enter **40/11** in the line height field, and Macaw will do the math for you!

Now attach this `<h2>` to the bottom of the header box. Switch to the Outline (Opt-O/Alt-O) and drag it underneath the `<h1>` (this is optional—just so the outline order reflects the order of the elements as you see them). Change its positioning to Absolute, its horizontal origin to Center, and its vertical origin to Bottom. If you see a blue border around any of these positioning settings, hover your mouse over them and reset them to the current settings with a ⌘-click/Ctrl-click (see **Figure 7.20**). Double-click outside the `<header>`, or hit the Escape key, to return to the main canvas editing context.

**Figure 7.20** If any settings have changed unexpectedly, you can reset them by holding ⌘/Ctrl and clicking the one that's correct.

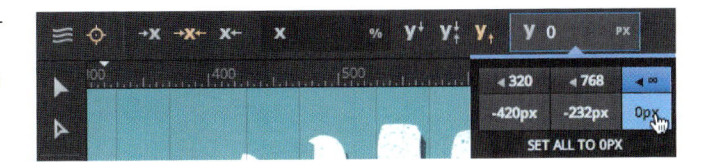

Now, of course you don't want to show this <h2> in the two larger breakpoints. To hide it, use the visibility icons in the upper right of the Inspector (or in the Outline). Because you already have the date and location available in the main header text, you'll use the small dot, for display: none. This causes the page to act as if the element doesn't exist—you could also use Hidden (the outlined eye icon) if you wanted the <h2> to affect other elements for layout purposes while staying invisible.

Switch to the small breakpoint, select the <h2> with Direct Select (A) by holding the ⌘/Ctrl key while clicking with regular Select, and change its visibility to visible again (the result is shown in **Figure 7.21**). Assuming you're doing this from the Inspector, this should outline the visibility settings so you can see that the element is only visible in the small breakpoint (if not, you can fix those now).

**Figure 7.21** The small breakpoint header after the subheader has been set to visible.

Now you just need to adjust the <h1> heading, and you'll be all set. It needs a new background image and to be resized. Select it, and then in the Backgrounds palette, click the plus sign to add another background. You can't swap out images across breakpoints in Macaw; you need to add them and hide the ones you don't want at each breakpoint. Import MacawfrenceHeader-sm-2x.png, center it on both dimensions, set its size to Contain, turn off repeating, and click OK.

Hide the other background image by clicking the eye icon next to it. The two background image boxes should show a preview of the image and are probably both outlined in blue, indicating that the visibility settings are different. Hover your cursor over one of them to see the popover.

There is a small preview of the background image in there (see **Figure 7.22**), which is empty for breakpoints where that image is not displayed. As with others, you can copy the settings of each background image from one breakpoint to another.

Now set the `<h1>` height to 110px, its vertical origin to Top, and its top margin to 0 to get it out of the way of the `<h2>`, which should look like **Figure 7.23**. Check the other breakpoints to make sure everything has behaved, but at this point, the header should be done. Lock it in the Outline if you want to; you may want to make more tweaks later, but for now let's move on.

**Figure 7.22** The popover showing the background settings for each breakpoint, including a tiny preview of the image.

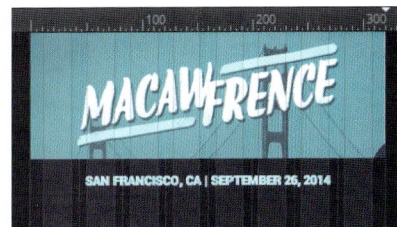

**Figure 7.23** The small header, with everything finished.

> **NOTE** Be sure to save your work at every reasonable opportunity. Macaw autosaves a recovery copy of your project when you preview, but you need to save your own work.

## Building the Navigation

Switch back to the default breakpoint, and if `<nav>` is locked, unlock it. If it needs to be converted to a container again, convert it using ⌘/Ctrl-G and double-click to enter it for editing. Add a text box for the first menu item, About. You can just click once in the menu area and type the word, double-clicking the canvas or pressing ⌘-Return/Ctrl-Enter when finished. Set the text to Roboto, size to 25px, weight to 900, and specify uppercase.

There's some extra letter spacing in the mock-up, so let's add that. In the advanced Typography settings, the first field is letter spacing. Set that to 2px (pixels is the only available unit for letter spacing in CSS). You can type this into the field, or hover your mouse over the field's icon, when the cursor changes to left and right arrows (see **Figure 7.24**). Click and drag left (to decrease) or right (to increase) the value. You can also hold Shift to change the value in increments of 10, but for letter spacing, that's probably going to be way too much!

**Figure 7.24** Mousing over the icon like this one for letter spacing will turn the cursor to arrows, letting you click and drag to change the value without typing.

There is a brushstroke used to indicate the active page, which can also be used for the hover behavior on these links; add that as a background image. The filename is nav-active-2x.png. Set its position to bottom, center it, and turn off all repeats. For the size, Macaw will detect the actual size and insert it; this is a 2x image, so click the @2x button to make Macaw cut the displayed size in half for you. **Figure 7.25** shows the settings.

**Figure 7.25** The background settings for this navigation item.

The background is currently overlapping the letters, and it's cut off on the edges, so give the item a minimum width (110px) and height (42px) to make sure it fits comfortably. This menu item turns out to be not quite as wide as the stroke, so set its text alignment to Center. You're going to create a few of these, so it's a good candidate for a global style.

With the menu item selected, click the stamp icon in the lower left and then click the plus button. The Global Style Properties dialog box will appear. Give the style a sensible name like "nav item." Check each of the sections of the dialog box to make sure the styles being captured are good to reuse. Any styles that aren't currently used are unchecked, and you can uncheck any others that shouldn't be captured. You can also modify captured styles. In this case, click the Backgrounds tab. When you save the style this way, the background stroke will always be shown by default. For inactive menu items, of course, that won't be the case, so click the eye icon next to the background, making the "off" state the default and leaving the check box selected, as shown in **Figure 7.26**.

**Figure 7.26**
Background settings captured in this global style.

You could go further and make a component of this item, but you only need two more, so instead duplicate it (⌘-D/Ctrl-D) and drag the other two into rough position. The duplicate will stick to your mouse cursor, so you can move it into place and click to put it down. Green guidelines will appear to help you maintain their vertical alignment. Change the text on each of these to **Details** and **Contact**, but hide the background image by clicking the eye icon in the Backgrounds palette.

Now you can add the social icons. Again, each could be added as a single image, but for better SEO and accessibility, you're going to use image replacement again. You're also going to add a pinch of web development pixie dust in the form of CSS sprites. A *sprite* in this case means multiple images are combined into a single file, so your web server needs to serve up only one image instead of several, making your page load more quickly.

Add a point text box that says "Like Macawfrence on Facebook" and make the text white so you can see what you're doing. The icons are 36-pixel-by-36-pixel squares, so set the height and width accordingly. Add a background image, importing social-icons.png. As you can see, the Facebook and Twitter icons tile over and over, so the trick is to set the position such that the correct icon shows. For the Facebook icon, this is easy; it's the left- and topmost icon in the file, so its default position is correct. Just click the @2x button to tell Macaw this is a 2x image, turn off the repeats (see **Figure 7.27**), and click OK.

**Figure 7.27**
Background settings for the Facebook icon.

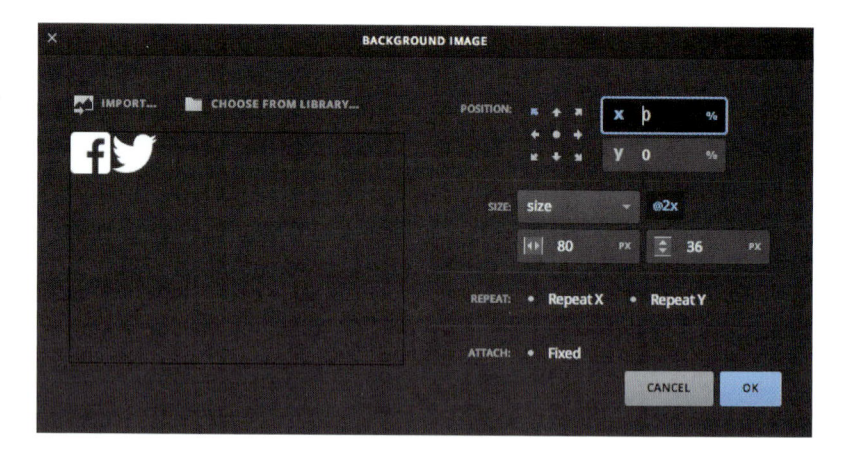

Now add the image replacement CSS settings: a text indent of 56px (if the box were to scale up somehow in the browser, this is a little extra protection against the text showing), and under Advanced set White-space to Nowrap and Overflow to Hidden.

Drag it roughly into place and then duplicate it (⌘-D/Ctrl-D) to create the Twitter link. In the Backgrounds palette, double-click the image name to open the backgrounds editor, and change the positioning so the Twitter icon is the one visible. There are only two icons, so the top-right arrow will work. Click OK to save.

The icon is just a little bit cut off, so change its width to 44px by dragging right on the width icon in the field, or by just typing it in. Now double-click the icon, which will cause its text to appear. Change it to

**Chapter 7:** Building a Website: Part 1    **111**

Follow Macawfrence on Twitter. **Figure 7.28** shows the final placement of the items.

**Figure 7.28** The navigation items in their final places.

All five items are now available, but they need some attention in the Outline. They're all `p.text`, and they all have warnings. You'll deal with both issues at once. Double-click the first item, which should be the Twitter icon. Type **a.twitter** (making this a link with the class of `twitter`—you'll add the actual link a little later); then instead of Return/Enter, press Tab on your keyboard. This will select the next item in the Outline, with the tag editor still active. Type **a.facebook** and press Tab again. Run down the remaining menu items this way; be sure to give them sensible classes.

> **NOTE** Strictly speaking, you don't need these classes on these items. Writing HTML and CSS by hand, we need classes and IDs to make sure our styles (and JavaScript) target the right items. In Macaw, we don't have to keep track of any of that (Macaw will auto-generate any classes it needs to make your designs look how you specify), so the classes mainly help figure out what's what in the Outline, which is a totally worthy job for them (just different).

Drag the five menu items into order in the Outline, with About on top and Twitter on the bottom. Then click About on top, Shift-click Twitter on the bottom to select them all, and set their top margins to 34px and left margins to 0 in the options bar. If there were any positioning foibles with these menu items while you were putting them together, they should be fixed now. Sometimes working with the contents of one container can cause others to shift around. We don't expect it to have happened here, but it's possible the main container could have moved, making the menu look too tall. If you see that, press Escape to get out of the `<nav>` container, unlock section.main, select it either on the canvas or in the Outline, and reset its top margin to 0.

> **NOTE** You may have to do this for all breakpoints, which thankfully is easy to do with the ⌘-click/Ctrl-click trick. Making good decisions about where to place everything is not easy, and Macaw sometimes loses the thread.

To fix the placement of the menu items, refer to the large mock-up. Here, the five items are more or less centered overall, with even spacing between them. Let's place the left- and rightmost items, and let Macaw place the other ones. With the regular Select tool (V) active, double-click the `<nav>` container. You could use direct selection, but entering the container helps prevent you from accidentally touching anything else. It also means the positioning guides are usable (with direct selection outside of containers, they do not appear).

Move About into place, just eyeballing it so its left edge is just under the middle of the first *A* in Macawfrence. Move the Twitter icon so its center is right between the *N* and *C* in Macawfrence. The rest of the items can be sort of wherever (a somewhat extreme example of which is shown in **Figure 7.29**).

**Figure 7.29**
An example of "wherever."

Select all five—while you're inside a container, Edit > Select All (⌘-A/Ctrl-A) will select all items in that container—and switch to the Inspector (Opt-I/Alt-I). You can edit multiple items like this using

**Chapter 7:** Building a Website: Part 1    113

any active fields in the Inspector, but you're interested in the Align palette at the top, shown in **Figure 7.30**.

**Figure 7.30** The Align palette, which appears when multiple items are selected on the canvas.

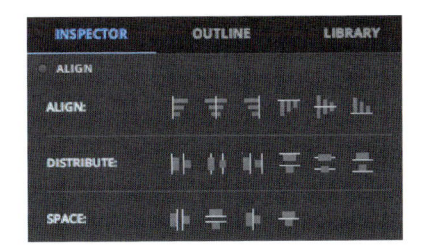

We could try distributing the centers horizontally, the second button from the left in the Distribute row, but the widths of the items vary so much that it wouldn't give us what we're looking for. What you really want is in the Space row. The first button will make the space between all items even. As you can see in **Figure 7.31**, this is just right. If your items started out as wacky as in Figure 7.29, you'd probably want to align the items as well using one of the buttons in the Align row.

**Figure 7.31** After aligning and spacing the items, they look much better.

If you use the resize handle to squeeze and expand the page, you can see that the items don't stay centered the way they obviously should. We want them to stay centered as a group, so let's group them and center that group. Select them all again and choose Elements > Tight Group (⌘-G/Ctrl-G). Give the container a sensible tag (`div.menu` is good for now), set its horizontal origin to center, and try resizing the canvas again. You'll very likely see the items wrapping as shown in **Figure 7.32**, which you also don't want.

**Figure 7.32** Unsightly wrapping in action.

There are different ways to deal with this depending on the behavior desired. Currently, the menu group has a flexible width, so it changes as the viewport changes. Changing that to pixels would stop it from flexing and maintain the same spacing at all sizes that this breakpoint applies to. If a flexible width is desired, you could change the positioning of the elements inside to absolute, which would stop the menu items from flowing around one another. This is an area where you and the designer need to talk and determine the right course of action. Of course, if you *are* the designer, working with Macaw lets you make decisions like this on your own.

In this case, setting a fixed width for the navigation is what the designer intended, so just select the menu container and change the units on its width from percent to px. Now the items will maintain their precise widths, but the whole block will stay centered in the `<nav>` area. Press Escape until you're backed out to the canvas for editing.

## Medium breakpoint

Switch to the medium breakpoint. Things could be a little messy when changing breakpoints, depending on what Macaw has done and how you've reacted to it as you've been working. **Figure 7.33** shows what we saw.

**Figure 7.33** We've seen worse, but this isn't good.

Several adjustments are needed: The type needs to be smaller, and the spacing and positioning need to be fixed. Deal with the spacing first so you can see what you're doing. Select the left edge of the menu container and drag it to the left edge of the third column as shown in **Figure 7.34**. With its origin in the center, this will expand the menu block on both directions, making it eight columns wide, as it is in the mock-up. Now double-click it so you're editing just the menu items; doing so causes the menu to be outlined, and you'll see a breadcrumb view of where you are in the Outline in the footer (see **Figure 7.35**).

**Figure 7.34** The left edge of the menu, aligned with the correct column in the grid.

**Figure 7.35** This breadcrumb-like footer shows up when you're editing inside a container, helping you track what you're working on. Click parent items to the left to go up to that level.

Select the first three and change them as follows:

- Height: 28px
- Minimum width: 80px
- Font size: 16px
- Background size: Contain

Select the Facebook icon and change it to be 24-pixels-wide-by-24-pixels-tall, and change its background size to 53-pixels-by-24-pixels. For the Twitter icon, the dimensions should be 28-pixels-wide-by-24-pixels-tall, with the background size also 53-pixels-by-24-pixels. Adjust the vertical spacing of the menu items to taste, and you should end up with something like what appears in **Figure 7.36**.

**Figure 7.36** Navigation items after being adjusted.

## Where did 53px come from?

The original size was 80 pixels by 36 pixels. The new height setting was 24px, which is two-thirds of 36 (24 / 36 = 2/3, or 0.66…). Two-thirds of 80 is about 53 (80 x 0.66… = 53.33…).

Try making the canvas narrower and you'll likely see wrapping again. Once again, you have to decide what to do. Let's try absolute positioning this time. Select all five items and change them to Absolute in the options bar. The first time you try this, you might see the menus go a little crazy, as shown in **Figure 7.37**. If that happens, undo it (⌘-Z/ Ctrl-Z) and try it again. In our experience, this has always worked. **Figure 7.38** shows the result.

**Figure 7.37** That... is not what I meant.

**Figure 7.38** That's better.

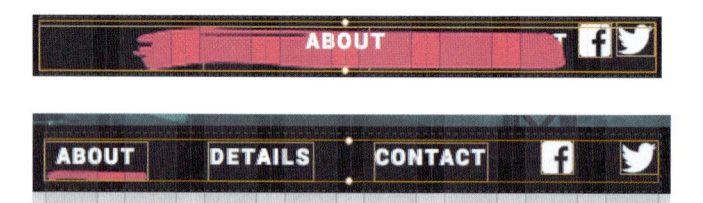

There's one more adjustment to make: the height of the `<nav>` container. It's 50px in the mock-up, so select it in the Outline and make this change. Adjust the vertical placement of `div.menu` so it looks good.

Try resizing now, and you'll see there's no wrapping, but the menu items run into each other before you hit the next breakpoint. There are several ways to deal with this, but here are a few:

- Set a minimum width on the menu container so it never gets narrower than our inter-item spacing can handle. This will result in horizontal scrolling in the space between that minimum menu group width and the next smaller breakpoint, and horizontal scroll bars are unsightly. Next!

- Adjust the width of the container, the font sizes, the spacing, anything you can to make these items fit between breakpoints. This approach will certainly work, but if you or the designer you're working with has already gotten everything working just right in that mock-up, you might not like the compromises you have to make at both ends of that breakpoint's range to make it work across the whole thing. In this case, 768px down to 320px is a pretty long way and won't fly.

**Chapter 7:** Building a Website: Part 1    117

- Adjust the position of the breakpoints or add a new one. Designing in a static tool like Photoshop, it's not hard to miss some areas where another breakpoint would be helpful, and creating yet another "pixel painting" can be daunting. In Macaw, it's comparatively easy; there's still work to be done to move everything around in a new breakpoint, but this kind of work is what the tool is meant for, so it's definitely easier. In this case, you can use a set width on the menu container, and then add a breakpoint just before hitting that width.

Select `div.menu` in the Outline, or on the canvas, switch to the Inspector and change its width from percent to px. In our copy, that width ends up being 475px. Click the canvas to show the breakpoints, and create a new one at 480px (which will be known from this point forward as the "medium-small" breakpoint). We'll leave the rest of the adjustments for the navigation (and to the header, if you like) at this breakpoint as an exercise for the reader. It will be very similar to the work you did on this medium breakpoint. Refer to the example Macawfrence project to see how we adjusted.

## Small breakpoint

The small breakpoint has a significant change in the navigation, with a stack of four blocks. First, make enough room that they can all fit. In the mock-up, that's around 200px, so select `<nav>` and set its height to 200px. The other major containers will move down to accommodate.

> **NOTE** It's simple adjustments like this that can make you love Macaw.

Next, double-click `<nav>` to edit its children, and select `div.menu`. Drag it to the top of the `<nav>` container so its top margin is 0, then drag the bottom until it's 15 pixels from the bottom (or set its height to 185px manually). It should look like **Figure 7.39**. Double-click `div.menu` to start working with the actual menu items.

**Figure 7.39**
The containers are ready.

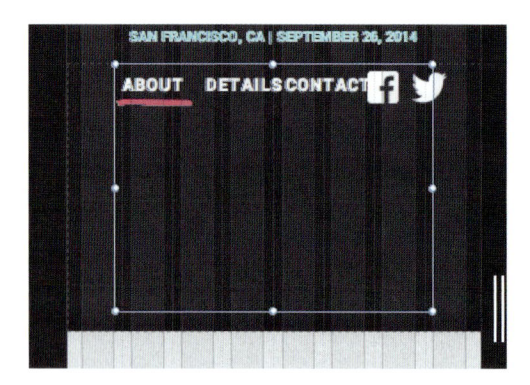

First, drag each menu item roughly into place: About on top, social icons at the bottom. Adjust each of the text menu items as follows:

- Positioning origin: Center
- Height: 36px
- Minimum width: 110px
- Font size: 21px (yes, you'll make these items bigger at this small size—larger tap targets are good!)
- Background image: Copy the settings from the default breakpoint, which will reset from Contain to the actual size of the image.

For the social icons, change the Facebook icon to a 30-pixel-by-30-pixel square, and the Twitter icon to a 36-pixel-by-30-pixel rectangle. Each should have their background size reset to 66-pixels-by-30-pixels (we'll spare you the arithmetic this time).

After all these size adjustments, some spacing adjustments are probably needed unless you got lucky. Make sure the About item is right up against the top of the `div.menu` container and that the social icons are right at the bottom. Then select each of the text items, along with one icon, and use the even vertical spacing button in the Align palette (second from the left) to evenly space them out, resulting in **Figure 7.40**.

**Figure 7.40** The small menu after clicking the vertical spacing button, over which you can see the cursor in the figure.

Use the resize handle to compress the window a bit and see how everything is behaving (see **Figure 7.41**). The social icons don't stay perfectly centered, so as an exercise you can group the social icons and adjust them so they stay centered. We've done this in example project file, but save it as an exercise when you've finished this chapter; there is more to discuss on the navigation below. There are other issues you might deal with at very small sizes, such as the date and location subheader starting to wrap and disappear, but in a world where cell phones are getting bigger (again), this is a fine place to stop for our purposes.

**Figure 7.41** The small menu in its finished state. Or is it?

## The Importance of Preview

Although Macaw is built on a real web browser, it's not wise to merely trust what you see on the canvas. As with so much else in software, testing is important. If you need to support an older browser, testing your work there is crucial. Also, Macaw has bugs (as does all software), and you might need to work around them. Publishing your work to the preview window and trying it in browsers is critical, and fortunately Macaw makes this pretty easy.

Try publishing what you have so far now using File > Publish or ⌘-P/Ctrl-P (the fact that this isn't Print takes some getting used to). This opens a browser window (using the same engine as Google Chrome), with a few extra features not in the usual browser toolbar (the buttons are shown in **Figure 7.42**). You can use this window to test your project in different window sizes, and you can see the HTML, CSS, and JavaScript Macaw has generated for you. The folder icon will open the published site folder, where you can see the actual files.

> **NOTE** **Macaw will overwrite everything in the published site folder every time you publish. Do not place any files in there!**

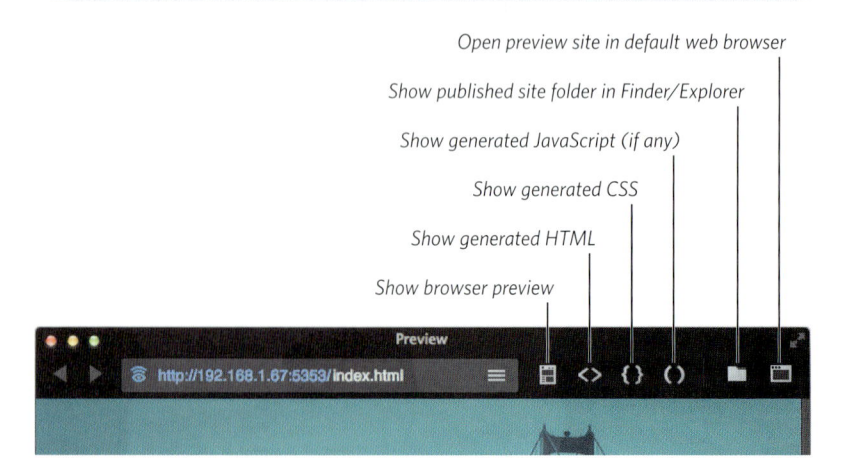

*Open preview site in default web browser*
*Show published site folder in Finder/Explorer*
*Show generated JavaScript (if any)*
*Show generated CSS*
*Show generated HTML*
*Show browser preview*

**Figure 7.42**
The preview window with buttons highlighted.

**Chapter 7:** Building a Website: Part 1     **121**

The window button on the far right opens the project in your default browser. Try that now. There's a problem to fix already; as you can see in **Figure 7.43**, the title of the window is "index," which is totally meaningless and would be terrible for SEO (search engines give a lot of weight to the title of a page).

**Figure 7.43**
The Macaw preview site opened in a regular web browser. Note "index" as the page title.

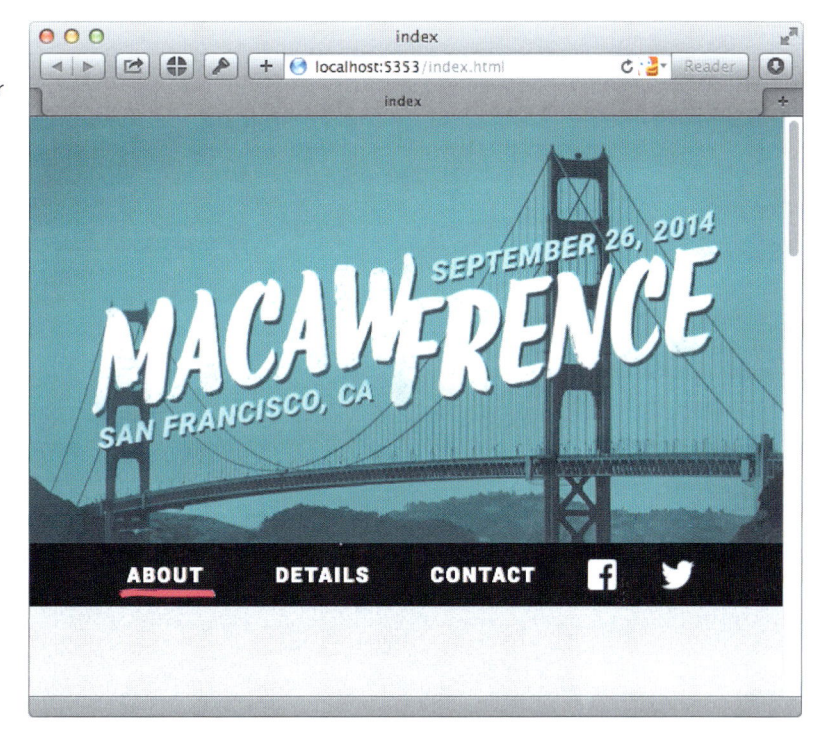

Let's change that now. Keep that browser window open to your Macaw project, but switch back to Macaw. Click the canvas so nothing is selected and show the Inspector, and you'll see Page Title palette at the bottom. Change that to **Macawfrence**. Save the project and publish (⌘-P/Ctrl-P) again. Notice that your browser automatically reloads with the fresh content. Pretty neat, but it gets better. The preview window probably shows a URL like this:

http://192.168.1.1:5353/index.html

**NOTE** This is what Macaw calls "Remote Preview", and is a setting in File > Publish Settings. If that is turned off, preview will still work, your URL will start with file://. See Chapter 11 for more on Macaw's publishing options.

This should be accessible from any device on your local network: phones, tablets, iOS or Android simulator software, virtual machines running other operating systems, other computers, Internet-connected soda machines, any device on your network. Type that URL into any of those devices, and you can preview your site. And every time you publish your site, Macaw will tell every single device to reload the fresh copy without any action from you.

This is your cue to say "cooooooool."

Another thing the preview window can do is shrink smaller than a typical browser can, making it easier to test your smaller breakpoints. Let's try squishing the window down small enough to see the smallest breakpoint, which might look like **Figure 7.44**.

There are two big problems here: The date-location subheader has jumped to the top of the window, and the social icons have been shoved off the screen to the right. We're pretty sure the first problem is a bug that will be fixed, maybe even by the time you read this book, but the workaround is quick to show, and might be useful anyway. The second issue may or may not be a bug, but still needs to be fixed.

The subheader issue is easily fixed. Select h2.date-location, and change its vertical origin from bottom to top. Preview again, and boom, it's fixed. Try resizing the window, and the only problem is the subheader's text starting to overlap the navigation menu at very small sizes. Feel free to fix this if you like.

**Figure 7.44** Uh-oh. The header and navigation are both wrong.

The second issue is a little more subtle, but it can also be solved with positioning adjustments. When items look like they're getting shoved around like this, and they have pretty well-defined positions that aren't affected by what's around them, it's often useful to try absolute positioning as a solution.

Select the Facebook icon (use Direct Select if needed) and change its positioning to absolute. Set its origin to the bottom and set the bottom offset to 2px (a pixel or two is enough to avoid buggy behavior here). Do the same with the Twitter icon, but also set its horizontal origin to right. The resulting placement and settings are shown in **Figure 7.45**.

**Figure 7.45**
The Twitter positioning settings with workaround applied.

## A note for more advanced users

If you're a savvy web developer, you can use the Open in Browser button in the Preview window to open the page in your favorite browser and then use Firebug, Chrome Developer Tools, or any of the other front-end development tools you already know to look at the chain of CSS rules applied to an item. Once you've figured that out, you can go back to Macaw and figure out another way to achieve what you're trying to do. At the time of this writing, the specific issues with the social icons were CSS rules from a larger breakpoint where absolute positioning was used, which were not being properly overridden in the generated CSS. Switching to absolute positioning here was a step in the right direction. As Macaw continues to mature, these bugs will surely be squashed, and the need for tracking down workarounds will diminish.

Preview again, especially on a phone or phone simulator, to see how this all worked. It isn't a perfect solution—if the window gets quite small, the icons start to overlap, but it is better, and it might be good enough.

Now you've seen how important publishing and previewing in real browsers is, as well as some relatively easy workarounds for quirky behaviors. Be on the lookout for these issues and know that you can fix them with a little ingenuity or just a bit of trial and error.

## Next Steps

In this chapter, we blocked out the major areas of the page and then started filling in the content for the header and navigation areas. We also looked publishing and preview and how it's important to check work often. In the next chapter, you're going to finish building this page, getting into the main and secondary content areas. As you continue on and things start to come together, the speed at which you'll be able to work through these pages (both those you're reading and those you're building) will continue to increase.

# 8

# Building a Website: Part 2

In the previous chapter, you started your first website in Macaw, building out the major sections of the home page and filling in the (largely) shared header and navigation. In this chapter, you'll finish the home page. The main content area is in two parts: The first shows highlights of what to expect at the Macawfrence, and the second shows a testimonial quote, with little circles indicating there are more of them. The highlights are easy to build and test in Macaw; the testimonials are more of a challenge. You'll work through both, picking a strategy for dealing with the part that can't easily be built in Macaw.

## Highlights

Reviewing the mock-ups, you can see that the highlights are set in three columns (fitting nicely in the grid) until you get down to the small breakpoint, when they become one column. They're similar, so you could build a component, but because there are only three of them (and they're not used anywhere else in the project), you'll just make copies. You can add the illustrations to the project in at least a couple of different ways. One option is to add them as standalone images, just dropped onto the canvas. With this strategy, you can later swap them out easily, whether in the Macaw project or in the published HTML, by replacing a single `<img>` tag. Alternatively, you can add the illustrations as background images for the headers. This approach is semantically virtuous—you're tying the images directly to the text whose meaning they enhance—but adds the small complication of the extra CSS (if all future editing happens in Macaw, this is less of a concern). We like to be semantically virtuous, so we'll go with that. You'll create one of the highlight blocks and then duplicate it and edit the copies.

### The trade-off of performance and maintainability

Using background images lends itself nicely to the image sprite technique you used earlier on the social icons in the navigation bar. Although sprites cut down on HTTP requests (which is great for making pages load faster), they can make maintenance more difficult. With sprites, when you want to update a single image in the design, you need to prepare the image, open the sprite file, place it correctly (assuming it's the same size), and possibly update the CSS that goes with it (and other sprites) if the size has changed. With conventional, single images, you just update one file and that's it. Which way you go will depend a lot on who is maintaining the project going forward (how web-savvy they are) and how they're doing so (for example, in Macaw, from the published HTML, or some other way).

If `section.main` is locked, unlock it. This element isn't a container at the moment, but we're going to build things on top of it and nest them later using the Outline (one of many ways to manage containment in Macaw). Select the Text tool (T) and create point text for the Speakers header with the following styles:

- Font: Roboto
- Weight: 900
- Size: 35px
- Color: #171f37 (we have a swatch for this)
- Text alignment: Center

Make the box four columns wide in the grid, and give it a sensible tag, like `h3.speakers` (the class is most helpful in the Outline so you can see what's what). **Figure 8.1** shows all the settings in action.

**Figure 8.1** The header as defined so far, with all relevant settings.

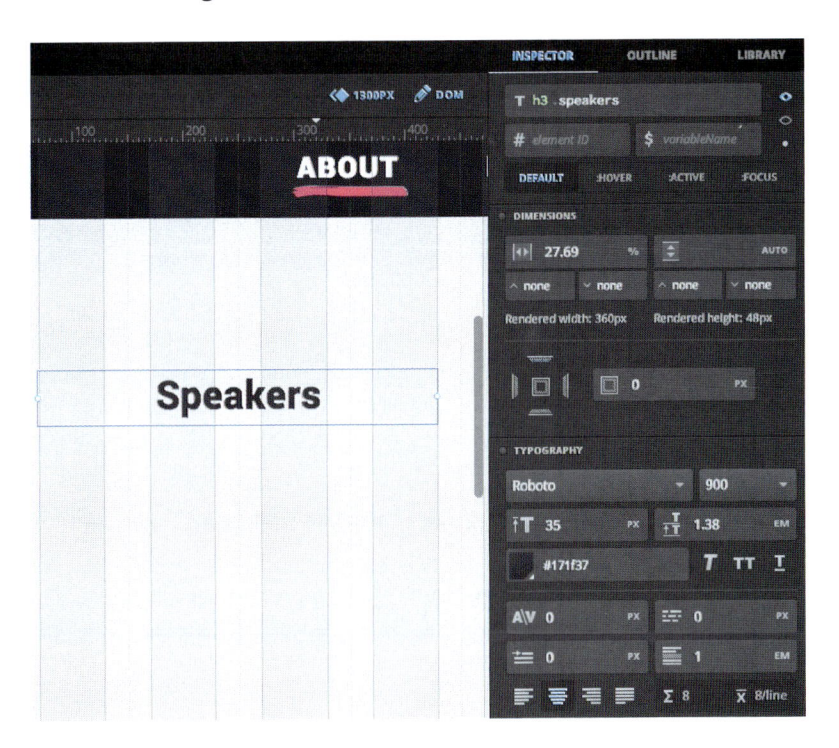

To make room for the image in the background, you need to add some padding to the text box. Padding is part of the Dimensions palette but appears only when applicable to the current selection. It looks similar to the first section of the Borders palette (see Figure 8.1, just to the right of the header on the canvas). You can add padding to any side by clicking one of the outer edges or to all of them at once with the inner square selected. There needs to be padding on top for this header, so click the top edge and then type **160** (pixels is always the unit here). As you can see in **Figure 8.2**, this creates a bunch of room above the text for the background image.

**Figure 8.2** With top padding, the text is apparently pinned to the bottom of its box.

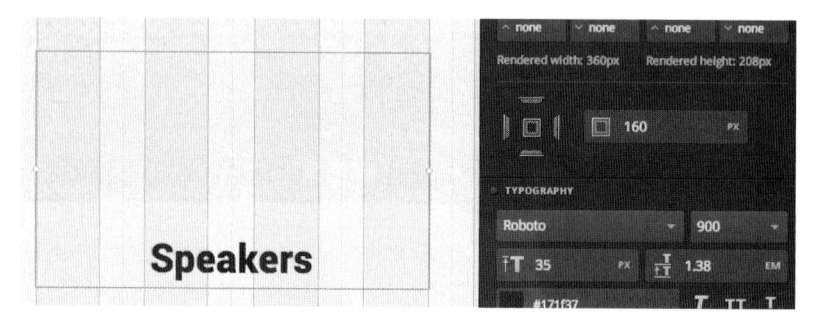

Now add the image. In the assets folder, you have a choice of SVG or PNG files. SVGs are well supported in recent versions of all web browsers, and they're completely resolution independent, so you don't need to worry about Retina and older conventional displays. As long as the browser supports them, they'll look great at any size and resolution. As an added bonus, the files are generally much smaller too (compare highlight-speakers.svg and highlight-speakers.png—the SVG is one-third the size). If compatibility with older browsers is important, you need to use something else, so we've provided PNGs as a fallback so you can compare the files in use if you like. We'll use the SVGs here. Macaw treats them like any other image, so add highlight-speakers.svg as a background image, top-center aligned, repeating disabled, as shown in **Figure 8.3**.

Now you can add the text block below the header. The assets folder has Text.txt, which contains all the text in the mock-up, to save you some typing (Macaw can also create dummy text for you; see the "Our friend Lorem Ipsum" sidebar).

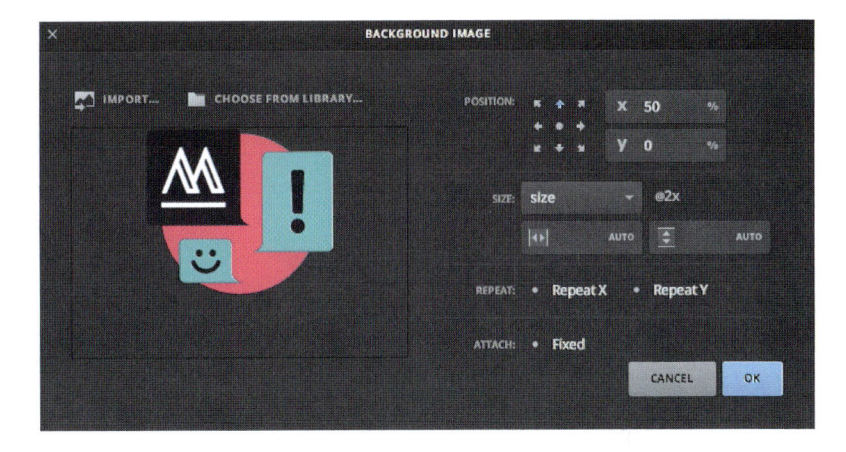

**Figure 8.3** The settings for the speakers background image.

## Our friend Lorem Ipsum

Using dummy, or filler, text is a long and mostly proud tradition in web design. Although it's always best to have real content ready before beginning design and development, in the messy real world that's not always possible. "Lorem Ipsum" text is the most common form of filler text, and Macaw can generate that for you in any text box using a special word followed by the Tab key.

The special word is "lorem" followed by a number, followed by p (paragraph), s (sentence), or w (word); followed by Tab, with no spaces anywhere. Here are some examples:

- lorem3p<tab> will create three paragraphs.
- lorem2s<tab> will create two sentences.
- lorem6w<tab> will create six words.

This is a pretty slick way to fill in any areas of a page that will need some text but you don't have any of the real stuff ready. Even though we've provided all the text you need for this page, give it a try!

Copy the text for the speakers section from the Text.txt document and then drag out a text block on the canvas that's the same width as the Speakers header (use the guidelines to snap it to the grid). Paste in the text and style as follows:

- Font: Roboto
- Weight: 400
- Size: 18px
- Line height: 1.38em
- Text alignment: Center
- Color: #171f37 (we have a swatch for this)

The box will have a default height of Auto, which we want because it allows the rest of the page to flow around it, but it will have a minimum height of whatever you originally created. You don't need a minimum height on this block, so delete it. Give the box the tag `p.highlight-text`; the result will look like **Figure 8.4**.

**Figure 8.4** The speaker text, and its header, together at last.

These two elements go together, so wrap them in a container by selecting and grouping them (⌘-G/Ctrl-G). Give the container `div.highlight` for its tag, with an ID of `#speakers`. Set its height to Auto—that way, if text inside ends up needing to be longer at some point later, or if it needs to expand vertically as its width gets smaller at smaller breakpoints, the container can stretch vertically to fit everything.

### *A brief intermission for global styles*

There's an existing global style for the navigation items, but other than create it, you didn't do much with it. We'll expand on this a bit now. Using the Direct Selection tool, select the header text in this highlight block and create a new global style for it with the stamp icon. Call the style **highlight header** and check the settings. Everything should be fine, except maybe the background image. You don't want the same background image on every occurrence, so deselect that part (the transparent background color is fine to keep). Click Save.

Select the highlight body text and save a global style for it as well. Call it **highlight text**, and check the settings. You might need to adjust the Geometry setting to make sure the width is 100% (now that the box is in a container, this is what you want), but everything else should be in order.

Now that these styles are in place, duplicate the block and place the copies in their respective places, with their tops aligned. Update the text, background images (highlight-workshops.svg and highlight-parties.svg), and tags of each so the second one is Workshops and the third is Parties. The result should look like **Figure 8.5**.

**Figure 8.5** The highlight blocks are placed, with updated text and background images.

One of the joys of global styles is that you can change the style, and everywhere that it's used will update right away. Click the canvas so nothing is selected (or at least none of the blocks we've been working on), and then click the stamp icon. Every style we've defined so far appears here (see **Figure 8.6**).

**Figure 8.6** Three global styles are defined here, with none used on the currently selected element.

Double-click the Highlight Text style to open its editing dialog box. Click Typography, and try increasing the type size. All three blocks update immediately, even before you click Save (see **Figure 8.7**).

**Figure 8.7** The type size has been increased to 24px, and all three blocks update.

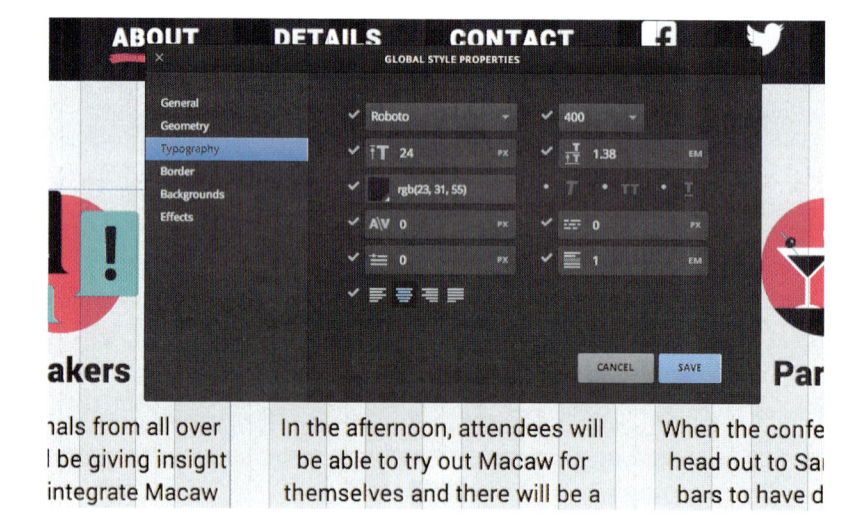

This is great, because once the style is defined, you can experiment with other treatments of the text (or whatever other properties the style captures—you can even add new ones you didn't originally capture) without having to reapply those styles manually. We were just experimenting, and you don't need to save anything, so click Cancel.

Global styles can be overridden. Using the Direct Selection tool, select the highlight text in the speakers block, and change its color to red in the Typography palette (you can use the Color Picker, or just type **red** in the color field). Click the stamp icon, and you'll see that the style has been overridden, as shown in **Figure 8.8**.

**Figure 8.8** The highlight text global style has been modified on the selected element.

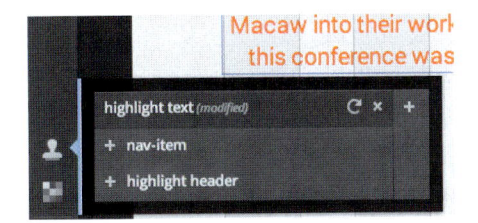

Clicking the circle-arrow/refresh button will throw away any aspects of the global style that have been modified on the selected element. In this case, that would change the color back to normal. However, if you double-click the highlight text style and boost the type size as you did before, you'll see that the red text also gets bigger with the others. Even when you override parts of a global style, the parts that aren't overridden continue to update. This behavior is a nice touch. You're all done with global styles for now, so click that refresh button to revert the highlight text back to normal.

### Back to highlights

Switch to the Outline (Opt-O/Alt-O), and note that the highlight blocks have warnings. They need to be moved inside the container where you want them: `section.main`. So move them in there—you can also order them by dragging them so that the speakers block comes first—but the main thing is getting the nesting correct.

> **NOTE** It's probably preferable, in general, to convert an element to a container first if needed, and then open it and add elements. Working this way seems to cause fewer unexpected behaviors and warnings with element positioning. We'll do that with the secondary content section, and other sections later in the project. That said, using the Outline to create containers is also possible, so we're covering both methods so you'll know how each works.

In fact, because these three highlights can be considered one unit together, group them as well. Select each one (doing this from the Outline might be easiest), and use Elements > Tight Group (⌘-G/Ctrl-G). Set the new container to be `div.highlights`. This new group will likely use the margins from the containers to set its boundaries, which is a little strange. Look at the borders of the container in **Figure 8.9** and note the extra space.

**Figure 8.9** The new container encompasses spacing that we really want outside of it.

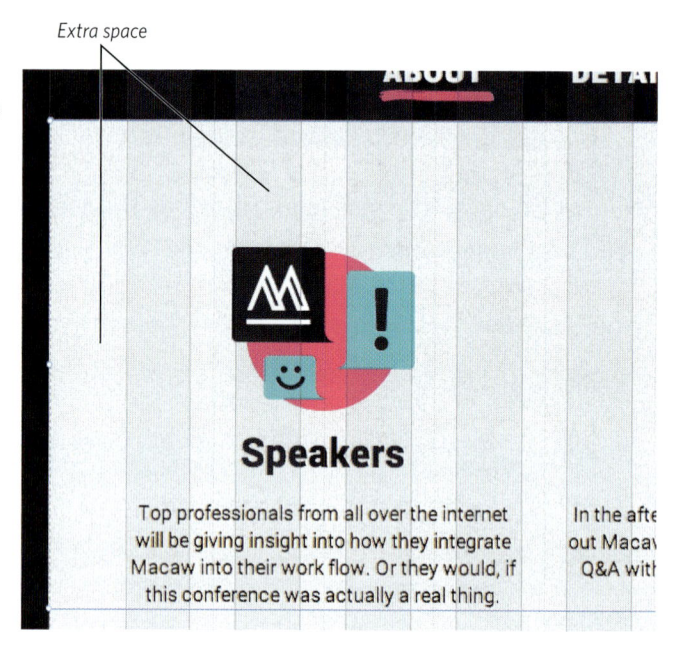

To fix this, double-click the container to open it for editing (you can also use the Direct Selection tool, but you can end up selecting too deeply—this way is more predictable); then select all three `div.highlight` boxes. They may or may not have the same top margin, but whatever it is now, we want them all to be 0, so change it to 0. This will shift all three boxes to the top. You'll want to copy this setting to all breakpoints using the Copy All (⌘-click/Ctrl-click) feature as well (see **Figure 8.10**).

The extra space on the left side comes from the left margin on the speakers block. Select it, and set its left margin to 0, copying that setting to all breakpoints as well. Go back up a level to `section.main` by double-clicking outside the container, clicking `section.main` in the footer breadcrumb, or pressing the Esc key.

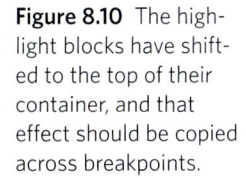

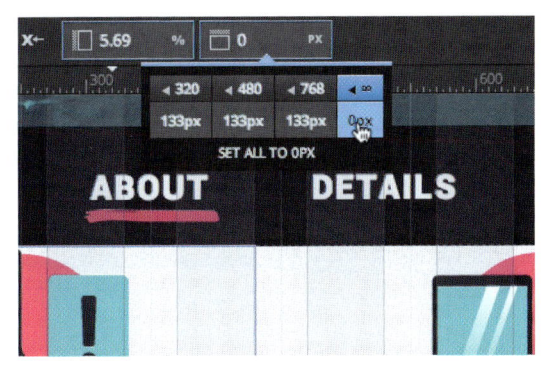

**Figure 8.10** The highlight blocks have shifted to the top of their container, and that effect should be copied across breakpoints.

Finally, we need to clean up the positioning and spacing of these blocks. First reset the width of the container to that of the grid by dragging the left edge to the first column edge, and set its positioning origin to Center (and copy that setting to all breakpoints). Set its top margin to 75px. Now it looks good, but the highlight blocks are a little out of whack (see **Figure 8.11**).

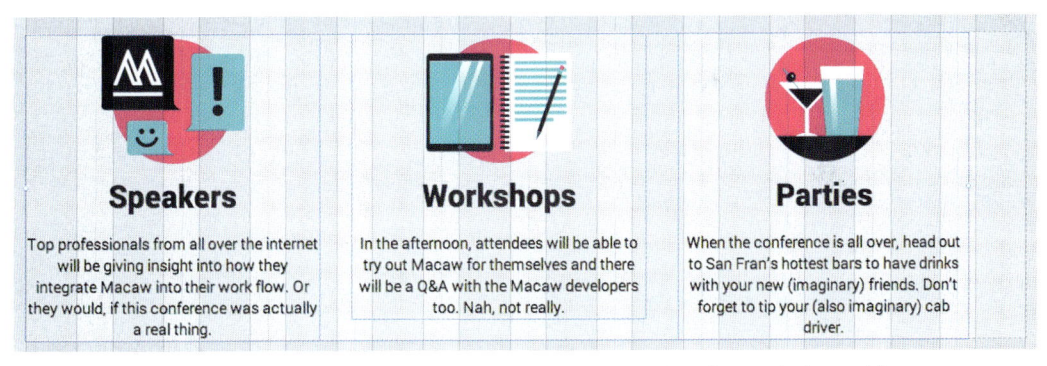

**Figure 8.11** The three blocks are supposed to be four columns wide, lined up with the grid lines. Obviously they are not.

Their widths were originally set without a container and need to be changed. Resetting the positioning of elements is something you'll need to do often; fortunately, it's not a lot of work (especially being able to copy settings across breakpoints). Double-click the highlights container one more time, and reset the positioning of the highlight blocks so they're where they belong, as shown in **Figure 8.12**.

**Figure 8.12** Everything reset and in place.

### Medium breakpoint

First, check the mock-up. The highlight block has the same relationship to the grid, and each highlight block still spans four columns. Because the grid is different at this breakpoint, some resetting will be necessary.

You might see some surprises, like **Figure 8.13**.

**Figure 8.13** The main section has shifted around, as have all of its contents.

After cleaning up the margins of `section.main` and the highlight blocks, we just needed to reset the width of the highlights container and slightly adjust the contained highlight blocks to get everything into position. The mock-up shows slightly tighter spacing between the highlight block and the menu (50px instead of 75px in the larger breakpoint), so update that. After shifting everything around, we end up with **Figure 8.14**.

**Figure 8.14** Everything in its place.

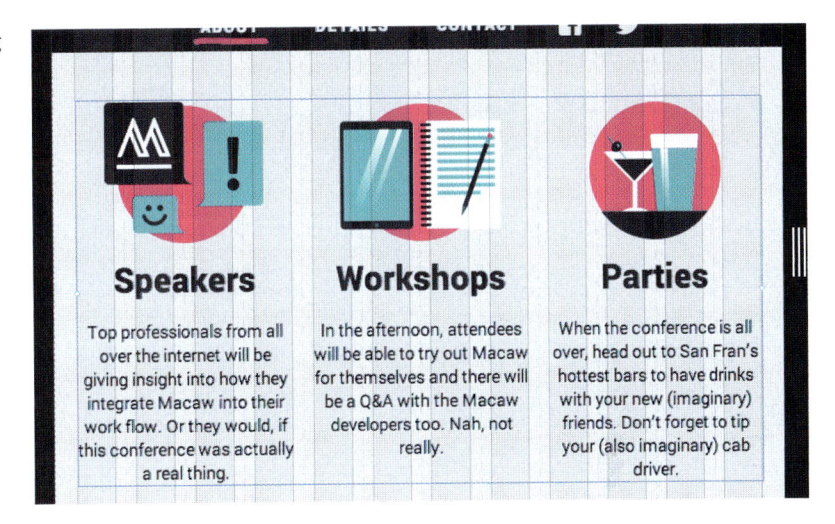

## Dealing with layout surprises

When Macaw recalculates the positioning of elements, it needs to do so across breakpoints, and sometimes it just doesn't do what you expect. Fortunately, these problems can be repaired without a lot of pain by starting with the parent element, resetting its positioning settings and/or dimensions as needed, and then going down the Outline and fixing any other problems. In this case, we saw negative margins applied to `section.main` and some very large top margins applied to the highlight boxes. You can try to catch some of these problems in advance by checking for blue outlines around the positioning settings of each element. Checking for blue outlines is especially helpful when you're fixing problems after the first breakpoint switch like this—as you fix the problem areas, check for blue outlines and obviously out-of-place values (for example, width is set to 33%, and it's 245% in another breakpoint—large positive or negative values are most likely not going to be correct). If you see that kind of thing, copy the corrected value to that problematic breakpoint, and you'll be less likely to see problems when you switch again.

Also note that locking elements will not necessarily stop these reflow issues from occurring. Locking will stop you from making accidental selections, but if Macaw needs to move things around to fit new elements, it will do so.

A few other style changes are also needed: the type size and images are a bit smaller. The type is all controlled by global styles, so at first you might be tempted to change those. However, global styles are truly global, not independent of breakpoints; in other words, if you change the highlight text global style in the medium breakpoint, it will change the text in the large breakpoint too (which is not good). So we'll need to override the parts that change. Select all three headers and make these changes:

- Top padding: 140px
- Font size: 22px

Then select each individually, open the background settings, and change the width from Auto to 150px, leaving the background height set to Auto, which will shrink them down slightly.

> **TIP** You may occasionally notice the Direct Selection tool not selecting deep enough into your containers. We're not sure why this happens, but you'll find that holding the ⌘/Ctrl key can help make sure you're able to dig deep.

Finally, select each highlight text block and reset the text size to 14px. Tighten up the spacing between the headers and text by shrinking their top margins slightly to 10px. They are now as designed in the mock-up (see **Figure 8.15**).

**Figure 8.15**
The highlight blocks with type and background images reset.

> **NOTE** It's a little bit of a bummer to have to override global styles this way. We hope a future version of Macaw makes global styles breakpoint-aware in some way. You may decide it's more sensible only to capture properties that are genuinely global in your global styles, or to capture everything and override as we're doing here.

### *Medium-small breakpoint: no mock-up*

Without a mock-up, we will skip over the medium-small breakpoint for the moment. Because we're building from mock-ups, we're first dealing with what we know, and we can copy or otherwise modify those styles for the intermediate breakpoint later. This is not a 100 percent ideal Macaw workflow—because it is currently built to work from the largest breakpoint downward, Macaw will copy style changes downward automatically (unless those styles are overridden). If you skip one, changes you make when returning it to it could be propagated downward to smaller breakpoints, which would need to be revisited and possibly reset. Fortunately, switching breakpoints and copy styles is pretty easy in Macaw, but it can mean a bit of extra work.

Ideally, we'd like to be able to set up each successive breakpoint from largest to smallest, letting the style changes propagate downward (meaning the amount of revisiting smaller breakpoints to fix issues could be reduced, at least slightly). Without a mock-up for the medium-small breakpoint, it is still possible to do work that way, but for our purposes in this book, we want to work through the areas that we know and copy changes back up the chain of breakpoint command if needed. Using Macaw in the real world, you'll encounter situations like this where you don't have as many mock-ups as you have breakpoints, so knowing how to work in a less-than-ideal way (from Macaw's perspective) is still worthwhile.

### *Small breakpoint*

The highlights break down into a single column here, as wide as the grid, with a much smaller gap at the top of 25px. Select `div.highlights` and change its top margin to 25px, and then adjust its width (if needed) so it's as wide as the grid. Then double-click to edit the highlight elements.

# Getting Started with Macaw

Select all three of them, making them 100% wide, with a 0 left margin. The contents are centered, so you don't need to change their positioning origins to Center (you can; it's just not necessary). At this point, you should see something like **Figure 8.16**.

**Figure 8.16** The highlights are starting to go into place.

They're all butted up against each other now, so add a little padding to the bottom: 25px. Manually spacing items out like this in CSS could be done with margins too, but in Macaw padding is the way to go. The visual result is the same (see **Figure 8.17**). This padding can be copied to the other breakpoints too.

**Figure 8.17** Adding some bottom padding to each of these blocks creates the spacing we need.

**Chapter 8:** Building a Website: Part 2     **141**

Now we need the adjustments for the illustrations and type. Select the three headers and change their top padding to 180px and the font size to 27px. The background images will need to be resized individually to 195px (arbitrary resizing with no side effects—isn't working with SVG nice?). Finally, select all three highlight text blocks and boost their font size up to 16px, using the same 10px top margin as in the medium breakpoint. With multiple selections like this, you don't get the blue borders and popovers that show what the settings are at other breakpoints, so just type them in. At this point, the highlight blocks are finished in this breakpoint (see **Figure 8.18**). Publish and preview the site to make sure everything you've touched is working well so far.

**Figure 8.18** The highlights are finished at the small breakpoint.

### Medium-small breakpoint: all yours

We'll leave the medium-small breakpoint as an exercise for you to complete on your own. In the order we've built this project, it should start with the same settings as the medium breakpoint, which could be adjusted to work (although at its smaller end, the three columns get very smooshed-looking). The small breakpoint settings work a little better, although closer to its large end, the lines of text start to get a little long. You could go with a 2-column + 1 below layout, or move the illustrations to the left of the text. One possible solution is shown in

Figure 8.19 (and is included in the example project), but feel free to experiment. Having a very different layout at each breakpoint is kind of a pain when building a site by hand—using Macaw, you can let it manage the complexity for you, and just design what works best at each size.

Figure 8.19 One way to go in the medium-small breakpoint.

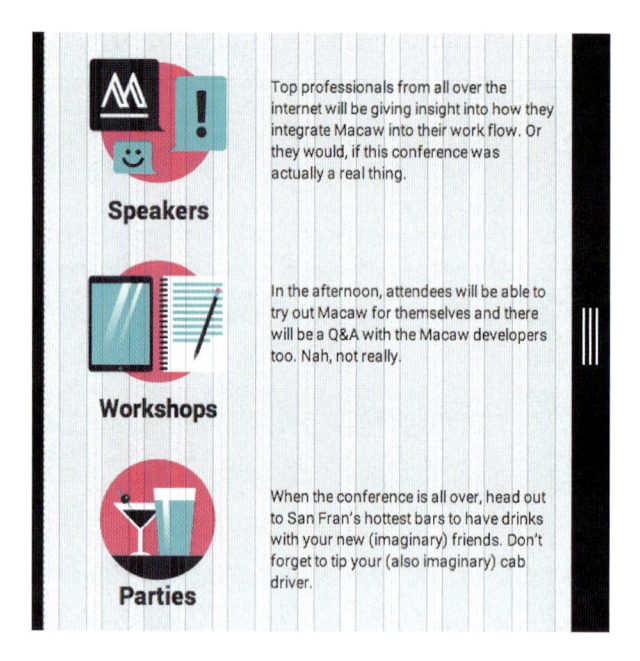

> **NOTE** Be sure to keep checking the other breakpoints. The small breakpoint in particular may pick up changes you made for its medium-small sibling, and it may have to be reset.

## Testimonials: A Challenge

The testimonials area presents a challenge: It calls for a kind of interactivity that Macaw doesn't natively handle: rotating through blocks of content, which is built using JavaScript usually in the form of a jQuery plugin, or through custom JavaScript if you're quite savvy. There are at least three strategies we could use:

- Just mock up the first quote as shown in the mock-ups, and leave the actual crafting of the markup as a postpublishing task. If you're a relative beginner with JavaScript, this is easily the most sensible option. To end any possible suspense, this is the way we'll go, but if you're savvier or just like to hack, other possibilities exist.

- Find a jQuery plugin, publish it somewhere accessible via HTTP (either on the Internet or in your local development environment), and integrate it into the project using the Head & Tail publish settings (File > Publish Settings or ⌘-Shift-P/Ctrl-Shift-P) or embedded scripts using View > Show Scripts. The interactivity will certainly not be visible on the canvas, but being able to style the markup in Macaw might be worth the trouble for more advanced users. This is interesting enough to bear inclusion in Appendix D, but awkward enough not to simply recommend for most people.

- Wrap up a block of custom HTML (which can include `<script>` tags, or anything you want) and use the Embed tool to include it. Macaw will insert anything you place in an embed block verbatim in the published document, but it will not include a preview on the canvas. (Macaw does preview some embedded content, but not custom HTML blocks.) If you can stand seeing something like **Figure 8.20** on the canvas, embedded blocks will be fine. Using external files in the second approach can be better for maintainability, and if you're relying on external hosted libraries, it is your best option. But if you want to keep as much code as possible in the Macaw project directly, this approach will work.

**Figure 8.20** Custom HTML blocks are not previewed on the canvas. Macaw doesn't know where that HTML has been—who knows what you put in there?

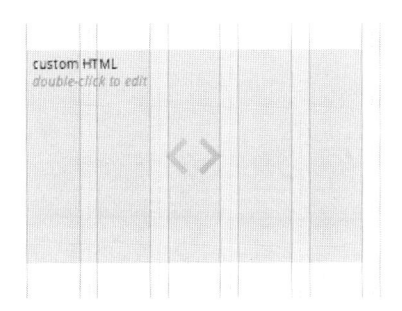

### Current solution: mock it up

Soldiering on with the "just mock up the look" approach, switch to the default breakpoint (Shift-\) so you can add some elements. Create a text block for the quote, extending through the gutters of the middle six columns, as shown in the mock-up. Here are the specs:

- Font family: Roboto
- Font weight: 300
- Font size: 28px
- Line height: 1.25em
- Text align: Center
- Color: #171f37 (remember the swatch)
- Height: Auto
- Minimum height: 150px
- HTML tag: blockquote (good semantics, and again we don't have to worry about default browser styles because of Macaw's CSS resets)
- Bottom padding: 20px

Next, create a second text block immediately below that block quote for the attribution. Drag it to the same width. If you have View > Toggle Positioning Guides enabled, you'll see helpful guidelines showing when you're aligned with the left and bottom edge of the block quote (see **Figure 8.21**), although of course you can reposition and resize it after creating it.

**Figure 8.21**
The positioning guides show up before creating an object.

Here are its specs:

- Font family: Roboto
- Font weight: 900
- Font size: 30px
- Color: #171f37 (swatch!)
- Text align: Center
- Height: Auto

Give this object the tag `p.attribution`.

Next you can create the pager (the three dots indicating which quote is shown). Duplicate the attribution text block and place the duplicate immediately below. Double-click the block to edit it, and replace the text with three bullets (Opt-8/Alt-0149), and then change the specs as follows:

- Font: Helvetica
- Size: 50px
- Line height: 1.25em (you can use line height instead of padding to create the space around the bullets—either way would work, but this keeps as many settings as possible in the Typography palette for convenience)
- Color: #2db1ba (make a swatch for this; it's also used in the site footer)
- Letter spacing: 2px

At this point, the result should look like **Figure 8.22**.

**Figure 8.22** The pager bullets in place and almost finished.

One of these bullets needs to indicate the currently shown quote. You might have noticed that text styles can seemingly only be applied to the entire text block at once, and only when you're not editing the text. However, it is possible to style sections of a text block; you just have to select a portion first. Once you do that, you can create a node, which essentially means wrapping that portion of text in an HTML tag, which can then be styled how you like. Select the first bullet in the pager block, and then click the SPAN button shown in **Figure 8.23**.

**Figure 8.23** A selected portion of text may be wrapped in a span, an em, or a strong tag, and subsequently styled.

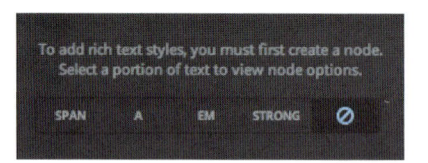

Once the text is selected, the Inspector will repopulate with all of its styling options, as shown in **Figure 8.24**. With the tags/nodes available, you can create links, regular and strong emphasis (you'll need to apply italics or bold manually—Macaw resets all default styles), and arbitrary styles using the `<span>` tag as we're doing here. For now, all you really need is to change the color of the bullet to #e21a64 (save a swatch for this just in case). You'll often see the keyword "inherit" when editing nodes, which means that style should inherit its value from the parent element (the one inside which this node was created).

**Figure 8.24** The Inspector shows the many options available for styling the new node.

**NOTE** *Node* is a term from the Document Object Model. It's a little technical, but if the term is new to you, at least it's short, and commonly used in the web development world. You can't touch the node beyond selecting a tag at present (that is, you can't add classes to it, or otherwise see it in the Outline), and nodes can't be nested in other nodes (that is, no links inside `<span>` tags).

Although the other bullets will presumably be clickable when the quotes block is finished later, we'll assume the clickability of those bullets will be handled by JavaScript, and therefore not manually create `<a>` nodes for the other two bullets. Give this pager the tag `div.pager`, and it's now all set.

Now we'll literally wrap everything up. Select the quote and attribution elements and group them into a container (⌘-G/Ctrl-G); call it `div.testimonial`. This container is just big enough to wrap the elements, but that isn't going to be quite right—we still need extra room on both sides for the big juicy quote marks. Those could be their own elements dropped onto the canvas, but then you end up with more movable parts to worry about (and they don't even appear in the small version). Instead, we prefer to wrap the entire quotes block in another container that spans the full width of the grid, and apply the quote marks as background images. So now select the testimonial and pager, and use Elements > Full-Width Group (⌘-Opt-G/Ctrl-Alt-G) to create another wrapper for everything that spans the entire canvas.

Before we add the quote marks, situate everything where it needs to be in the Outline, and polish the elements' positioning. Switch to the Outline and change the tag of the outer wrapper to `div.testimonials`. Drag it into `section.main`, below `div.highlights`. The negative margin warnings should go away at this point. You can also drag the block quote above the attribution element if you like.

**NOTE** Sometimes warnings don't disappear immediately. If you think you've fixed the issues but still see warnings, switch to the Inspector and back to the Outline quickly (Opt-I/Alt-I and Opt-O/Alt-O are great for this). If the warnings are still there, and you're not purposefully using negative margins, you still have some positioning gremlins to zap.

Try resizing the canvas if you haven't already, and you'll probably notice the quotes overlapping the pager and the secondary content block below, as in **Figure 8.25**.

**Figure 8.25** We resize because we care. We care to catch issues like this.

Overlapping behavior like this often indicates areas where one or more elements have their height fixed where it should be Auto. Because we created a container, that's a good place to look. Indeed, `div.testimonials` has a fixed height, so change that to Auto (for all breakpoints). Its child `div.testimonial` will also need the same treatment. Now check the top margin of `div.testimonials`. Make sure it's a reasonable value (for example, 54px and not 54 million pixels or -3201px), and copy that value to all breakpoints. In our build, these changes fixed that overlapping nonsense, but there are a few more things to clean up. You want Macaw to do as much work for you as possible, but it's critical to check that the work done has accomplished what you want, and to help give Macaw the best chance to act correctly.

We want the quotes and pager to stay centered, so change the positioning origin of `div.testimonial` and `div.pager` to center across all breakpoints, and change both of their top margins to 0 (again for all breakpoints). Double-click `div.testimonial` and make sure the quote and attribution are both set to 100% width inside their container and that their margins are all zero. These changes help make sure the container is doing all the positioning work, while the children just fill all available space (basically we're trying to give Macaw less to worry about).

Now let's add the quote marks as background images. Select `div.testimonials` and add a background image to it (import `quote-begin.svg`). Turn off all repeats, and then set its X position to 13.25% and its Y position to 30px (as usual, change the unit first, then the value).

Then add a second background image to the same element, `quote-end.svg` this time. Turn off the repeats, and set its X to 86.75% and Y to 30px. Once you do, the quote marks should be lined up with the same column guides as the mock-up, and also with the second line of the quote, as shown in **Figure 8.26**.

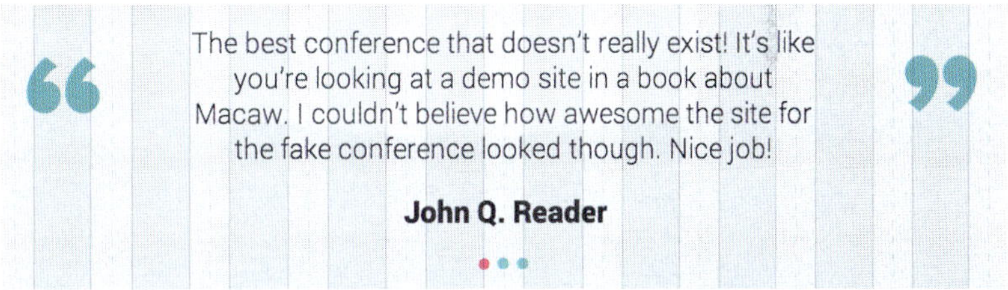

**Figure 8.26**
The testimonial quote machine with quote marks added.

**NOTE** Using a sprite here would be good, but we decided not to do that because Macaw's background image palette shows the names of the files used, and it's nice to be able to tell which image is which. If you're working in an environment where every last milliliter of performance matters, we're assuming you have a post-Macaw pipeline that will help optimize all the HTML, CSS, and images Macaw produces, or that maybe your requirements are too advanced for Macaw to be an appropriate fit for that project. For everyone else, this small trade-off in favor of maintainability could be worth the extra HTTP request.

With all of these changes made, we can remove the minimum width from `section.main`—with all the content in place, it's no longer needed.

Resizing the canvas, publishing and previewing, you should see some pretty sensible behaviors. A fluid grid means that things have the chance to look at least pretty good at almost any size. Now, of course, we want to do better than pretty good—so we'll make some refinements for the other breakpoints according to the mock-up—but this section is in good shape.

### Medium breakpoint

Switching to the medium breakpoint, you'll see it really does look fine. We can do better, though, so let's do that. First fix the quote marks so they're closer to the edges of the page. Change the positioning of the quote—set its X to 5.5% and its height to 45px (leaving width set to Auto). For the background image, quote-end.png, set X to 94.5% and height to 45px (see **Figure 8.27**).

**Figure 8.27**
The settings for the background quote-end.png in the medium breakpoint.

Then stretch the width of `div.testimonial` so it spans the middle eight columns into the middle of the gutters on each side (Macaw will snap to the middle of a gutter). Change the font size of the block quote to 21px, set its bottom padding to 14px, and remove its minimum height by setting it to 0 or deleting it (copy that removal across all breakpoints—we only used that for the initial mocking up).

Set the font size of the attribution to 22px and the line height of the pager to 1em. This will result in **Figure 8.28**, which should stand up well to resizing.

**Figure 8.28** The testimonials block resized for the medium breakpoint.

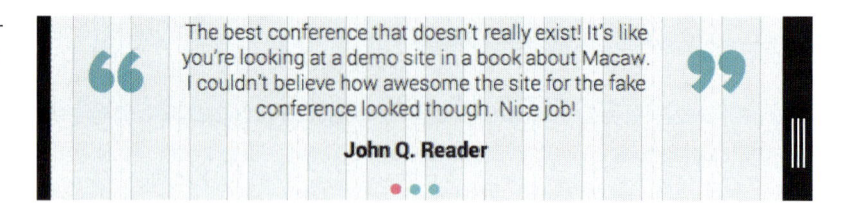

### Small breakpoint

Once again, we're skipping the in-between breakpoint and going straight to the small one since that's what we have a mock-up for. This one is a little different from the others: The quote marks are gone, and there's a background gradient applied instead. Let's start with those changes, and then apply a few others.

Hide the two background images by clicking their eye icons. Add a new background gradient with the following settings:

- Angle: 90°
- Left color: transparent (click the swatch with a line through it, drag the opacity slider all the way to the bottom, or type **transparent** in the text box)
- Right color: rgba(0, 0, 0, 0.1) (that's 10 percent opaque black)

Macaw is clever enough to hide this gradient at the larger breakpoints, but you can switch to them and confirm that if you like. Select `div.testimonials`, set its top margin to 0, its top padding to 35px, and its bottom padding to 15px. This brings it closer to the highlights but leaves a bit of whitespace on the top and bottom. Next select `div.testimonial` and make it as wide as the grid, and change its font size to 21px. Check that the pager has a top margin of 0. With all of these changes in place, you should end up with **Figure 8.29**. Try resizing and previewing, of course, to make sure everything is copacetic.

**Figure 8.29** The testimonials block fixed for the small breakpoint.

As in previous sections, how you adjust the medium-small breakpoint is up to you. The example project shows one solution; it mostly keeps the behaviors from the medium breakpoint, with a few adjustments.

Once you've finished these modifications, you can lock `section.main` and continue.

# Secondary content: "Meet the Developers"

This section is pretty straightforward given what we've done so far, with a big image of text for "Developers" and regular text for the other pieces. Making sure the background image behaves correctly will take a little bit of attention, and there's a text shadow on "in your dreams," but overall we're dealing with previously explored territory.

First, switch to the large breakpoint (Shift-\), unlock `section.secondary` if needed, and check its positioning options. Specifically, its top margin might be wacky. If it is, reset it to 0. It's not currently a container, but you can convert it using ⌘-G/Ctrl-G (Elements > Tight Group). Now double-click `section.secondary` to open it for editing. Then add three text boxes, each the width of the page, for "Meet the" (tag: `h3.meet`), "Developers" (`h3.developers`), and "(in your dreams)" (`p.dreams`).

For positioning, we'd argue that the elements sit on top of each other starting from the bottom—that is, the distance from the bottom of the photo to "in your dreams" stays more consistent than the distance from the top to "Meet the," so we'll position the elements to use the bottom of `section.secondary` as the origin, which means absolute positioning (static can't do it, and we don't need fixed).

In the Outline (the items may have shifted out of view, so this approach is easier), select `p.dreams`, change its positioning to absolute, its horizontal origin to center, and its vertical origin to bottom, with an offset of 50px. Set its font settings as follows:

- Font: Roboto
- Weight: 700
- Size: 20px
- Color: #e21a64 (there is a swatch for this)
- Italics and Uppercase buttons turned on

To add the shadow, scroll down in the Inspector to the Effects palette. In the current version of Macaw, the available effects are Drop Shadow, Inner Shadow, Text Shadow, and Opacity. Drop and Inner Shadow both apply to the entire box—we want the shadow to apply to the text only, so click the plus and choose Text Shadow. The parameters of a CSS shadow are a little different from those of Photoshop (the angle is 180° opposite, for one thing), so a direct translation from Photoshop is not possible. Macaw tries to offer similar controls, but as a result, the options shown are not all free parameters—an adjustment to one can cause the others to shift. You'll sometimes need to play with the options to get the look you want. **Figure 8.30** shows settings that work well here, but experiment with changing the angle and watch how the other text boxes change, and vice versa.

**Figure 8.30** A shadow with an angle of 300°, X offset of 2, and Y offset of 3 looks good.

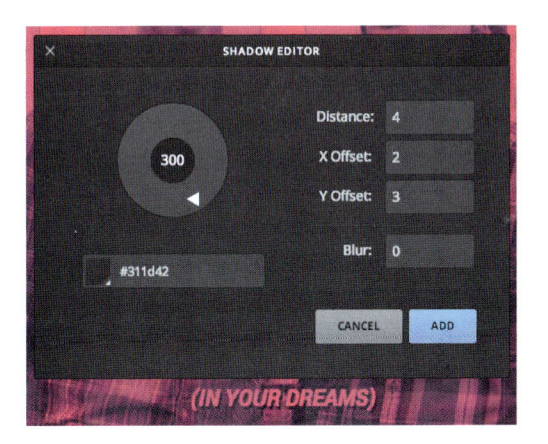

Next select `h3.developers`. Set its positioning to absolute, X and Y origins center and bottom, with a bottom offset of 90px. Change its height from Auto to 150px. Add a background image (`developers-2x.png`) with no repeats, positioned at center-bottom, and click the 2x button to tell Macaw it's a 2x image and to resize it accordingly.

To make the regular text go away, change the text settings as follows:

- Size: 1px
- Indent: -300px

Because `developers` is 100 percent wide and the text is short and set small, this is enough to get it off screen at any reasonable size.

Now select `h3.meet`. Set its positioning to absolute, X and Y origins center and bottom, with a bottom offset of 240px. Change its font settings as follows:

- Font: Roboto
- Weight: 700
- Size: 50px
- Color: white
- Letter spacing: 2px
- Uppercase turned on

The results should look like **Figure 8.31**.

**Figure 8.31**
The developers block, with everything set correctly.

### Medium breakpoint

Looking at the mock-ups, the adjustments this section needs at each breakpoint are relatively minor by the standards we've seen so far. Select `section.secondary` and set its height to 390px (the height will get a little smaller at each breakpoint to allow the background image to show everyone in it).

Select `p.dreams`, and in the options bar set its bottom position to 35px and its font size to 15px. With the reduction in font size, the shadow will need some adjusting as well, to bring it a little closer. In the Effects palette, double-click the Text Shadow effect, and change the distance to 2, X offset to 1, and Y to 2. The angle will shift slightly as you do this, which is fine.

Next up is `h3.developers`. Set its bottom position to 70px and its height to 100px. The background image will be way too big for the small container, so double-click that to edit it, and change its size to Contain, which will make sure it always fits but can also make the image smaller if the width of the header gets too narrow. So when using Contain, be sure to check the small end of your breakpoint to be sure everything works how you want. In this case, "Developers" starts to get just a little bit smaller around 500px. In this case, that's fine, but this could be an opportunity to make other adjustments.

Finally, select `h3.meet` and change its bottom position to 170px and its font size to 35px. The end result is shown in **Figure 8.32**.

**Figure 8.32**
The developers block reset for the medium breakpoint.

### Small breakpoint

Same drill here—just some slight changes to make everything sit better at this small size. Change the height of `section.secondary` to 177px.

For `p.dreams`, set its bottom position to 20px and its font size to 20px. The text shadow can be adjusted so the distance, X offset, and Y offset are all 1px (this will shift the angle slightly).

For `h3.developers`, set its bottom position to 44px and its height to 65px.

For `h3.meet`, set its bottom position to 95px, font size to 20px, and line height to 1em (for text that's meant to stay on one line, you can always do this—in Macaw, it makes the selection border tighter around the text, meaning snap guides will be closer to the top and bottom). With these changes, you'll have **Figure 8.33**.

**Figure 8.33** The developers block reset for the small breakpoint.

Once again, we'll leave the medium-small breakpoint as an exercise for you, the reader, though as exercises go, this one will probably be pretty quick. When you're finished, you can lock `section.secondary` and move on.

## Footer: Pleasantly Easy

The last piece of the home page to be built is the footer, which is very simple on this site. To get started, switch to the large breakpoint and unlock `<footer>`. Convert it to a container if needed using ⌘-G/Ctrl-G, and double-click it for editing.

Create a single line of text that says "Photography from Unsplash.com," and set its top margin to 40px, left margin to 0, and width to 100%. Style the text as follows:

- Font: Roboto
- Weight: 400
- Size: 18px
- Color: #2db1ba
- Alignment: Center

Set its tag to `p.credit`. Next, duplicate that text block and drag it 20px down. Macaw shows you a margin indicator while dragging (see **Figure 8.34**) that helps with this step.

**Figure 8.34** After duplicating an element, Macaw shows this positioning guide to help you place an element precisely.

Change the text to "Copyright © 2014 Nobody" (for the copyright symbol, press Opt-G on a Mac, Alt-0169 on Windows), set its tag to `p.copyright`, and style it as follows:

- Weight: 700
- Size: 16px
- Color: white
- Uppercase turned on

Unsplash.com is a link to the free photography website, so let's create that link. Double-click `p.credit` to edit its text, and select Unsplash.com. In the Inspector, click the A button to create that node, and a new Anchor palette will appear (see **Figure 8.35**).

**Figure 8.35**
The Anchor palette appears after you create an A node (a link) in a text block.

Fill in `https://unsplash.com/` in the HREF field. Leave Target set to Self to allow the link to open in the same window, or change it to Blank to force it to open a new window or tab.

> **NOTE** The specific photo used is of the San Francisco Bay Bridge, and you can find it here: http://unsplash.com/photos/n7n-nkadHRM.

Notice that the link doesn't get underlined automatically—as with all default browser styles that Macaw resets, you must do this yourself. The Underline button in the Typography palette will do this, or if you prefer to use borders, you can add the underline that way. **Figures 8.36** and **8.37** show each of these options, though of course you'll probably just need one.

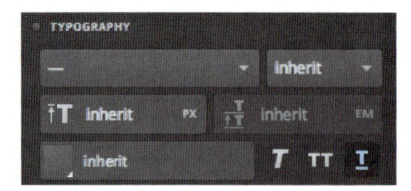

**Figure 8.36** The underline option—just clicking the underline button—is easy but doesn't provide as much control. The underline is the same color as the text and can't otherwise be styled easily.

**Figure 8.37** Using a bottom border instead, you can change the color, opacity, weight, and style.

Links also have states, shown as a button group below the Node Tag selector (see **Figure 8.38**). Hover (for when the mouse is over a link) and focus (for when a link has keyboard focus, via the Tab key or other means) are good ones to pay attention to. Each state may be styled independently. Change at least the `:hover` and `:focus` states by removing the underline and changing the color of the link to the brighter aqua (#74f6ff; you should have a swatch for it). Preview the project to see these link changes in action.

> **NOTE** Although it's good to change the color of a link in response to these states, it's better to change other properties as well, so people with less-than-perfect eyesight have a better chance of seeing the changes. That's why we've disabled the underline here, but of course there are lots of other possibilities to consider depending on your audience.

The footer is ready to go, so let's make the adjustments for the other breakpoints.

**Figure 8.38** The states button group. The state currently being edited is shown in blue, and any states that have been edited are shown in white (as is the default here).

### Footer fixes for other breakpoints

The rest of the breakpoints can use the same settings. Change to the medium breakpoint, and update the height of `<footer>` to 120px. Leave some whitespace (or maybe bluespace?) at the bottom of the page, but not too much.

For `p.credit`, change its top margin to 35px and its font size to 14px. For `p.copyright`, change its top margin to 10px and its font size to 13px. The result of these changes is shown in **Figure 8.39**. Check the other breakpoints to confirm that they are using the same settings.

**Figure 8.39** The footer modified for all smaller breakpoints.

# A Full Page: Done!

With that, it's time to do the dance of joy because you've just built an entire responsive page in Macaw! You're going to add a couple more pages to the project coming up, but having worked to this point, you have a tremendous amount of knowledge and can build anything you want. Take a break, go look at some cat videos on the Internet, or take a walk outside—go on, you crazy kid!—and meet us in Chapter 9.

# 9

# Building a Website: Part 3

In the previous two chapters, you built the common elements for the whole website and finished the first page. In this chapter, you'll build the next page: Details. Once again, the first step is to review the mock-ups and clarify what you're putting together.

## Review the Mock-ups

The Details page has a little bit of information on the conference, with big, picturesque links to other sections not included in this project, and an embedded map of the location.

The other main thing worth noting is that in the large and medium breakpoints, the header is different on these two pages. The location and date are treated differently from the home page, and the Macawfrence logo is the same one used on the small breakpoint.

## Create a New Page

We'll start with the Details page. You could create a new page using ⌘-N/Ctrl-N or File > New Page, but you'd be starting completely from scratch, without the breakpoints, grid settings, or anything else you've built up so far outside of the assets and components in the Library. There's a lot we'd like to reuse, so a copy will be better. Click the page menu in the upper left and mouse over the index page. A couple icons will appear on the right side, as shown in **Figure 9.1**, letting you either make a copy of the current page or delete it. In this case, we want to make a copy, so click that icon to open a new tab, with a page called index-copy.

**Figure 9.1** The page list shows all pages in the current project and lets you duplicate or delete any page using the copy and trash can icons.

The default name (index-copy) is not what we want. To rename it, open the page menu again, but this time right-click index-copy. As shown in **Figure 9.2**, a context menu appears, offering everything you can do with the page, including renaming it. Choose Rename Page, and change the name to **details**. You can also rename a page by double-clicking the text of the name in the page menu (double-clicking the nearby whitespace won't work).

**Figure 9.2** Right-click a page in the Page menu to show this context menu, which offers options for doing everything you can with a page.

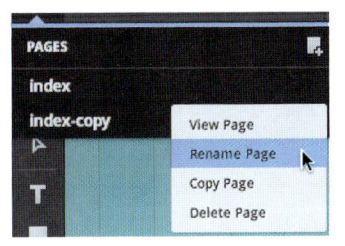

Finally, change the page title. Click the canvas so nothing is selected, and change the title in the Page Title palette to **Details - Macawfrence**.

> **NOTE** A page's name is the name of the HTML file Macaw will generate. As such, while you can type whatever you want in the text field, it will be converted to a web-safe format (using all lowercase, substituting hyphens for spaces, and dropping most punctuation). The title of the page, which is shown in the browser title bar and in search engine results, is unrestricted.

## Revise the header

With the new page created, we can revise the header to match the mock-up. Some modifications will be needed for the date and location, but we can start with the parts that involve styling and positioning. Switch to the default breakpoint (Shift-\), unlock `<header>` in the Outline if it's locked, and change its height to 250px. Double-click it to edit its contents.

Now select `h1.macawfrence`. It has two background images, but we're only going to need one of them on this page. Delete MacawfrenceHeader-2x, and then set MacawfrenceHeader-sm-2x to visible by clicking its eye icon. Double-click it to change its settings, changing its size to Contain and its positioning to left and center, and disabling any repeats. Change the element height to 230px. Now the element needs to be repositioned and resized horizontally, so change its horizontal origin to left, and drag it so the left edge aligns with the left edge of the second grid column. Drag the right edge out until the background image fills the box completely, right around the beginning of the seventh column (see **Figure 9.3**).

**Figure 9.3** The Macawfrence header resized and repositioned on the Details page.

The date and location header provides a small challenge. We already have a header, currently only shown in the smallest breakpoint, but the text is slightly different (text can't be changed with breakpoints at all in Macaw, and only in limited ways in CSS using :before and :after pseudoselectors). Also, the designer wants the text to resize smoothly the way the Macawfrence header does as the window gets smaller. There are ways to get this behavior using advanced CSS techniques (for example, viewport units) or JavaScript libraries (for example, FlowType.JS), but they are not supported in Macaw directly. The easiest way to get the desired behavior is to use an image.

We'll use the existing h2.date-location and apply the background image to it in the larger breakpoints. We could create a new element, but it would be redundant. Select h2.date-location and click the eye icon to make it visible. Change it as follows:

- Positioning origins: right, center
- Height: 90px
- Background color: transparent
- Text alignment: left
- Text indent: -9999px (or use the image replacement technique from Chapter 7)

For the background image, import Macawfrence-dateloc-2x.png, positioned center and right, size set to Contain, with repeats turned off. Drag the header so it's aligned with the right edge of the second-to-last column on the right, as shown in **Figure 9.4**.

**Figure 9.4** The date and location header, placed where it belongs for now.

If you try resizing the canvas, you'll see that the two pieces of the header do not move together, so we need to add a container. Select the two headers and group them, giving the new container the tag `div.hgroup` (as of this writing, the HTML5 `hgroup` tag has an uncertain future, so we'll use an old-school alternative) and setting its positioning origin to center. Double-click it to edit the two headers.

Check that `h1.macawfrence`'s width is a percentage and that it has no minimum width. For `h2.date-location`, you might not need to make any changes. Now the header should resize smoothly.

## Medium breakpoint

Switch to the medium breakpoint (Shift-[) and change the header's height to 182px. Select `div.hgroup` and change its top margin to 0, its height to 182px, and its width so it spans all 12 columns (you can use ⌘-E/Ctrl-E to do this). Double-click it to edit the two headers inside. Set the height of `h1.macawfrence` to 182px, its left position to 0, and its width to the span of the left seven columns (around 57%). Switch to the Outline, select `h2.date-location`, and click the eye icon to make it visible. Set its right position to 0, make it as wide as the right five columns, and then make it tall enough that the background image fills the box.

With these changes in place, the header should look like **Figure 9.5**.

Figure 9.5  The header reconfigured for the medium breakpoint.

## Medium-small breakpoint

We leave this as an exercise for the reader once again. You can adapt the medium breakpoint settings, use the small breakpoint, or some variation.

## Small breakpoint

The header for the small breakpoint is laid out identically to the home page, but with the addition of `div.hgroup` and the other changes from the previous breakpoints, there is some reconfiguring to be done. Start with `div.hgroup` and reset it to the same size as its container. Use ⌘-E/Ctrl-E to expand it to the width of the canvas. Set its top margin to 0 and its height to 150px.

`h1.macawfrence` is mostly fine; it needs just a couple of tweaks. Set its horizontal origin to center and its vertical origin to top, with a value of 8px. Use ⌘-E/Ctrl-E to expand it to the width of the container (and therefore the grid).

Next, select `h2.date-location`. Hide the background image, and set the background color to #171f37 using the Swatch tool (S). Set its vertical positioning origin to bottom and the value to 0. Make it 40px tall, 100% wide. To restore the text, set the text indent to 0 and the alignment to center.

With these changes in place, the header is all set, as shown in **Figure 9.6**.

Lock `<header>` once again, and we'll move on to the navigation.

**Figure 9.6** The header reset in the small breakpoint.

## Revise the Navigation

Now that we have more than one page, we need to update the navigation menu by activating the links and giving them more meaningful hover and focus states. Start by switching to the Outline, unlocking `<nav>` if needed, and double-clicking the container icon next to `div.menu`. Doing so will open that container for editing directly without having to double-click its parent elements first.

This is the details page, so we want its link to have the "I'm the active page" indicator, not About. Select `a.about`—it has the `nav-item` global style assigned, but overridden. Click the circle arrow to revert it to the default state (that is, no background image). We would like the stroke to appear on mouse hover or keyboard focus, so click `:hover` in the Inspector (see **Figure 9.7**). In the Backgrounds palette, click the eye icon to show the background image again. Do the same thing for the `:focus` state.

**Figure 9.7** Clicking `:hover` activates styles that will apply to an item when the mouse is over that item.

Now select `a.details` and enable its background image, making it look active. The background image doesn't reach the edges of the word "Details" at the moment, so update that by editing the background image and changing its width from 105px to 100% (leaving the height as is). Stretching an image can look a little unsightly at times, but with a relatively small stretch like this, it still looks good. Make the same changes for `a.contact`, showing its background image on hover and focus and resizing the background image as needed.

Switch to the medium breakpoint and check the links' hover and focus states. Start with the default, and then look at `:hover` and `:focus` for each link in turn. Depending on the size of the text, you may find that the background image sizes need to be adjusted—the Contain setting can be a helpful first try as the items get smaller, but if you need to, you can tweak the sizes manually. We found that the changes made here cascaded downward nicely to the medium-small and small breakpoints, so try previewing the project now and making sure each of the links behaves correctly. If there are problems at any breakpoint, fix them up, starting with the largest breakpoint with an issue and working downward (because Macaw will cascade corrections downward).

## Adding links

The menu is almost ready now, except the links don't actually go anywhere yet. In the Inspector, below Effects, is the Links palette. Details is the current page, so clicking it doesn't need to do anything, but About should be activated as a link to the index page. Select `a.about`, and then click the page selector in the Links palette to show all pages in the project (see **Figure 9.8**). Choose index, which will fill in index.html in the link field.

**Figure 9.8** The Links palette includes a page selector for linking to pages in this project.

## Linkage

The link field can contain anything that works in an `href` attribute in HTML. For linking to external websites, `http` and `https` work, but so do `mailto:` links for email addresses, or even `javascript:` links if you need to use those (hopefully you don't, but if you do, they will work).

Links may be added to any element in Macaw, whether or not you've given that element an `<a>` tag. Non-anchor tag elements with links will have a JavaScript `onClick` event added to them to make the element behave like a link. This is not recommended—if something is a link, it should pretty much always use the `<a>` tag.

Links are consistent across breakpoints, so although you should feel free to preview and check that they work everywhere, you don't have to. However, changing the menu on one page does not update it on another page, so open the index page in the Page menu, or just click its tab if you still have it open to switch to it. Select `a.details` here, and link it to the Details page using the page selector. Then run through the same drill as on the Details page, making sure the `:hover` and `:focus` states are set up correctly for each link (once we've created the Contact page, we can return to these pages and add it easily).

At this point, the menu is all set, so we can lock it and move on to the content area.

# Build the Content Area

We're going to keep the separation between the main content section and the secondary section on this page (Contact won't need it). The main section will have the big text block and the grid of four images, and the secondary section will have the embedded map. We'll start with the main section.

## Big text box

Unlock `section.main` if it's locked, and switch to the large breakpoint (Shift-\). We could just delete everything contained in the section, but that would collapse `section.main` into a regular element. Instead, we'll just delete one of the elements we don't need, leaving the container open. In the Outline, double-click the box icon next to `section.main` to open it for editing; then select and delete `div.highlights`. A big space will be left where it was—in that space, add a new text box (don't worry about its size yet) and fill it with the sample text (copy and paste it from Text.txt in the assets folder). Set it up as follows:

- Font: Roboto
- Weight: 300
- Size: 28px
- Line height: 1.25em
- Color: #171f37 (swatch!)

The last sentence in this block is smaller and italicized, so double-click the text box for editing, select that last line, and add a node. Use `<em>`, since this line is a bit of emphasis—that will not give you the default italics a browser gives you, so click the italics button in the Typography palette, and set its text size size to 20px (you cannot use relative sizes directly in Macaw at this time).

> **TIP** If you create multiple nodes in a block of text, Macaw uses the same styles for all of them, which is handy if you've created a lot of links in a single block, for example. Along with global styles, a way to share styles between text blocks is to use Edit > Copy Visual Properties (⌘-Opt-C/Ctrl-Alt-C) and Edit > Paste Visual Properties (⌘-Opt-V/Ctrl-Alt-V). This will copy all the active styles from one element to another. When you paste, text blocks will pick up all the styles from the original text block, including those of the embedded nodes. For moving styles around, global styles are often a better choice, especially if you think you'll want to edit the styles later, but at worst you might need to create and apply a global style after the fact.

With the text in place, you can position the box. Set its horizontal origin to center, and use Elements > Expand (⌘-E/Ctrl-E) to make it as wide as the grid (if you already did this, it will appear as if nothing happened, which is fine). Set its top margin to 0, and if it has a minimum height, remove it. Give it the tag `p.details`.

Now the text block is butted up against the top of the section, which we don't want. We could create space using margins, but this time, just to try something different, we'll use padding on `section.main` instead. Hit the Esc key to go back up an editing level, in this case to the main canvas. Select `section.main`, and in the Dimensions palette, set its top and bottom padding to 75px. Now it should be all set, as shown in **Figure 9.9**.

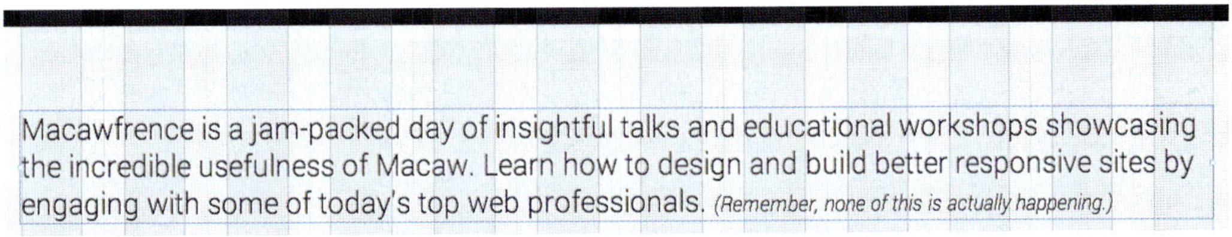

![Figure 9.9 screenshot showing details text box]

**Figure 9.9** The details text box, formatted and positioned according to the mock-up.

## The image grid: first image

These could be set up as background images, but considering these are links with which you might directly interact (and, let's face it, because we haven't covered it yet), we'll use regular images for this section. The idea will be to import and place the images, and then wrap them in links and any containers we need to make the layout behave as desired.

Switch to the Library and click the Import button. Import the four images that start with "details" (for example, `details-agenda-2x.jpg`). Drag `details-speakers-2x` onto the canvas, between the old `blockquote` and the new details text box. It will come in comically large (see **Figure 9.10**).

**Figure 9.10** An image this big is not overly useful.

Select it and switch to the Inspector (Alt-I/Opt-I), and you'll see the Image palette. This palette is mostly informational, but it does have a 2x button, which you should click to bring this image under control. At this point in the process, it's possible that `p.details` and the leftover block quote will seemingly disappear or otherwise get displaced in apparently weird ways. The block quote can be deleted at this point, since we don't need it anyway, and the speakers image establishes the rest of the space needed in this region. As for `p.details`, select it in the Outline and restore its margin settings to the correct values (and copy those values to other breakpoints). If the other breakpoints have sensible values, you can copy those instead of typing.

Now check that all negative margins are gone from the image and the paragraph, and drag the image into place, aligned with the left edge of the grid, six columns wide. Give it a top margin of 65px. The image should be 75px from the secondary content area below because `section.main` has a setting of Auto for its height, and there is the 75px of padding you added earlier, as shown in **Figure 9.11**.

**Figure 9.11** The speakers image, placed and spaced correctly.

This image still needs tag work. By default, Macaw gives it the tag `img.image`. We don't need the class (it will be wrapped in a link with a class of its own shortly), so you can delete that. In the Advanced palette, however, there is the `alt` attribute, which is only shown for images (see **Figure 9.12**). The `alt` attribute is used in contexts where the image is not displayed or used conventionally (for example, for screen readers, search engines, and any browser with images turned off), so it's important to set it on every image. Speakers will be sufficient here.

**Figure 9.12** The `alt=` field in the Advanced palette appears only for images. Always set it, and set it to something meaningful.

We don't have pages to link these images to, because of course the conference doesn't really exist, but let's still establish these images as links for whenever they'll be needed. Note that Macaw doesn't show the Links palette when an image is selected; you need to wrap the image in an `<a>` tag yourself. The easiest way to do this is via the Tight Group command (⌘-G/Ctrl-G). With one element selected, that simply wraps the element in another div, which can be changed to a link. In this case, use the tag `a.speakers`. Referring to the Outline (see **Figure 9.13**), you now have `a.speakers` with `img` inside it—we're using the nesting of the elements to help know what's what here, which is why you could remove the class from the `img` tag.

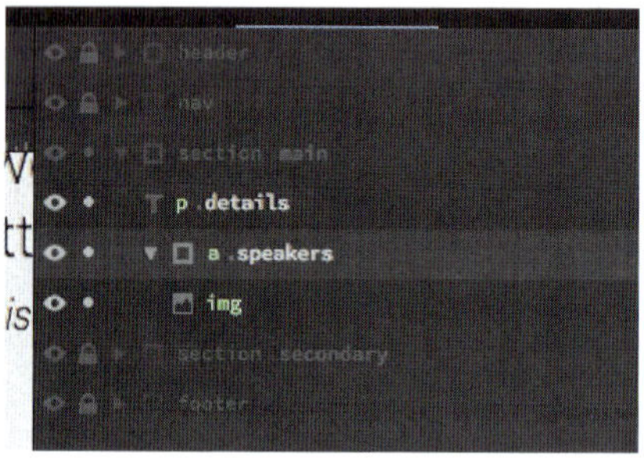

**Figure 9.13**
The image is wrapped in a link with a class, which helps keep everything clear.

Now that the image is wrapped in a container, it should scale with that container. Select the image and set its width to 100% (it probably started out at 560px—just change the unit from px to % and that should be enough). Finally, select `a.speakers` and set its height to Auto so that it will stay only as large as the image it contains. Try resizing the canvas to see the resulting behavior; as you can see, the image shrinks with the canvas.

## Image grid: the other three

The other three images are a stacked group that will stay that way throughout, so they will definitely want a container of their own. With the Container tool (G), drag a square the same size as the speakers image but spanning the rightmost six columns. Hold the Shift key when dragging to constrain your drawing to a square (just as in most graphics apps), and watch for the green guidelines to help you. When finished, give it a sensible tag like `div.more-details`, and double-click it to open it for editing.

Switch to the Library and drag in `details-workshops-2x`. As before, select it, and in the Image palette, click the 2x button to bring it down to size, though it will still be a little too large for the container. To fix this, you could drag it to size, but instead, change its width to 100% in the Dimensions palette. Set its `alt` attribute to "Workshops" in the Advanced palette. Use ⌘-G/Ctrl-G to wrap the image in a container, setting the tag of that container to `a.workshops`, and remove the `.image` class from the image. Set the top and left margins of `a.workshops` to 0 and its width to 100% and its height to Auto, with no minima or maxima. At this point, the result will look like **Figure 9.14**.

**Figure 9.14** The workshops image is ready to go.

**TIP** Sometimes Macaw will set a value to something really close to what you want, but not exactly. While we were building this project, the width of *a.workshops* kept getting reset to 100.06%. After clearing up possible issues with margins, a solution was to set the width manually to 99.99999%, which Macaw handily reset to 100%.

For the most part, we'll follow the same steps with the final two images. Add `details-agenda-2x` next, as a square on the lower left of the container. First click 2x to bring it down to size and then shrink it further to span three columns. Add `details-parties-2x` in the same way but this time span the other three columns on the right-bottom edge. At a minimum, the workshops image will need to be repositioned, so find it in the Outline and adjust the margins of all three images until they're in place. Copy these margins to all breakpoints. Set the `alt` attribute of each image (Agenda and Parties). Surround each image with a link (`a.agenda` and `a.parties`). Be sure that the links each have their heights set to Auto, and then set the width of the images inside to 100% each, and remove the `.image` class.

# Take a Break: More on Images

Macaw has some nice image-handling features that we haven't discussed yet: in-app cropping and responsive image swapping.

## In-App cropping

Macaw lets you take an image from your Library and crop it right on the canvas. Just double-click the image and you'll get crop handles on each edge, which you can drag into the image to set a custom crop (see **Figure 9.15**). Double-click outside the image to save the crop.

**Figure 9.15** When you're cropping in Macaw, resize handles appear along each edge of the image.

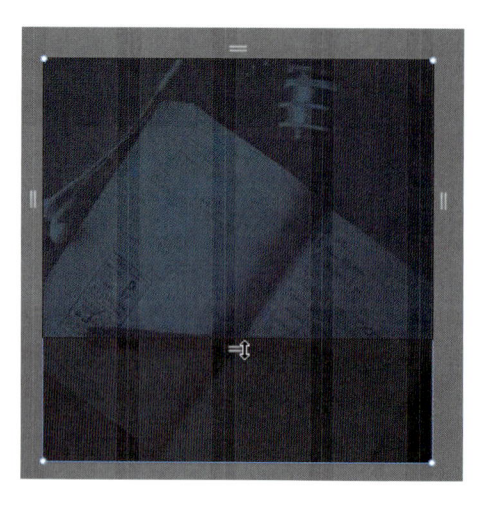

**NOTE**  Generate Optimized Images must be turned on in Publish Settings (⌘-Shift-P/Ctrl-Shift-P) for this to work. If you double-click an image on the canvas and the setting is not turned on, Macaw will ask you to turn it on.

When publishing (and previewing), Macaw looks at all the cropped versions of images and saves copies with your custom crop applied, but the original is always preserved. This is pretty sweet, and moreover, it's nondestructive. If you want to change the crop later, you can double-click the cropped version, and the whole image will be there ready to recrop. If you drop the same image onto the canvas multiple times, you can crop each one differently; Macaw generates separate image files for each one in the published website.

This behavior is especially helpful when you're prototyping a page—there's no need to use another app for cropping your images. The Macawfrence project we've been working on is being built from comps, so we haven't needed this feature. And of course, maybe you prefer to use your favorite image editor to prepare your images in advance. If you're a control freak who doesn't trust Macaw to make perfect crops of your perfect images, you could return to your favorite image editor after going through the cropping process in Macaw and create a new, cropped version to drop into the project.

## CSS transforms and filters

Macaw also supports CSS transforms and filters, which let you use CSS to perform real-time alterations of the positioning, size, and look of items on the canvas. These effects include rotation in two or three dimensions, scaling, blur, color inversion, and much more. These effects can also be animated, but the CSS involved must be written outside Macaw after publishing. This topic is complex because it involves writing CSS, and the options are therefore available in the Advanced palette. In **Figure 9.16**, you can see an example. The top and bottom images are the same file, cropped in Macaw. The top image has been rotated with a CSS transform, and then blurred and brightened using CSS filters. The syntax for those transforms and filters is shown in the Advanced palette.

**Figure 9.16** The image on top is the same file as the original below, but it has a rotation CSS transform and two CSS filters (blur and brightness) applied to it.

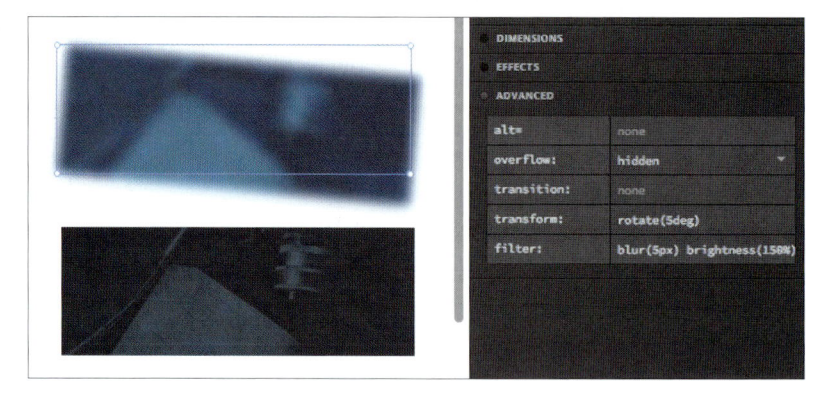

Browser support for filters is not ideal (as of this writing, Internet Explorer doesn't support them at all), but the support for transforms is broad. Because these effects are made with CSS, they are applied in real time in the browser, so there's no need to generate new images, in Macaw or otherwise. More information is available in Appendix B.

## Device-specific images

Another image-handling feature Macaw offers, but that we haven't used, is swapping images based on the pixel density of the device. In the never-ending quest for better performance, web developers have been hoping for ways to deliver different image alternatives to users based on factors like pixel density of the device (for example, is this a Retina display, a Retina HD display, an old-school desktop display, or something else?), whether the user is on a slow connection, and so on. Connection detection is tricky, but Macaw has a JavaScript plugin that can swap between 2x Retina-sized images, and regular 1x-sized images. Moreover, given a 2x image, it can generate the 1x-sized version for you, so you only need to provide the big one in your project. Generate Optimized Images must be turned on in Publish Settings (⌘-Shift-P/ Ctrl-Shift-P) for all of this functionality to be available.

That sounds like a good thing, and until more browsers support technologies like the `<picture>` element or `srcset` attributes on `img` elements, JavaScript-based alternatives are the only option to make this specific functionality happen broadly.

Okay, so why haven't we used it in this book? The book *Retinaify Your Web Sites & Apps* recommends a different method: SVGs when possible, and either highly optimized PNGs or large but low-quality JPEGs where photographs are used. You can read more in that book (see Appendix B to learn more about it), but basically as of this writing, that's the technique we prefer, so that's what we've used here and in other projects. Depending on the requirements of your site, you might prefer to use the built-in Macaw tools. They do exactly what they say, so feel free to experiment with them and see what works best for you.

## Back to Work

If you resize the canvas smaller now, you'll see a couple things: there is too much whitespace below the images, and though the images squeeze down nicely, the bottom edges of the images don't line up perfectly unless we're exactly at the width of the largest breakpoint. Both issues are shown in **Figure 9.17**.

**Figure 9.17**
When made smaller, the left and right images go out of alignment, and there is too much whitespace below them.

The first issue is easy to fix: make sure the height of `div.more-details` is set to Auto so it will be only as big as it needs to be. The second issue is a little trickier—the problem is that the distance between the workshops image and the two below it is a set number of pixels, whereas the images scale fluidly as the page expands and contracts. Ideally the distance would be set in a relative measure (this is not possible in Macaw), or the images below would not care about their distance from the workshops image above. Using relative units for vertical margins and positioning is not possible in Macaw, so we need a way to make sure the two smaller images stay aligned with the bottom edge of the biggest image. Essentially, they need to be inside the same container; the big image can be statically positioned and determine the height of the container, whereas the two smaller images can be absolutely positioned, pinned to the bottom edge. So instead of wrapping the three right-hand images in a container, place all four in a single container.

> **NOTE** We're engaging in this bit of pedagogical inefficiency to show how you can recover from decisions that don't work out as you expect once you start resizing and experimenting. If we were omniscient, we wouldn't have much use for a helpful piece of software!

To get all four elements inside one container, we could drag `a.speakers` into `div.more-details`, but that would wreak positioning havoc. It's much better to use Macaw's Elements > Ungroup command (⌘-Shift-G/Ctrl-Shift-G), which will remove the container while preserving positioning as best it can, and then select the new set of elements to group together. So do that now: select `div.more-details` and ungroup it; then select all four links (`a.speakers` through `a.parties`) and group them. Retag this group as `div.details-grid`.

Now you can reset the positioning of these elements so they'll stay put. `a.speakers` can stay as is: static with a left origin. Workshops can be kept static but changed to a right origin. (However, this is optional—the left margin is flexible, so it will look right either way. It's all in how you want to think of its position.) `a.agenda` should be set to Absolute, with a vertical origin of bottom, and a bottom position of 0. `a.parties` should be set to Absolute, with a vertical origin of bottom (position: 0) and a horizontal origin of right (position: 0—as with workshops, this is optional). With these changes, everything is in place and works well regardless of how the window is resized (until the next breakpoint, of course).

For the finishing touch, each image will need a drop shadow. We'll create a global style for this and apply it to each link. Select a.speakers; then in the Effects palette click the plus button and choose Drop Shadow. We've used Text Shadows already, but this time we'll use Drop Shadow, which applies a drop shadow to an element's positioning box. Use the settings shown in **Figure 9.18**.

**Figure 9.18** The settings for the image shadow: angle 270°, color rgba(0,0,0,0.2), distance 10, Y offset 10, blur 30.

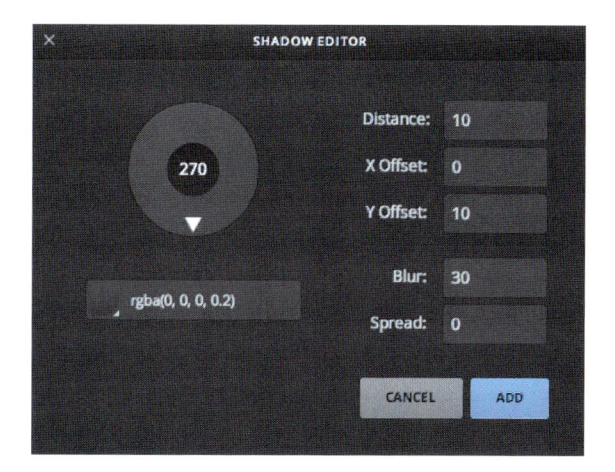

Click the stamp icon to create a global style and call it **image shadow**. Deselect everything except the shadow in the Effects tab and click Save. Then select the other three links, click the stamp again, and click the plus next to *image shadow*. This will apply the shadow to each of the images, and will allow you to go back and edit the shadow later if needed.

## Medium breakpoint

Switch to the medium breakpoint (Shift-[). To match the mock-up, we need to make a few changes:

1. Set the top and bottom padding on section.main to 35px.

2. For p.details, use Elements > Expand (⌘-E/Ctrl-E) to make it as wide as the grid. Reset its font size to 21px and the smaller text inside it to 14px.

## A small bug, and a solution

Preview the page now and squish the preview window down enough to see the smallest breakpoint. In the version of Macaw as of this writing, the Agenda image is being pushed unexpectedly under the Parties (see **Figure 9.21**). There's no such thing as perfect software, but hopefully by the time you read this, the bug will be fixed. Tracking down an issue like this is a big part of a web developer's job and is best done with tools like Firebug in Firefox, the Developer Tools of Google Chrome, the Web Inspector of Safari, or the F12 Developer Tools of Internet Explorer. The specifics of how to use tools like those could consume entire books (or at least long articles) of their own, and you'll find more information in Appendix B.

**Figure 9.21**
Look closely at the left edge of Parties and you might see a bit of Agenda.

Suffice it to say the problem here is that, in the change from absolute positioning in larger breakpoints to static positioning at this breakpoint, some styles were not sufficiently overridden. This failure to override caused Agenda to pick up CSS from an earlier breakpoint. If you experience this bug, here's one possible solution:

1. Select `a.parties` and change it from absolute to static positioning. Its horizontal origin should still be set to right, with a margin of 0. Basically it should stay right where it is, but it should be static instead of absolute so it stays in the document flow. Either `a.agenda` or `a.parties` needs to be static in order for the auto height on `div.details-grid` to work correctly (changing the height to a static value at this breakpoint is another possibility you could play with), but using auto gives you more flexibility.

2. Select `a.agenda` and change back to absolute positioning, with its vertical origin set to bottom again and its left set to 0 (in our build, this left positioning setting is what wasn't being overridden properly).

Preview after making these changes, and now everything should correct on the canvas and in the preview window. As Macaw matures, issues like this should go away, but getting comfortable with the tools in browsers that can help find issues like this, and being enough comfortable in Macaw to try different solutions to those problems, are valuable skills.

## Secondary Content: Embedded Map

The secondary content area on this page contains an embedded map pointing to the Moscone Center in San Francisco, a big venue for Macaw's first fake conference. There are text blocks similar to what we used for Meet the Developers, so there will be a relatively small amount of work here.

First let's lay some groundwork. Unlock `section.secondary` and remove its background image by hovering over it in the Backgrounds palette and clicking the trash can icon. Set the background color to very light gray (for example, #e4e4e4)—this will be a better background for the darker text while the map loads.

Double-click `section.secondary` to edit it, and then select `h3.meet`. Change its text to **Location:**, update the color to #171f37 (from the swatch), and change its tag to `h3.location`. Select `p.dreams`, change it to `p.someday`, change the text to **(maybe someday)**, and change the color of its shadow to white.

Select `h3.developers` and change it to `h3.moscone`. This is a header with offscreen-indented text, so editing it as is may be tricky. If you double-click it, Macaw will try to show you the text by scrolling way over to the left, at which point you can press ⌘-A/Ctrl-A to select it all and change it to **Moscone Center**—but you're editing blind. For those who prefer to see what they're typing, a better choice is to temporarily set the font size to something reasonable (for example, 16px) and the text indent to 0 (moving the text back into view as in **Figure 9.22**), change the text, and reset those values when finished.

**Figure 9.22** After you reset the font size and indentation values, hidden text is made visible again for editing.

With the text updated, double-click `developers-2x` in the Backgrounds palette to edit it. Import moscone-center-2x.png and set the size to Contain; leave the other settings as is. We could have deleted the old image and added the new one, but most of the settings are the same, so this way is a little faster. Change its height to 120px, and then move it and `h3.location` into position according to the mock-up. The result looks like **Figure 9.23**.

**Figure 9.23** The text overlays for the map, properly sized and positioned.

Embedding a map is easy using the Embed tool (M). Drag a small box in the container, and a dialog box will appear with various embeddable options: custom HTML, a URL for embedding a website or page, video IDs for embedding YouTube or Vimeo videos, and finally what we're interested in now: maps. The embedded map is simply a query to Google Maps, so any query that would work in Google Maps will work here. That can be an address, longitude and latitude coordinates, or simply "Moscone Center, San Francisco, CA." Enter that in the dialog box (see **Figure 9.24**), click Embed, and you'll see the embed box change to show the location you entered as well as a map icon (see **Figure 9.25**). Macaw does not preview embeds directly on the canvas, but it will show them on publish/preview.

With the embed set, it needs to be positioned. Set its positioning to Absolute (top and left set to 0), 100% wide, 550px tall. Switch to the Outline, change its tag to `div.map`, and drag it below the text blocks. Publish the page now, and you'll see the map live and in color, behind the text.

**Chapter 9:** Building a Website: Part 3

**Figure 9.24**
The Embed Options dialog box, with the default embed block in the background.

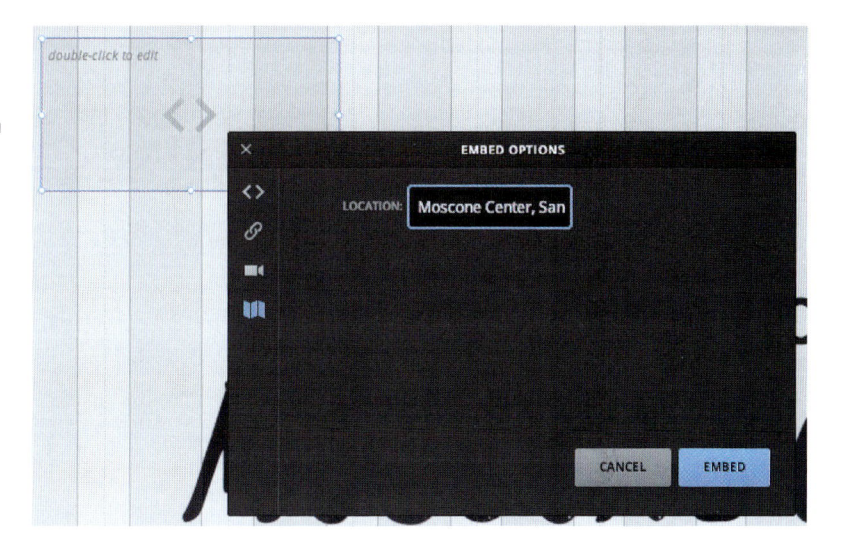

**Figure 9.25** Embeds containing a map show the location entered and a map icon.

Of course, that map doesn't look exactly like the map in the mock-up. Macaw's built-in map embedding function uses the same tools that sharing a map from the Google Maps uses. If you want to customize this further, you'll need to look at other options from the Google Maps JavaScript API, using the Custom HTML embedding option instead of the built-in map embedding. That process is beyond the scope of this book, but links to the relevant pages are available in Appendix B.

One more little touch for this map is the gradient along its top. Inner Shadow, available in the Effects palette, would seem to be the solution for this, but if you try it, you'll see that the map doesn't show it. Instead, we need to add an empty element just for a gradient.

Select the Element tool (R) and drag a new element along the top of `section.secondary`, 100% wide and 40px tall. Set its position to Absolute, and use 0 for both its left and top origins. Set its tag to `div.shadow`, and use the Swatch tool (S) to set its background color to transparent. In the Backgrounds palette, add a gradient that goes from transparent on the left to rgba(0, 0, 0, 0.2) (20% opaque black) on the right, with an angle of 90 degrees. Preview this and you'll see it works, looking something like **Figure 9.26**.

**Figure 9.26** The gradient looks like an inner shadow over the top edge of the map.

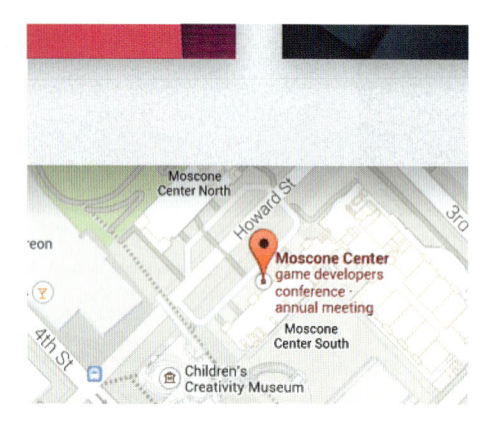

This overlaid gradient also means that users can't interact with the map while their mouse is over it. If you'd prefer to make the map noninteractive, you could add another div (the same width and height as the map) above it in the Outline. That way, the map wouldn't respond to clicking, scrolling, or other events. We think it's fine to allow interacting with the map once loaded, so we'll leave it as is.

Taking a look at the other breakpoints, it turns out the only change needed is cutting the height of the map down to same height as `section.secondary` (390px for medium, 270 for medium-small, and 177px for small) and making `div.gradient` a little smaller as needed. Any further adjustments are up to you, but now that's two pages down, one to go!

# Next Steps

In the next chapter, we're going to build the contact page. Yes, that's right, the last page in the project!

# 10

# Building a Website: Part 4

In the previous three chapters, you built the first two pages in this Macaw project. In this chapter you'll build the last page: Contact. If this website were going to be for a real event, there would likely be more pages, but once this one is built, everything we planned for will be done and you'll have learned everything you need to know to go and conquer the Internet with Macaw.

## Review the Mock-ups

This page's main event is a form—we can lay this form out in Macaw, but making it work requires extra code on a web server. This extra code could be something provided by your web host, a block of custom PHP you write or find online, or a snippet of HTML that's tied into an external service (for example, MailChimp). The point is that Macaw is very good for laying out and styling forms, but the actual processing will be a post-publishing step (just as it would be with any other design tool).

Reviewing the mock-ups, we see that the Contact page shares the same header and other shared regions as the Details page, although the secondary content area is gone. The form fields have quite a bit of custom treatment in the form of gradients and inner and drop shadows that we'll need to account for. The way the fields collapse into one column at the small breakpoint is something we'd need to think about more if we weren't using Macaw (since we'd have to plan our containers according to whether the items were considered to be laid out in columns or rows). With Macaw, we can just move the fields wherever they need to go with each breakpoint, which is rather liberating. With this initial review finished, we can proceed to the build.

## Create the Page

Duplicate the Details page by using the Copy button in the Page menu; then double-click details-copy and rename it to **contact**. The new page is opened immediately. You can close the tab for the Details page; although you can have as many pages open in tabs as you like, Macaw will run fastest if you keep open only the pages you're actively working on.

The header is exactly the same as the Details page, so you can leave it completely alone. Unlock `section.secondary` and delete it. The footer will stay where it was, so you'll need to unlock it and set its top margin to 0 so it will attach itself to `section.main` again (and copy that setting to all breakpoints). Click the canvas so nothing is selected, and change the page title to **Contact - Macawfrence**.

The navigation menu needs the following updates, which are just old hat to you as an experienced Macaw user, and are therefore left as an exercise for the reader:

1. Move the active page brushstroke from Details to Contact.

2. Update the Details menu item so it reacts to `:hover` and `:focus`, and links to the Details page.

3. Update the Details and Index pages so they link to the Contact page.

4. Check each breakpoint to make sure the changes have propagated correctly. You can do this in the preview and revisit any breakpoints that need adjusting afterward.

With these updates finished, let's move on to building the form.

## Build the Form

Unlock `section.main` and double-click to edit its contents. Start by swapping out the introductory text in `p.details` (copy and paste it from Text.txt in the assets folder if you want to save some typing). Change its positioning origin to center, and make it eight columns wide. No further changes are needed there.

Next, select `div.details-grid` and delete it. Create a new container (G) that spans the middle eight columns, with a positioning origin of center and a top margin of 40px (copy both settings to all breakpoints). Give the container the tag `form.contact`. Set its height to Auto with a minimum height of 800px so you'll have room to work while you're filling it in. Then double-click the container for editing.

Each of the form elements we'll create is going to need a label, the field itself, and a container so we can drag the two of them around together easily. If this project were going to be larger, with form elements appearing on many pages, we could consider making components of these form elements. For our purposes here, we'll simply duplicate the ones we need (though we'll still use global styles). Keep in mind that on large projects, components can be helpful for often-used elements like form controls.

## Build and style the first field

We'll start with the First Name field. Form elements are created with the Input tool. N is the keyboard shortcut to select the tool; Shift-N will cycle through the available types of form elements (text fields, text areas, select boxes, check boxes, and radio buttons). You can also click and hold the tool icon in the toolbar to show a pop-up selector of all the available form elements to select one directly. Select the text box tool (the default for the Input tool) and drag one from the left edge of the form container. Make the text box span four columns. Don't worry too much about positioning yet; we're just laying some groundwork.

When a form element is initially created, it uses some default styles Macaw provides, not those provided by the browser and operating system. Text fields, after creation, prompt you for the placeholder text that will be shown before the user's input is added. Use **first name** here for the placeholder, and then make some changes to the field's appearance as follows:

- Height: 40px
- Font: Roboto
- Weight: 400
- Size: 16px
- Color: #171f37 (swatch)
- Background color: white (swatch)
- Border: 1px wide, color #cecece (you can make a swatch for this, although it might be hard to tell apart from the white one)
- Border radius: 4px

> **NOTE** The text that appears in the field will be used for the placeholder, but the color of the placeholder text will be whatever the browser provides. You'll see this when you preview the page. Once the user has filled in any given field, the color used in the Typography palette will appear. Other font settings will apply equally to the placeholder and entered value.

At this point, you'll have a field that looks like **Figure 10.1**. Give this field the tag `input.form-text` (which helps us know that this is a text field when looking at the Outline—there's also an icon, but it's very small). You can also add an ID like `fld-text-firstname`, which is used in forms to associate `<label>` and form elements together using the label's `for` attribute. At this time Macaw doesn't support that attribute, so the ID doesn't serve much of a purpose in Macaw itself. You could manually add the `for` attributes later as a postpublishing step (and as a step to having accessible forms, we recommend it—you learn more about accessible forms in Appendix B).

**Figure 10.1** The first text field with its initial styles applied.

Along with the visual settings that most elements have, form inputs have their own options that appear in the Input palette when a form element is selected (see **Figure 10.2**). For text fields, you can set the name (that is, the key representing this element that will be passed along to the server when the form is submitted, along with the value the user entered) and the type. The type determines whether the field is a plain-old text field, a password field that masks the user's input, or one of the newer HTML5 types (`email`, `url`, `search`, and `number`; other types might be added in future versions). With this First Name field, the default text field type is the right choice, but set the name to **firstname**. According to the HTML spec, the name can contain pretty much anything, but we recommend just using lowercase letters and underscores—depending on how the form will be processed later on the server, you may have naming conventions you have to follow.

**Figure 10.2** The Input palette in context, just above Dimensions in the Inspector.

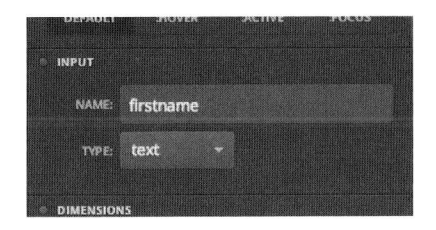

The other, newer field types can cause different useful behaviors in browsers—for example, showing a different keyboard on a mobile phone when the field type is `url`, making it easier to enter the slashes, colons, and so on that are not as easily accessible on the regular onscreen keyboard. Matching the field type to the sort of data expected is good practice, and we'll follow that as best we can in Macaw.

Let's finish up the styling of these form elements. We still need to apply a gradient, so add one in the Background palette with the following settings:

- Angle: 90 degrees
- Right color: #eeeeee
- Left color: white
- Repeat X checked, Repeat Y unchecked

Drag the left color stop over to the left about 20 percent of the way. **Figure 10.3** shows the result.

**Figure 10.3** Gradient settings for the background of the text fields, and a text field with that gradient applied.

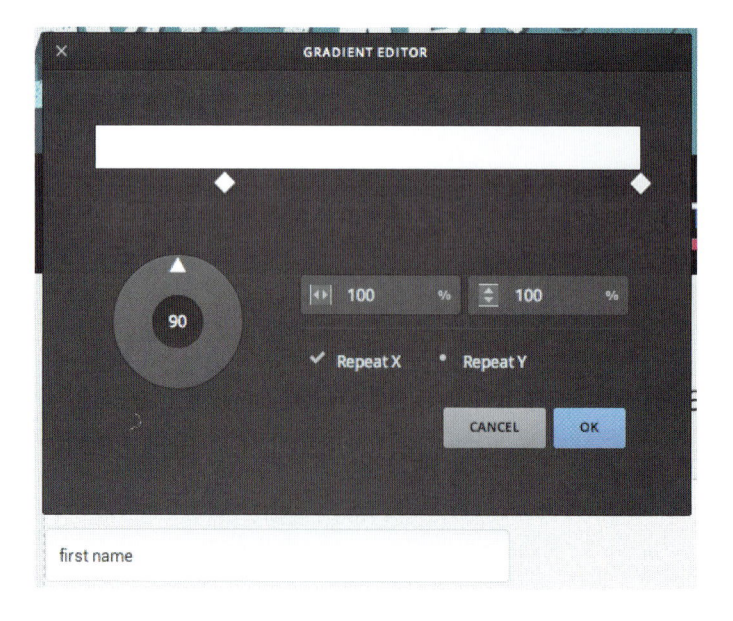

One more touch: The fields have a small inner shadow that looks like a light border along the top. In the Effects palette, add an inner shadow with the following settings:

- Angle: 270 degrees
- Distance: 1
- Blur: 0
- Spread: 0

The result is **Figure 10.4**, which looks remarkably like what Photoshop can create, with no background images required. CSS can't do everything, but what it can do is quite useful.

**Figure 10.4** The final look for the text field.

Make a global style for the field called **form field**. Save all the settings except the width.

Now this form needs a label. Use the Text tool (T) to create one right above the form; make the text box span the same four columns. Give it the tag `label` with the following styles:

- Font: Roboto
- Weight: 900
- Size: 20px
- Color: #171f37 (swatch)

Create a global style for this as well called **form label**; leave out the width but capture all the other settings. Now select the label and text field and group them by pressing ⌘-G/Ctrl-G. Set the tag for the new container to `div.form-item.first-name`, indicating both that this is a grouped form element and that it's the first name field. The resulting group appears in **Figure 10.5**. Check the height of the group and copy the height setting to all breakpoints if there's a blue border.

**Figure 10.5** The text field, and its label, together at last.

## Create the other text fields

Now that we have one form element ready to go, we can refine its positioning and start adding more of them. Set the top and left margins on `div.form-item` to 0 to place it in the upper-left corner of the form container. Then make five duplicates (⌘-D/Ctrl-D) for the other five text fields (Last Name, Company, Website, Email, and Phone). There should be 25px of space between the fields vertically, which is pretty easy to do with the guides shown in **Figure 10.6**.

**Figure 10.6**
The positioning guides are your friend.

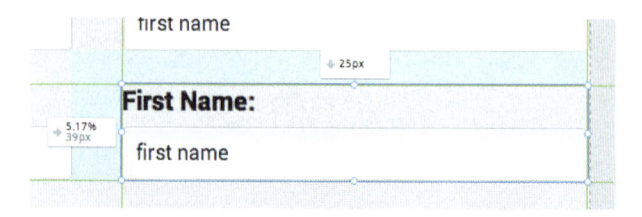

**TIP** You can select and duplicate multiple items at the same time. The only reason we didn't do that here is the lack of positioning guidelines when your selection contains more than one element (one selected container with many items inside it is considered one item for this purpose). Making multiple duplicates, and then aligning them afterward using the Align palette, might be preferable to you if you're making a lot of duplicates at once.

With the duplicates created, you can go through each one. Change the classes and IDs (of the individual elements and their containers), field names and types, labels, and the placeholder values so that they match the mock-up. Most of this process bears no special explanation, but here are a few things to note:

- The first name, last name, and company fields don't need placeholder values, so remove those.

- The website field should use the `url` field type. It's a good idea, when showing sample URLs anywhere, to use example.com/org/net, which are reserved for this purpose and help guarantee that you won't accidentally send anyone to a real website. So www.example.com would make a good placeholder.

- The email field should use the `email` field type. We recommend <anything>@example.com for the placeholder.

- The phone field should use the `tel` type if available. As of this writing, `tel` is not available in Macaw, so the example project uses `text` as the field type. The placeholder can help guide users to enter data in the expected format, for example, *xxx-xxx-xxxx* (although hopefully the form processor will accept data in a variety of possible formats).

- The smaller label text for "optional" is 18px with a weight of 400.

**Figure 10.7** shows the results after all six fields are laid out and set.

**Figure 10.7** The first six form fields are in place and ready.

## Add the radio buttons

Create the label first to establish the space where the radio buttons will go. Use the Text tool (T), add the text, apply the form label global style, and drag it into place (25px below the Email field),

Check boxes and radio buttons are special in Macaw: unlike the other field types, they are created as a small group of elements: the radio button or check box with a span tag serving as its label, both wrapped in a `<label>` tag, which binds the span tag to the radio button, and ensuring that the text and the radio button are both clickable.

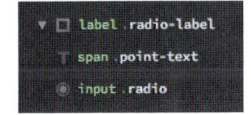

**Figure 10.8** The three elements comprise one radio button form widget.

Select the Input tool and change it to the radio button element with the mouse or by pressing N or Shift-N until it comes up (the little circle icon). Drag and draw a box, and you'll see the radio button with Label next to it. Switch to the Outline and you'll see the three new elements, as shown in **Figure 10.8**.

Use the Direct Select (A) tool to select `span.point-text`, and change the text to **Email**, the font to Roboto, and the weight to 400. Then select the radio button itself and look at the Input palette. You can set a name and a value—each radio button in a group must have the same name and different values (the same goes for groups of check boxes). Here, change the name to **contact_method** and the value to **email**. Drag the radio button into position, with its left margin set to 0 and its top margin set to 12px, and make it as wide as one column and one gutter, which is more than enough to fit the whole word.

Now duplicate `label.radio-label`, the entire radio button widget, for the phone option. Keep it aligned vertically with the first one, with its left edge against the second column of the container. Change the span text to **Phone** and the radio button's value to **phone**. Try previewing the page now and confirm that the radio buttons cannot be selected at the same time (if they can, their names are different and should be made the same). Finally, select the overall label and the two radio button widgets, and group them (⌘-G/Ctrl-G). Give the group the tag `div.form-item.contact-method`. The result should look like **Figure 10.9**.

**Figure 10.9** The radio buttons, grouped and in position.

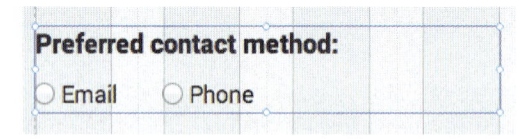

## Add the select box

As before, create a label for **Inquiring about…**, using the label tag and the form label global style, 25px below and left-aligned with the Phone field.

Change the Input tool to the select element using Shift-N or the mouse, and drag and draw below the label a new select box that spans four columns and that's 40px in height. Select boxes have default styles applied by Macaw, including a background image for the up and down arrows on the right side. We're going to override those styles with some of our own, but first look at the Input palette. There's a name field, as all form elements have (use **inquiry** for this one), but there's also an option with a plus next to it (see **Figure 10.10**). Select that initial option by double-clicking it (or by right-clicking and choosing Edit) and change it to **Please choose…**. Click the plus sign to add more options—as many as you care to have (an example is shown in **Figure 10.11**).

**Figure 10.10** The Input palette for select boxes shows one default option.

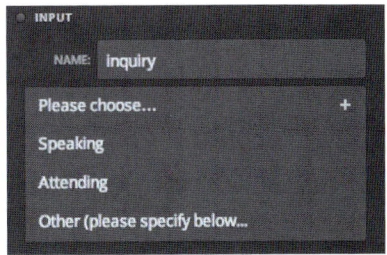

**Figure 10.11** Each option added will show up in the select box. Hover the mouse over any option to show a trash icon for deleting it.

To style the select box, we want something similar to the existing form field global style. To speed the process along, use the Direct Selection tool to select one of the text inputs and use Edit > Copy Visual Properties (⌘-Opt-C/Ctrl-Alt-C) to copy its styles. Then click the select box and choose Edit > Paste Visual Properties (⌘-Opt-V/Ctrl-Alt-V). The same styles will be applied, but without being referenced to a global style.

> **NOTE** As mentioned earlier in the book, if you want to really get granular with global styles, you can. You could make a global style that captures nothing but the border radius for these form elements, so it can be applied and adjusted globally every time. As with anything that might help productivity, it's up to you to decide where to draw the line between "This is great, and I'm saving myself time later" and "This isn't good, I'm just wasting time now. In a project this small, it doesn't matter very much."

For the adjustments, start with the Backgrounds palette. Edit the gradient by reversing its angle to 270 degrees, changing the right color stop to #dcdcdc, and dragging the left color stop all the way to the left.

Next you'll add a new background image. Import `dropdown-arrow.svg` from the assets folder. Set its position to 97% for X and 50% for Y, change the height to 5px (leaving the width as Auto), and disable the repeats.

In the Effects palette, edit the inner shadow by increasing the Distance setting to 2px. Finally, add a new drop shadow with an angle of 270 degrees, a distance of 1px, and a blur of 1px. The result should look like **Figure 10.12**. If you were going to create more of these, it would be a good idea to save a global style for select boxes.

**Figure 10.12** The select box with all custom styles applied.

Group the label and select box and give the container the tag `div.form-item.inquiry`. For consistency's sake, make sure this select box group and the radio buttons group are the same height.

### Add the last elements

This form just needs the big text area and submit button. First, create the **Message:** label 25px below the radio buttons. Apply the form label global style and changing the tag to `<label>`.

Change the Input tool to text area by pressing N or Shift-N or by clicking the icon; then drag and draw the text area to the full width of the form container. Make it 240px in height, and give it a 5px top margin. Copy the visual properties of one of the text fields and paste them onto this text area, as you did for the select box. In this case, the gradient needs modification, but pretty much everything else is fine. Edit the background gradient; keep all the settings but move the left color stop most of the way to the right until the text area looks like it does in the mockup, as shown in **Figure 10.13**.

Along with the name field (use **message** for this), the Input palette has a resize setting. This is a relatively new CSS property (not supported in Internet Explorer as of version 11) that determines whether the text area should be arbitrarily resizable in the browser and in which dimensions. The default is None, meaning the text area will be exactly the size drawn. The other three settings will let the text area resize horizontally, vertically, or both. For our purposes, None is good. Group the label and text area into a container with the tag `div.form-item.message`.

**Figure 10.13** The gradient settings needed, and a little bit of the message field with the settings applied.

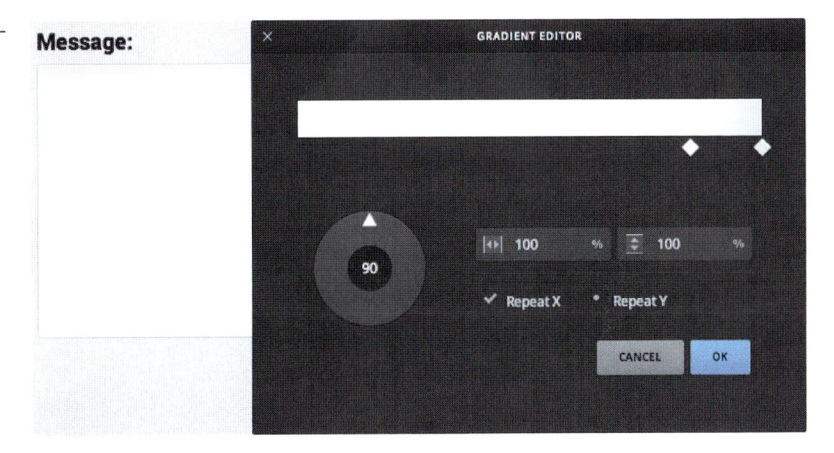

The last element we need is the submit button. Use the Button tool (B) to create one below the message field; align it with the right edge of the form container. After drawing it, you'll be able to fill in the text (**Submit**), and finish typing the same way as with any text field (pressing ⌘-Return/Ctrl-Enter or double-clicking outside the button). Set its positioning origin to right. To style the button, we'll copy and modify the styles from the select box (it's a little faster than starting from scratch). With the box selected, choose Edit > Copy Visual Properties (⌘-Opt-C/Ctrl-Alt-C), and then choose Edit > Paste Visual Properties (⌘-Opt-V/Ctrl-Alt-V) to copy the styles to the submit button. This will give you a button that looks just like the select box (see **Figure 10.14**).

**Figure 10.14** Submit button after we copied the visual properties of the select box.

Here are the changes needed to finish the button:

- Font: weight 700, size 20px, center-aligned, italics off

- Color: white

- Background: set the color to #e21a64 with the Swatch tool (S); then remove the background image and gradient.

- Border: set it to none, leaving the corner radius as is.

- Inner shadow: set the color #950037, and use the settings shown in **Figure 10.15**.

**Figure 10.15** The inner shadow settings for the submit button, with the results shown.

An additional nice touch for the submit button would be to give it a smooth hover state. Let's make it a darker pink and get a little fancy by adding a CSS transition to smoothly transition from the original color to the hover color.

With the button selected, click the `:hover` state in the Inspector. Click the background color, and choose one of the darker variations, one or two stops to the right (see **Figure 10.16**). Save a swatch for it (we ended up with #870f3c). Select the `:focus` state, and apply the same background color there. This change should propagate to other breakpoints, but you'll want to confirm that when checking them later.

If you preview at this point, you'll see the button change to this darker pink immediately when the mouse is over it. We can smooth this out using CSS transitions. With the button selected, look at the Advanced palette. One of the available options is Transition—enter **all 0.5s** here, as shown in **Figure 10.17**. This tells the browser that you want to see a smooth transition of all changing CSS properties to take place in half a second.

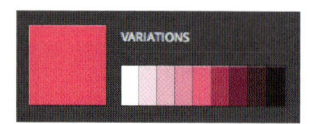

**Figure 10.16** The variations on the default pink. Click one just to the right of center to get a darker version.

**Figure 10.17** All available properties will transition over half a second with this setting.

**Chapter 10:** Building a Website: Part 4    203

Try previewing again and you'll see a smooth fade from hot pink to dark pink. Additionally, if you resize the preview window, you'll see that instead of snapping immediately to its new size when you hit a breakpoint, the button and its text will change smoothly. If you'd rather just see the background transition but nothing else, change the Transition value to **background-color 0.5s**. CSS transitions are a nice way to enhance a website. Read more about them in Appendix B.

There's no Input palette shown for buttons, because buttons aren't necessarily parts of forms—they can also trigger JavaScript behaviors completely unrelated to forms. To tell Macaw which type a button is, look at the Advanced palette (see **Figure 10.18**). When a button is selected, the first option is Type=, which sets that attribute on the button tag's generated HTML. If this option is left empty or set to Submit, Macaw assumes that the button will submit data to a server if it's part of a form (as it is here). If you want a button that clears out the entered values in the form, choose Reset as the type. Choosing Button as the type means the browser shouldn't necessarily do anything by default and that it should let JavaScript handle it. In this case, because we don't have a form processor to target, it doesn't technically matter, but because setting Submit explicitly makes our future intentions a little clearer, go with that.

**Figure 10.18**
The button type selector in the Advanced palette.

**NOTE**   You can change the button's tag to <input>, but Macaw will warn you that its appearance might change. One reason for this is that it's more difficult to override operating system default styles on <input> buttons. It's fine to use button tags for buttons, but if you must use an <input> tag for technical reasons, go for it.

Remove the minimum height from **form.contact**, since we have all the elements in place and don't need it.

## Positioning cleanup

Before moving on to other breakpoints, we should run through the form and check for possible issues. Check the margins for each form widget group; copy the current values to all breakpoints if you see negative values (to make things easier later—fewer elements end up in weird places).

The form does not fill the grid at this breakpoint. In fact, it's just a bit smaller (at 760px in our build) than the width of the medium breakpoint. So set a minimum width on both `p.details` and `form.contact` of 760px, thereby ensuring the form elements will always be at least as large as they are drawn here, unless the page gets wider. This minimum width will need to be removed in smaller breakpoints.

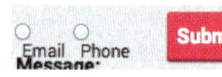

**Figure 10.19** Examples of form elements getting too small because their widths are set as percentages with no minima.

One issue you might see is some form elements getting too small as the page gets smaller, as shown in **Figure 10.19**. The problem is that the elements have their widths set as percentages by default, with no minima. Giving each one an explicit width (or at least a minimum) will fix it—just change the width unit on the submit button and the radio button's label wrappers to pixels.

With these changes in place, the form is in good shape in the large breakpoint, and we can move on to the others.

## Medium breakpoint

Switch to the medium breakpoint (Shift-[). The kinds of changes needed are well-traveled territory by now, but here are a few highlights:

- Remove the minimum width from `p.details` and `form.contact`. This change should be propagated automatically to the smaller breakpoints, but check it in the popover (as shown in **Figure 10.20**).

**Figure 10.20** After you change the minimum width from 760px to 0, the value should cascade downward automatically as it did here.

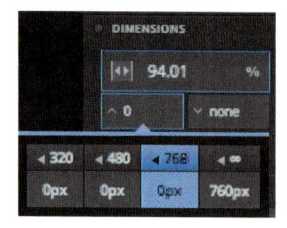

- Make `form.contact` the width of the grid by pressing ⌘-E/Ctrl-E.
- Reduce all of the label text size to 16px. You can select them all with the Direct Select tool and change them all at once in the Typography palette. The "optional" lines can be reduced to 14px.
- The labels on the radio buttons can be reduced to 14px and nudged down 2px to better align them with the radio buttons.
- Reduce the height of the text area to 185px.
- Reduce the font size of the submit button to 16px and its size to 100 by 40 pixels.

Other than that, it's a matter of repositioning the form widget groups, making each column six grid columns wide and aligning them as shown in the mock-up. Once everything is set, the page will look like **Figure 10.21**.

**Figure 10.21** A section of the page at the medium breakpoint.

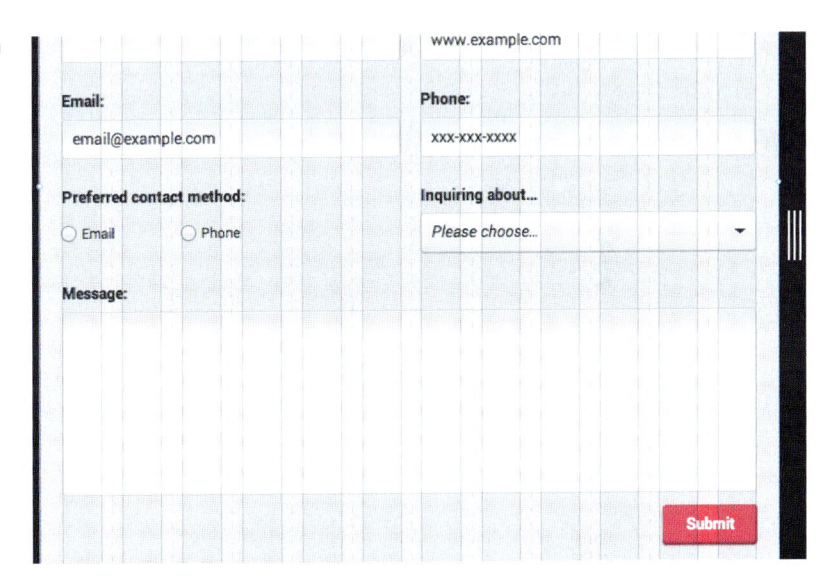

The medium-small breakpoint is left as an exercise for the reader, so we'll continue to the small breakpoint.

## Small breakpoint

In the small breakpoint, the form collapses to a single column that spans the full grid. First adjust `p.details` and `form.contact` so they're the width of the grid.

Most of the adjustments involve placing all the form widget groups in the right order, the full width of the grid, with about 10px of spacing between the groups. You are well equipped to take care of those adjustments now, but here are a few specific pieces not to miss:

- In our build, some elements had apparently disappeared off the canvas at this breakpoint. Switching to the Outline to select them works fine, but changes happen more quickly if you use the Select > Select Element Above (Opt-]/Alt-]) or Below (Opt-[/Alt-[) commands, which you can use without leaving the Inspector. For example, after selecting the First Name field group, use Select Element Above a few times until the next hidden `div.form-item` container is selected (the text field and label will probably be selected first); then set margins that will bring the elements into view.

- The radio button labels can be adjusted to the width of their content. A window isn't likely to get a great deal smaller than this breakpoint in actual use, but making the labels closer to the width of their content will help alleviate awkward wrapping. Set the height of `.contact-method` to Auto as well to help ensure that if the elements do happen to wrap, they won't overlap anything else.

- The submit button is full-width here, so its width can be converted from pixels to 100%. Making it full-width, but still set in pixels, could cause horizontal scroll bars to appear on the window if it gets any smaller (and we try to avoid those).

After all the adjustments are made, you'll end up with a page that looks like **Figure 10.22**.

**Figure 10.22** A section of the form at the small breakpoint, with everything the full width of the grid.

# That's It!

At this point, you have built every page on the site. Congratulations! We've gone through this whole exercise building a site from comps, but everything you've learned here should serve you well when prototyping or otherwise designing in Macaw from scratch. In the next chapter, we'll take a closer look at what a published project looks like.

# 11

# Preview and Publish

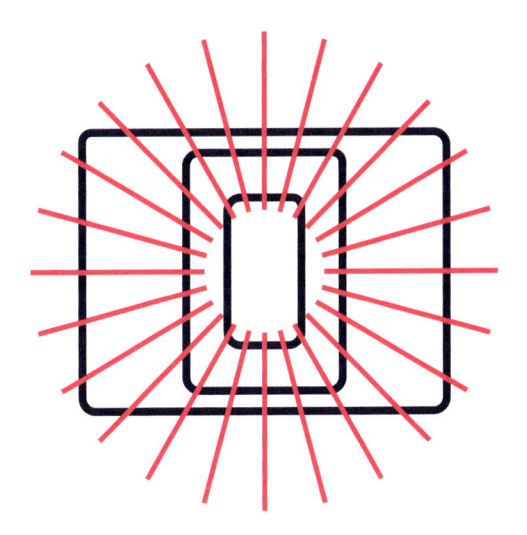

So far in this book you've learned enough to create websites and prototypes as Macaw projects on your computer. Of course, there's an important step we haven't discussed: where are the files that you put on the web when you're ready to graduate from project to website? In this chapter, we're going to take a closer look at what happens when you preview and publish a site and how to change those behaviors.

## Resulting Files

The first time you preview a site, Macaw asks for a location to save your project. If you've been watching the folder where you saved your Macaw project, you'll notice that, in addition to, for example, Macawfrence.mcw (the Macaw project file), a folder with the same name (but without the .mcw extension) is created. Every time you preview, Macaw is running through its publishing workflow, generating everything that represents your website project (HTML, CSS, JavaScript, and image files) in whatever state it currently exists. **Figure 11.1** shows an example for the Macawfrence project.

**Figure 11.1** The files Macaw has generated for the Macawfrence project.

| | |
|---|---|
| contact.html | 4 KB |
| details.html | 3 KB |
| index.html | 3 KB |
| ▼ css | -- |
|     contact-grid.css | 3 KB |
|     contact.css | 23 KB |
|     details-grid.css | 3 KB |
|     details.css | 17 KB |
|     index-grid.css | 3 KB |
|     index.css | 20 KB |
|     standardize.css | 9 KB |
| ▼ images | -- |
|     bg-bridge.jpg | 70 KB |
|     bg-devs.jpg | 253 KB |
|     details-agenda-2x.jpg | 51 KB |
|     details-parties-2x.jpg | 41 KB |
|     details-speakers-2x.jpg | 84 KB |
|     details-workshops-2x.jpg | 41 KB |
|     bg-sand.png | 4 KB |
|     developers-2x.png | 37 KB |
|     Macawfrence-dateloc-2x.png | 13 KB |
|     MacawfrenceHeader-2x.png | 139 KB |
|     MacawfrenceHeader-sm-2x.png | 49 KB |
|     moscone-center-2x.png | 60 KB |
|     nav-active-2x.png | 532 bytes |
|     social-icons.png | 886 bytes |
|     dropdown-arrow.svg | 676 bytes |
|     highlight-parties.svg | 2 KB |
|     highlight-speakers.svg | 3 KB |
|     highlight-workshops.svg | 5 KB |
|     quote-begin.svg | 963 bytes |
|     quote-end.svg | 1 KB |
| ▼ js | -- |
|     jquery-min.js | 94 KB |

**Chapter 11:** Preview and Publish       211

> **TIP** Never put any files in your project folder! Macaw overwrites the entire folder every time you preview your site, and any files it did not create will be erased. If you have a folder of extra files you want to reference from Macaw, keep them in a separate folder alongside your Macaw project file and published folder, and reference them using dot-dot-slash (../). For example, if you have a folder called extras next to your Macaw project and want to reference a file called myfile.png, its link would be ../extras/myfile.png.

As you can see, there is one HTML file per page, as well an an accompanying CSS file in the css folder. There are grid css files here (more on those shortly) and standardize.css, which is the reset stylesheet Macaw uses to zero out all default browser styles.

> **NOTE** Like many parts of Macaw, this reset stylesheet is open source, from a project called normalize.css. Open the file and look at the comment on the first line to see where it comes from. If you build websites outside Macaw and are looking for a good CSS reset, you could try this one.

All the images you've imported and used, and any that Macaw generates for you, are in the images folder. The js folder contains the popular JavaScript library jQuery, and if you've added any other JavaScript, or called upon Macaw to include its responsive image swapping plugin, those would appear here as well.

Publishing your site on the web is just a matter of copying the files (Macaw doesn't provide any direct-to-server publishing at this time). You could take the contents of this folder, upload them to a web server using the file manager available in the control panel on most web hosts, or with SFTP (please don't use vanilla FTP if you can avoid it—it's insecure and, frankly, crappy), and have a fully functioning website.

At least as fully functioning as it is when previewed on your computer. Parts like forms that require server-side or third-party interaction will require more work, of course, but that's beyond the scope of this book.

Let's take a look at the publishing options Macaw has, and how they impact your final, publishable files. Open the Macawfrence project if it's not already open, and choose Publish Settings from the File menu (⌘-Shift-P/Ctrl-Shift-P).

## Project Settings

These settings are saved with, and only apply to, the current project.

### Pages

By default, every page you've created in your project will be published. However, if there are pages that shouldn't be published yet because they're unfinished, or pages that shouldn't be published at all (like a scratchpad page where you experiment building up widgets to be used elsewhere in the project), you can uncheck them here to keep them from being included. In **Figure 11.2**, from the Macawfrence project, all pages are published.

**Figure 11.2**
The Project > Pages section of Macaw's publish settings.

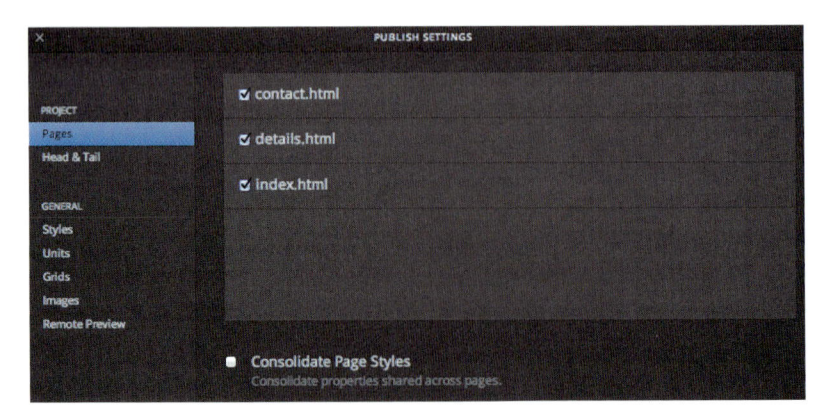

If checked, Consolidate Page Styles tells Macaw to generate a single CSS file that encompasses all styles used for all pages in your project. If you're planning to peek into the CSS while building a project, you might want to keep this unchecked, so you can more easily see which styles Macaw has built for each page. For a finished project, however, or if you're just not a tinkerer in that way, keeping this box checked is generally a good idea. Macaw will look through all pages and reduce as much redundancy as it can, making the overall amount of generated CSS smaller, in many cases by quite a lot. Also, in terms of reducing how many files a browser needs to ask for when loading your site, one CSS file is better than one-per-page; once the single CSS file is cached, it never needs to be downloaded again.

## Head & Tail

Here, Macaw gives you the chance to add your own HTML to the `<head>` tag, and before the closing `</body>` tag, of every page in the project. Macaw leaves some very dark comments to help guide you. Do not delete these; just fill in your custom markup after the comments. An example is shown in **Figure 11.3**. In it, a meta tag has been added to the `<head>` tag to prevent the old Internet Explorer image toolbar from appearing, and some fake Google Analytics code has been added to the footer (that is, before the `<body>` tag).

**Figure 11.3** The much brighter code here shows where your custom stuff would go.

This is the area where you can add custom meta tags for site verification or other SEO purposes (these are shared across all pages, so don't add page-specific meta tags here), references to external JavaScript and CSS files (for example, if you are integrating Macaw with Bootstrap, Foundation, jQuery UI, or other front-end toolkits), and so on. For more on custom integrations using Head & Tail settings, see Appendix D.

## General Settings

General settings are preferences at the level of the Macaw app, and therefore shared across all projects. If you change some settings and open an older project, when that older project is previewed and published, the new settings will apply to the generated files.

### Styles

These settings, shown in **Figure 11.4**, determine the form of the CSS Macaw generates for you.

**Figure 11.4** Macaw's Styles publish settings.

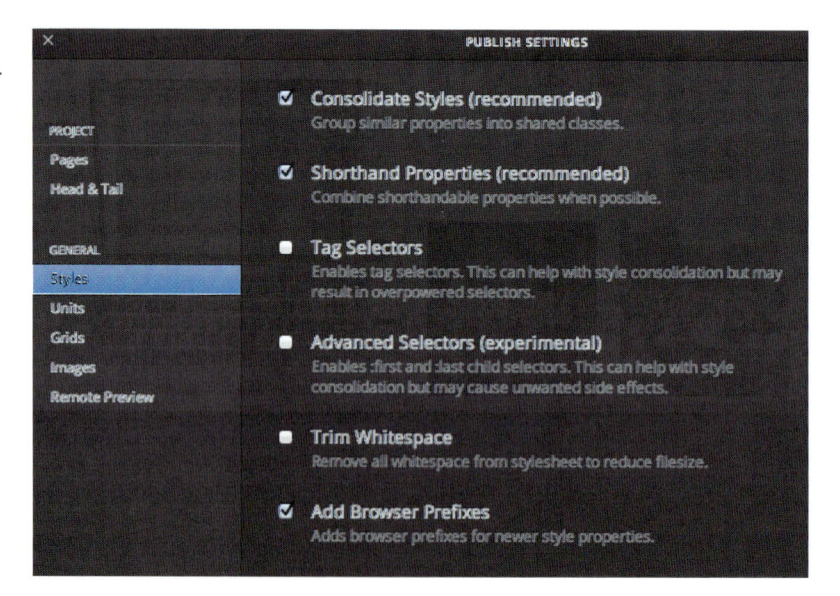

Consolidate Styles should be left on. As the Macaw documentation says, this option uses a powerful algorithm to consolidate styles based on the relationships existing between elements and generates far superior code when enabled. Enough said.

Shorthand Properties should also be left on. If it's turned off, Macaw uses more verbose CSS for things like borders and backgrounds, which is wasteful.

Enabling Tag Selectors lets Macaw use tags instead of just classes for selectors in its CSS. Turning this option on can make your CSS files smaller at the expense of some CSS being overly specific. If you're just sticking to Macaw for the purposes of your project's CSS, this option is probably safe to enable.

The Advanced Selectors option is currently experimental. It lets Macaw use more recent, though not as well-supported, CSS selectors. You'll see a warning about unwanted side effects, which might refer to bugginess (since the feature is experimental right now) or to compatibility with some browsers.

Trim Whitespace will remove whitespace from CSS files to make them smaller. If you don't have another CSS minification tool that can do this for you (like Grunt or gulp.js), and you're not planning to read the CSS Macaw generates, this is a good option to turn it on.

Add Browser Prefixes tells Macaw to add vendor prefixes (for example, -webkit, -moz, -o, -ms) to CSS selectors for newer CSS features. To maximize compatibility, turn this on. To minimize file size, and if you don't mind that your site might look less than perfect in older browsers, turn this option off.

## Units

There are two settings in the Units section, shown in **Figure 11.5**.

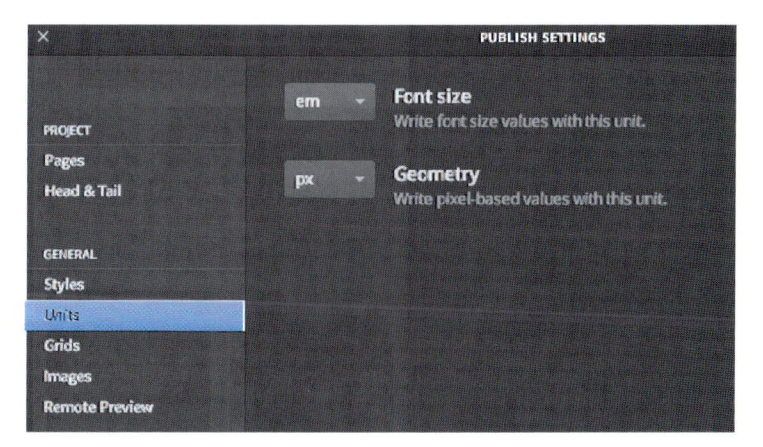

**Figure 11.5** Macaw's Units publish settings.

Font sizes are always set in pixels in the Macaw Typography palettes. The font size setting gives you the chance to tell Macaw what units to use in the generated CSS. Everything except px are relative units; for the best compatibility, em or percent are fine choices.

The Geometry setting allows you to convert pixel-based dimensions and margins into another unit after publishing. If you are fastidious with your breakpoints and want to make sure everything is just so, px may be the right choice here. If you want your final site to be as fluid as possible, and don't require a huge degree of pixel-precision in spacing, em or rem might be a better choice.

## Grids

There's only one check box under Grids: Publish Grids. When you select it, Macaw will generate a <pagename>-grid.css file for each published page that represents the grids used on that page. The files are linked in each relevant page, but otherwise are unused. If you want to share the grid system you created in Macaw with other web developers who don't use Macaw, these files could help. You can turn this option off to generate fewer files and make your site load faster.

## Images

Again, there's just one check box here: Generate Optimized Images. If you use Macaw's image cropping features, or if you want to use the image swapping JavaScript plugin Macaw includes to load separate images in Retina and conventional resolution environments, this option must be enabled. We generally prepare and optimize images before importing them into Macaw, so we keep Generate Optimized Images turned off.

## Remote Preview

Under Remote Preview you'll see one check box, Enable Remote Preview, which is enabled by default. With this feature turned on, Macaw runs a small web server that lets you view your project from any device on your local network using a special URL shown in the preview window (like http://192.168.1.50:5353). This web server also supports automatic reloading when the project is republished, so every browser on your computer, or any other device that's open to the special link, will automatically reload itself when you preview/publish your project. This is really cool, of course, but running it can slow Macaw down a bit. If you want to squeeze a little more performance out of Macaw, don't need live-reloading, or to preview on other devices this seamlessly, you can turn Enable Remote Preview off.

## Published and Done!

Once you've published your site for the last time (or the last time for now anyway—no website is ever done), you should copy the resulting folder somewhere safe, apart from the .mcw project file. Remember, Macaw will overwrite the folder on every publish! At this point, you can do whatever else might need to be done before publishing. Here are some examples, all on the somewhat advanced end of the scale:

- Run the image files through an image optimizer like ImageOptim for Mac or Caesium for Windows. If you're letting Macaw generate images for you, this is a good idea to help save bandwidth.

- Run the CSS files through their own optimizer(s). If you're code-savvy, consider using Grunt and gulp.js, which are JavaScript-based tools that can do all kinds of processing for you, to CSS files and just about anything else. There are also online possibilities like cssminifier.com.

- Convert your files into templates for your favorite CMS like WordPress, Drupal, or Joomla. The specifics will vary by the CMS, but if you know how to make a custom theme for a CMS, you can take the Macaw files and make one.

- If you want to keep your site static, the way Macaw generated it, but make deployment more automated, you can use a tool like Jekyll (jekyllrb.com). The Macaw documentation (docs.macaw.co) is deployed using Jekyll (at least we're pretty sure it is!).

All in all, the files that Macaw generates can be quite efficient on their own. You can make prototypes that might never see the public Internet, all the way up to full-blown websites. Go forth and publish!

# 12

## The Possible Future of Macaw

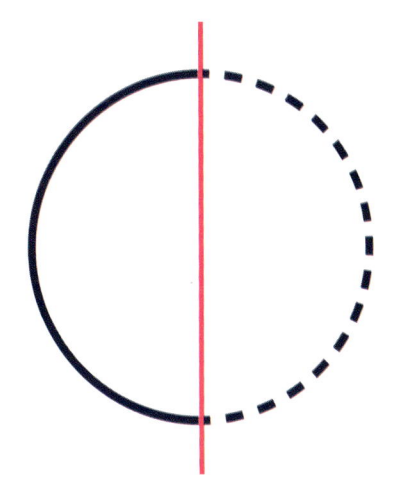

By this point, you've worked with Macaw enough to have seen that it is very capable. It is possible to build prototypes, pages, and sites in a way that is responsive and much easier than in any of the static-oriented tools from days of yore. Macaw can do a lot, but it's still a relatively young application, so there are a lot of things that could be added to it to make it even better.

In this chapter we'll discuss a sort of "wish list" of things we'd like to see added to Macaw, improvements to existing features that we hope get implemented, and anything else that could make Macaw even more useful than it already is.

> **NOTE** Any and all of the topics discussed in this chapter are purely speculation on our part and in no way constitute any foreknowledge or roadmap for inclusion in future versions of Macaw. We can dream, can't we?

# Big Things

There are a few big things that we think would be awesome if they were part of Macaw, and if you agree, some ways we've thought of to achieve similar results in the meantime.

## Mobile-first workflow

Many proponents of responsive web design are also fans of a "mobile-first" workflow. A mobile-first workflow simply means designing your projects for mobile phones or small devices first, and then expanding the design for tablets and larger screens. We know that introducing this methodology could add a lot of complexity for the built-in CSS generator, but we hope the developers come up with a way to do this that lets us choose to work from small-to-big as well as big-to-small. In the meantime, following a mobile-first way of thinking about the project from the beginning is still useful, even if building a project that way is not yet possible in Macaw.

## Integration of popular frameworks or preset components libraries

It'd be super handy if frameworks like jQuery UI, Bootstrap, Foundation, or others could be used in conjunction with Macaw. Many developers got into responsive web design using frameworks like these, so if Macaw can't tie in with them, many users won't even bother touching Macaw in the first place. For many developers especially, a drag-and-drop design tool that uses a popular front-end framework would be a truly Killer App™.

However, if direct integration with these types of frameworks would be too complicated, it would be great if Macaw had a built-in components library with a lot of the same stuff that those frameworks provide (especially UI widgets like tab groups, accordions, drop-down menus, and so on). If those could be dropped on the canvas, and styled using a special palette, that would be excellent for prototyping.

For now, the closest you can get to this is including hosted versions of the CSS and JavaScript files that the publishers of these frameworks make available in the Head & Tail section of Macaw's Publishing Options. You can't see the components on the canvas, but the published project can still include them. See Appendix D for more on integrating custom CSS and JavaScript.

## Linked image assets

Currently, image assets are imported into the project, and can be referenced without going out to the filesystem again. That is very handy, but it would be even better if the assets within a Macaw project could be added as linked files. That way, a user could just overwrite an older asset and it would automatically be updated within Macaw. Being able to update images the way we can update Smart Objects in Photoshop, or run them through file size optimizers like ImageOptim after importing, would be great for long-term projects that take days or longer to finish. This would be especially helpful for those using Macaw in a larger team environment with multiple designers and developers.

### Custom fonts, especially icons

Macaw's inclusion of Typekit and Google Fonts is great, and we can import our own custom fonts installed on our systems, but we cannot export CSS that uses those custom fonts directly from Macaw—we have to do that manually (see Appendix D). It would also be excellent to have built-in support for icon fonts, although this need is mitigated by Macaw's built-in support for SVG.

### Template files

It would be nice to be able to build a basic structure of a responsive site (a few breakpoints, base font sizes, some navigation capabilities) and save everything as a template Macaw file. We could then use this template file when creating future projects and a lot of the initial setup would already be done. (Admittedly, it is possible to work around this by making said basic responsive Macaw project, saving it as a regular file, and always duplicating the file when starting a new project. However, this approach has the potential for users accidentally saving over the initial file and doesn't have the ease of use of a true template file.)

Mac users who want this feature can get it right now using "stationery pads." If you've never heard of these, see Appendix B.

### Better component editing

It'd be sweet if components were more like Smart Objects in Adobe Photoshop or symbols in Adobe Flash. Being able to edit components directly from the library and have all the instances automatically update on the canvas would save a lot of time.

## Export/import/share components and global styles

Say you've spent a lot of time making a bunch of nice components or global styles that could be useful on other Macaw projects. Wouldn't it be great if you could export libraries of components or sets of global styles? You could then import these component libraries and global style sets into other projects. In addition, if the component libraries or global style sets are useful enough, you could share them online with other Macaw users for use on their Macaw projects.

It is possible to achieve something like this for components now by creating a dedicated Macaw project for them—just keep them on the canvas and use pages to group the various types. Because several projects cannot be open at the same time, copying elements from one library to another is a little awkward, but it is doable. As you start to build up a suite of goodies in Macaw, keep this in mind.

## Add custom states to elements

**Figure 12.1** Nav menu icon (sometimes called a *hamburger icon*).

Any element in Macaw can have different styles applied by using the built-in CSS hover, active, and focus states. Being able to create custom states (in the form of an HTML class) and toggle them in response to all the kinds of events JavaScript supports (clicks, taps, swipes, and so on) would be really helpful. Common responsive UI patterns, like navigation menus that are opened and closed via icons (**Figure 12.1**), could easily be built this way.

## Enhanced SVG styling

Being able to style any Scalable Vector Graphics (SVG) element directly in the inspector would be amazing. Styling things like color, stroke, opacity, and hover, would be helpful. It's great that Macaw allows importing of SVGs, but not being able to style them limits their effectiveness.

## Little Things

There are a handful of little things that caused us some hiccups in the learning process that we hope get ironed out in future updates to Macaw.

### Multiple open projects

Currently, there's no way to have multiple Macaw projects open at the same time. If you have a handful of elements or components in one Macaw project that you'd like to copy/paste into another project, you can do it—but it's pretty awkward compared to being able to copy and paste (or drag and drop) between two open windows.

### Swap an image from the library

Currently, the only way to update an image on the canvas is to delete it and put a new one in its place. If a selected image could easily be swapped with another asset from the library, it would make updating old image assets easier and keep layouts from reflowing and possibly going nuts.

### More global styles options

It'd be nice if the global styles palette showed which tabs have styles active. Then having the ability to toggle them all off in one click would make it easier to create granular global styles.

### Custom library folders

Macaw makes a couple default folders for organization in the library (one for images, one for components). As projects get large, this starts to feel a little cramped. Many developers use folder structures that are integral to tying in with content management systems and working with other team members, so it'd be awesome if Macaw let users create their own folders in the library and organize the files in a way that makes sense for their particular situation.

### Workspace customization

Many power users like to organize their palettes and toolbars to their liking (we both do!). It would be great if Macaw had this capability.

### Enhanced swatches

Saving solid color swatches is really handy, and we'd like to be able to save swatches for gradients as well. Being able to save swatches as sharable components would also be helpful.

### Use different background images at different breakpoints

In the current version of Macaw, all background images for all breakpoints need to be added to the desired element, and then the ones you don't want on need to be turned off at each breakpoint. The generated CSS only includes the ones it needs to, but from a UI perspective, it would be cleaner if different background images could be specified at different breakpoints.

## A Bright Future

Macaw is not perfect, but no piece of computer software is. To be honest, it's amazing that Macaw can do as much as it can having been around for only a short while. But its future looks bright. With a growing user base, constant feedback from active users, and a dedicated development team, Macaw will only get better from here.

Every major advancement in the web community (standards, CSS, web fonts, and so on) has come about because users demanded it. They were unsatisfied with the tools and capabilities available to them at the time, so they did what they needed to do to make things better. Kudos to the Macaw development team for creating the tool so many of us have only dreamed about.

Macaw is a tool that the web community has needed for a really long time.

We're glad it's finally here.

# A

# Helpful Shortcuts

Macaw, like other applications on your computer, has many built-in keyboard shortcuts that let you quickly access tools or commands. Using (and memorizing) the keyboard shortcuts that are most helpful to you can greatly increase your productivity and efficiency. We've listed some of the most useful shortcuts in this appendix, but there are more. To view a list of keyboard shortcuts directly in Macaw, select Help > Keyboard Shortcuts.

## Tool Shortcuts

| | |
|---:|---|
| V | Select tool (hold ⌘/Ctrl to toggle this to Direct Select) |
| A | Direct Select tool |
| T | Text tool |
| R | Element tool |
| G | Container tool |
| B | Button tool |
| N | Input tool |
| Shift-N | cycle through Input types |
| M | Embed tool |
| H/Space | Hand tool |
| I | Eyedropper tool |
| C | Show Color Picker |
| S | Show Swatches (to set an element's background color—an element must be selected) |

## View Shortcuts

| | |
|---:|---|
| Opt-I/Alt-I | Show Inspector pane. |
| Opt-O/Alt-O | Show Outline pane. |
| Opt-L/Alt-L | Show Library pane. |
| Tab | Toggle palettes. |
| ⌘-;/Ctrl-; | Toggle grid. |
| ⌘-U/Ctrl-U | Toggle snap (to the grid or other objects). |
| ⌘-'/Ctrl-' | Toggle positioning guides. |
| ⌘-Y/Ctrl-Y | Toggle outline mode. |

**Appendix A:** Helpful Shortcuts **229**

| | |
|---:|---|
| ⌘-W/Ctrl-W | Toggle wireframe mode. |
| Shift-[ | Switch to next smaller breakpoint. |
| Shift-] | Switch to next larger breakpoint. |
| Shift-\ | Switch to default (largest) breakpoint. Press this again to toggle back to the breakpoint where you started. |

### Other Helpful Shortcuts

| | |
|---:|---|
| ⌘-Opt-C/Ctrl-Alt -C | Copy an element's visual properties. |
| ⌘-Opt-V/Ctrl-Alt-V | Paste visual properties onto an element. |
| ⌘/Ctrl-D | Duplicate element. |
| ⌘/Ctrl-E | Expand an element to the width of the grid. Invoke again to expand to the width of the canvas. |
| ⌘/Ctrl-R | Set keyboard focus on the class name field for editing (in Outline or Inspector). |
| ⌘/Ctrl-G | Group selected elements into a container exactly as big as needed, or convert a single empty element into a container. |
| ⌘-Opt-G/Ctrl-Alt-G | Group elements into a container as wide as the canvas (or the container in which the selected elements reside). |
| ⌘/Ctrl-Shift-G | Ungroup elements, keeping them in position. |
| Arrow keys | Nudge 1px. |
| Shift-Arrow keys | Nudge 10px. |
| ⌘/Ctrl-Arrow keys | Nudge to grid (moves the edge of an element to the next gridline, according to the element's positioning origin). |
| Opt/Alt-Arrow keys | Pudge (increase element's size) 1px. |

| | |
|---|---|
| **Shift-Opt/Alt-Arrow keys** | Nudge 10px. |
| **⌘/Ctrl-Opt/Alt-Arrow keys** | Nudge to grid. |
| **Escape** | When editing inside a container(s), go up one level in the Outline. |
| **⌘-P/Ctrl-P** | Publish and preview page. |
| **⌘-Shift-P/Ctrl-Shift-P** | View publish settings. |
| **⌘-Opt-F/Ctrl-Alt-F** | Send feedback to Macaw developers. |

## Outline shortcuts

| | |
|---|---|
| **Tab** | Move down through items in the Outline. Double-click an element's tag first or press Cmd-R/Ctrl-R; then the Tab key will move down through each element in turn. |
| **Shift-Tab** | Move up through items in the Outline. |
| **Click element icon** | Scrolls the canvas directly to the item. |
| **Double-click container icon** | Scrolls the canvas to the item; opens container for editing. |
| **⌘-2/Ctrl-2** | Lock an element so it can't be selected (this works anywhere, but you can see the lock icon only in the Outline). |
| **⌘-Opt-2/Ctrl-Alt-2** | Unlock all locked elements (also works anywhere). |

### *Bonus for Mac users: custom shortcuts*

Some menu options do not have keyboard shortcuts, but Mac users can create their own for Macaw (or any other app) using the Keyboard preference pane of System Preferences. Instructions are available from Apple here:

support.apple.com/kb/PH13916

Windows doesn't have this function built-in, but you can try a third-party like Clavier+, which can create custom shortcuts that simulate the movement and clicking of a mouse to click open a menu and click the relevant menu item. It's not as easy to set up, but being able to create custom shortcuts could be worth it.

utilfr42.free.fr/util/Clavier.php

## Other Shortcuts and Quick Tips

| | |
|---|---|
| ⌘-click/Ctrl-click | In any style field or setting, if a popover appears, this will copy settings to all breakpoints. |
| **Arithmetic in fields** | Most text fields will accept arithmetic. Enter **2+2**, press Return/Enter, and Macaw will give you 4. This is especially helpful for aspect ratios: if you want a 4×5 box that's 150 pixels tall, type **150*(4/5)** in the width box to let Macaw figure out what the other value should be. |
| **Up or down arrow keys** | While any numeric text field has keyboard focus, you can press the up or down arrow to change its value by 1. Hold the Shift key to change its value by 10. |
| **Icons in text fields** | In any field with an icon, hover your cursor over the icon, and then click and drag left or right to change the value. Doing so is not as precise as using the arrow keys, but you can make large changes quickly. |

# B

## Further Reading

Macaw is a tool best employed with the backing of knowledge. In this chapter, we offer a lot of references in books and online to learn more about areas we touched on.

# More on Macaw

### Macaw Forums

http://forum.macaw.co

Though not publicized (as of this writing, anyway), these forums are a helpful place to go to learn more and talk about Macaw.

### Macaw Documentation

http://docs.macaw.co

The Macaw documentation site. There's a lot of detail in this book, but if there are areas on using particular tools that fall short, the Macaw documentation site can help. You can also make it better by contributing to it on GitHub.

### Macaw Videos

http://macaw.co/videos/

There aren't very many videos on the Macaw website, but the ones there are helpful.

### Designing and Building Websites with Macaw, by Adi Purdila

http://webdesign.tutsplus.com/series/designing-and-building-websites-with-macaw--cms-556

If you prefer to learn by video, this selection of short videos doesn't go deep, but it can be helpful.

# Responsive Web Design

### *Responsive Web Design*, by Ethan Marcotte

www.abookapart.com/products/responsive-web-design

This is the original—the one that started codifying the practices that Macaw uses to create responsive sites.

### *Responsive Web Design: Learn by Video*, by Tim Kadlec

www.peachpit.com/store/responsive-web-design-learn-by-video-9780321971142

This video course is a comprehensive overview on responsive web design. Tim also has a book available on Peachpit.com called *Implementing Responsive Design: Building Sites for an Anywhere, Everywhere Web*.

### *Articles on responsive design from A List Apart*

http://alistapart.com/topic/responsive-design

A List Apart is an online magazine, a clearinghouse for great information of interest to anyone building the web. Ethan Marcotte's original article that spawned his book appeared here, and they have kept publishing articles on responsive web design ever since.

### *Mobile First*, by Luke Wroblewski

www.abookapart.com/products/mobile-first

Although Macaw does not support mobile-first directly, we expect it will at some point in the future, and thinking mobile-first is increasingly important to web designers from all walks of life. Luke's book is a clarion call to work mobile-first, and how to start doing so.

# Making Good Mock-ups

A variety of applications are available for creating web design mock-ups, and within those applications you'll find even more ways to create a web design mock-up. Every designer has his or her favorite apps and favorite methods of working, so we'll just point out some popular apps and best practices here.

### Adobe Photoshop

www.adobe.com/products/photoshop.html

The most popular application for creating web design mock-ups is Adobe Photoshop. It's been around for a long time and has a ton of functionality.

### Sketch

http://bohemiancoding.com/sketch/

Sketch is a relative newcomer to the graphics application game, but its popularity is growing fast.

### Pixelmator

www.pixelmator.com

Pixelmator is a pretty popular alternative to Photoshop (at a much more affordable price).

### Adobe Fireworks

https://creative.adobe.com/products/fireworks

Fireworks is still loved and used by its diehard fans so we're mentioning it here to let those users know that we've thought about them. However, Adobe stopped making new versions of Fireworks in 2013, so if you're not already using it, picking up a more recent tool is probably a better idea.

### Tuts+

http://tutsplus.com

Tuts+ is a great site for all sorts of design-related tutorials, many of them for web design.

### Smashing Magazine

www.smashingmagazine.com

Another great site with tons of web design content. Their articles are less tutorial in nature and more about the practice of web design and the industry as a whole.

### Photoshop Etiquette

http://photoshopetiquette.com

A great resource on best practices when using Photoshop to design for the web. Following these guidelines is extremely helpful when you're returning to designs you've worked on in the past (so you can make sense of what you did), or when sharing files among teams.

For more tutorials on creating web design mock-ups, use your favorite search engine and enter **website design tutorial** (plus the name of your chosen application) into the search field and you'll get all sorts of links to helpful articles. Every site you design is going to be different, and you'll need to use different tricks to get desired effects. So work through as many tutorials as you can. The best way to learn is to just start making something!

# Front-End Web Developer Tools

Every major browser offers developer tools, which allow you to inspect a web page and find out what makes it tick. Though they're all different, once you understand one, most of what you learn is applicable to the others. Software like this is absolutely essential for the web professional or enthusiast.

For Google Chrome, there are the Chrome Developer Tools, which are built into every copy.

https://developer.chrome.com/devtools

For Firefox, there is a Web Inspector built in, but what you really want is Firebug. It is not built into Firefox, but it's an easy download. Firebug was the first software in this class and continues to be excellent.

https://getfirebug.com

For Safari, there is the Web Inspector, which shares the same DNA as the Chrome Developer Tools. It is also built into every copy of Safari, though it must be enabled in Safari's preferences.

https://developer.apple.com/safari/tools

Internet Explorer has the F12 developer tools, which have come a long way in recent years.

http://msdn.microsoft.com/library/ie/bg182326

## Other Areas of Interest

Here are some more topics we covered, along with helpful resources for each.

### Accessibility

Understanding accessibility for websites and apps is crucial. Not all of these techniques can be applied in the Macaw UI, but everything you can do (whether in Macaw or after publishing) helps.

http://alistapart.com/topic/accessibility

http://webaim.org/techniques/forms

### CSS transforms, transforms, and filters

Macaw supports all of these on every element, and while you can't see all of them easily on the canvas, the techniques are good to know, and you can flesh them out after publishing if needed. Here are a book, a video course, and a pair of interactive iBooks on the subject:

*CSS Animations and Transitions for the Modern Web,* **by Steven Bradley**

www.peachpit.com/store/css-animations-and-transitions-for-the-modern-web-9780133980509

*CSS Transitions and Transforms,* **by Joseph Lowery**

www.lynda.com/Dreamweaver-tutorials/CSS-Transitions-Transforms/101072-2.html

*CSS Transforms* **and** *CSS Animations***, both by Vicky Murley**

https://itunes.apple.com/us/artist/vicki-murley/id724992995?mt=11

## Retina-safe and responsive images

Eventually, standards will emerge and solidify to help make sure our websites don't chew up everyone's data quotas on mobile, while still looking gorgeous on big 4K and 5K displays. Until then, you need to know how to make images look good today.

**_Retinafy your Web Sites & Apps_, by Thomas Fuchs**

http://retinafy.me

This book contains the guidance that led to the way we handled images in this book.

**_Articles on responsive images from Opera_**

https://dev.opera.com/articles/responsive-images/

https://dev.opera.com/articles/native-responsive-images/

Opera has long been on the forefront of supporting emerging web technologies. These articles explain where responsive images are in late 2014, and what to expect soon.

Information on the HTML5 `<picture>` element, and enhancements to its older sibling, the `<img>` element, for the responsive web can be found on the Web Hypertext Application Technology Working Group (WHATWG) website.

https://html.spec.whatwg.org/multipage/embedded-content.html

## Better embedded maps

If the built-in map embedding is insufficient, you'll want to look at some other options. Google has a JavaScript API (application programming interface—basically an officially supported way of programming something) for creating maps using JavaScript instead of the embedded `<iframe>` method. There is also a Static Maps API if JavaScript is not appropriate. Both require a Google API key to use (as described in their documentation).

https://developers.google.com/maps/documentation/javascript/tutorial

https://developers.google.com/maps/documentation/staticmaps

There are other map providers as well, of course. Leaflet is an open source option based on JavaScript. There is a hosted version that you could add to your Head & Tail in Macaw to start using immediately.

http://leafletjs.com/download.html

## Hosted front-end toolkits

To use Macaw with additional JavaScript plugins, it's easiest to use versions available on the Internet. You can upload your own copy to a web hosting account you control, but many are already available through popular content distribution networks.

https://developers.google.com/speed/libraries/devguide

Google hosts many, many popular JavaScript toolkits, some of which (like jQuery UI) include CSS for user interface components.

www.jsdelivr.com

jsDelivr offers a wide variety of UI components, with a handy search engine to find what you're looking for.

www.bootstrapcdn.com

Hosted copies of Bootstrap and Font Awesome.

## Stationery files on OS X

Mac users can create template files from any document in the Finder. Just by clicking a check box in the Finder's Get Info window, you can turn a file into a template (and then revert it to a normal file if it needs to be updated). This can be very handy if you end up creating many similar Macaw projects.

http://support.apple.com/kb/PH13816

# C

## Troubleshooting

Sometimes Macaw can be a cranky bird. The software is still quite new, and problems sometimes happen. In this appendix, we'll suggest some tricks to try when you encounter unexpected behaviors.

## Save, Quit, and Restart

Macaw is, on some level, a *really* souped-up web browser. Just as web browsers can misbehave from time to time, so can Macaw. Just like a web browser needs to be quit and restarted from time to time to stay happy and healthy, so does Macaw. If Macaw ever starts to feel slow in any way, save your project, quit, and restart. On a reasonably fast computer, this takes just a few seconds, and usually any problems you might have had will go away.

If things go really haywire and Macaw crashes or you need to force-quit it (and possibly lose real work), keep in mind that Macaw saves a backup copy of your project in a temporary location every time you publish. The next time you open Macaw, it will notice that there's a leftover autosave and ask if you want to restore it (see **Figure C.1**). If it's restored, you'll have a new untitled project, so you'll need to save it again, overwriting the original copy if appropriate.

**Figure C.1** Macaw recognizes that an autosave exists and asks if you want to restore it.

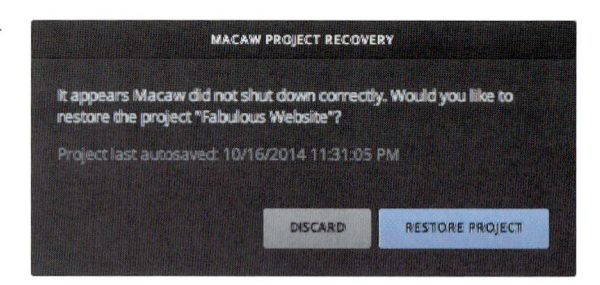

## Create a New Project, and Then Switch Back

Like any somewhat modern application, Macaw supports undo and redo. That said, sometimes in between times you save a project, it's possible to get the work into a state that's hard to undo from, due to too many little changes, or maybe some changes that can't be undone (or not easily). Ahem, we are speaking hypothetically, of course.

Macaw projects cannot be closed without quitting the application. That said, you can sort of fake it by creating a new project via File > New Project (⌘-Shift-N/Ctrl-Shift-N). Macaw will ask you to save your work before closing the project, but you can just close it. After the new, untitled project loads, use the File > Open Recent menu to switch back to your project in its last saved state, and then continue working.

## Send Feedback

We first heard about Macaw through its Kickstarter campaign in 2013, and just as the software was crowdfunded, refinements and bug reports have to come from us, the users of Macaw. Use the Send Feedback tool (⌘-Opt-F/Ctrl-Alt-F) to report bugs you find and odd behaviors you experience. It is, of course, not enough to simply say "something's not working—bye!" If something's broken, a developer is always more responsive if the report comes in a form that is polite and (most importantly) repeatable. The feedback tool was made easy to access so we would use it—so do!

## Post in the Forums

Along with reports direct to the Macaw team, don't miss the Macaw forums at forum.macaw.co. There are lots of Macaw users out there working with this new tool, and talking with one another can help. We've covered a lot in this book, but not everything. If something seems to be going wrong, it is helpful to have a community of other folks to talk with and try to figure out what's going on together.

# D

# Custom Integrations

In this appendix, we'll talk about some integrations you might be interested in: adding custom CSS, using custom web fonts, and adding JavaScript libraries to a Macaw project. The processes are a little more advanced since they can involve writing your own custom CSS and JavaScript and digging into that which Macaw generates.

## Custom CSS

Macaw removes a lot of the need to write CSS by hand, but there are some things that are either not built-in or not quite practical to use. Adding custom CSS to a project is pretty easy to do, but there are two tricky parts. Your custom CSS will not be displayed on the canvas, and you might need to finesse your CSS if Macaw's generated CSS overrides it.

In Chapter 7, we explored image replacement techniques for text. Like with many CSS patterns, people are constantly trying to find the best way that ties in accessibility, SEO, maintainability, and so on. The HTML5 Boilerplate project includes a version that is battle-tested but is too specific to be set in the Typography palette. Here is the CSS:

```
.ir {
    background-color: transparent;
    border: 0;
    overflow: hidden;
    /* IE 6/7 fallback */
    *text-indent: -9999px;
}

.ir:before {
    content: "";
    display: block;
    width: 0;
    height: 150%;
}
```

To use this, open Head & Tail in Publish Settings (⌘-Shift-P/Ctrl-Shift-P). Add the CSS to the `<head>` section, wrapped in a `<style>` tag, as shown in **Figure D.1**.

**Figure D.1** The image replacement CSS as added to Head & Tail.

```
<head>
    <!-- <title> and other generated code will appear above
    your static head code. -->
<style type="text/css">
body .ir {
    background-color: transparent;
    border: 0;
    overflow: hidden;
    /* IE 6/7 fallback */
    *text-indent: -9999px;
}

body .ir:before {
    content: "";
    display: block;
    width: 0;
    height: 150%;
}
</style>
</head>
<body>
    <!-- Page content will appear above your static tail
    code. This is a good place for analytics code, etc. -->
</body>
```

Once that CSS is in place, you can add the class to any element that should have its text shifted out of the way for the background image. With this specific CSS, you need to make sure the element has a height other than auto for it to work. On the canvas, you'll still see the text, but when previewed, it will be shifted away, leaving just the image.

**Figure D.2** shows the canvas with the class and height applied.

**Figure D.2** This heading has two classes: macawfrence and ir. The text still appears here but will go away when published.

As long as you're not bothered by the limitation of not being able to see your CSS on the canvas, this is a perfectly usable technique for incorporating custom CSS into your projects.

## Custom Web Fonts

By default, you can use any of the standard web fonts, a selection from Google Fonts library, and any Typekit fonts you have access to. If you have a custom font installed on your system that you'd like to use, you can enable it by selecting Show System Fonts in the Typography palette's Font menu (see **Figure D.3**). Once you've enabled your system fonts, you'll have a lot more options, as shown in **Figure D.4**. System fonts have a laptop icon next to them.

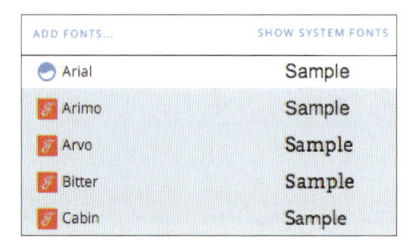

**Figure D.3** The Fonts menu before enabling system fonts, showing standard web fonts and Google fonts.

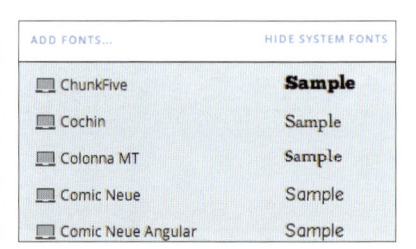

**Figure D.4** The Fonts menu after enabling system fonts, with many more available; system fonts use a laptop icon.

If all you wanted to do was use the fonts in Macaw projects that never leave your computer, you'd be done at this point. If you want to publish a project on the Internet and have fonts actually work, more setup is needed: the font files need to be accessible to the project, and CSS font-face rules are needed to let your CSS know where the fonts are and what they're called.

> **NOTE** We're assuming that you have properly licensed web fonts. Stealing fonts, or using fonts you have on a website without a proper license for that use, are both deeply uncool.
>
> Also, if the fonts you've purchased only come in web-accessible versions, not in a downloadable version you can install on your computer, you're not going to be able to use them in the Macaw UI. You can override Macaw's CSS with your own, but you won't be able to see those custom fonts on the canvas.

## Making fonts available

First, you'll need the web font files, which generally come as a set of files with extensions like `.woff`, `.svg`, `.ttf`, and `.eot`. If you don't have these but your font allows web embedding, you can generate the files (and the accompanying CSS) by using the Webfont Generator on Font Squirrel (a great site for good, free fonts).

www.fontsquirrel.com/tools/webfont-generator

**NOTE** We're using Chunk, a free font from The League of Movable Type, in this example. You can get it here: www.theleagueofmoveabletype.com/chunk.

Once you have those, create a folder next to your Macaw project file (and published files folder). Call it something web-safe (no punctuation or spaces), like **extras**. In **Figure D.5**, you can see an example of this setup, with the fonts nested inside another folder called fonts, but this is just a matter of preference.

**Figure D.5** A sample project, with an extras/fonts folder where the set of web font files live.

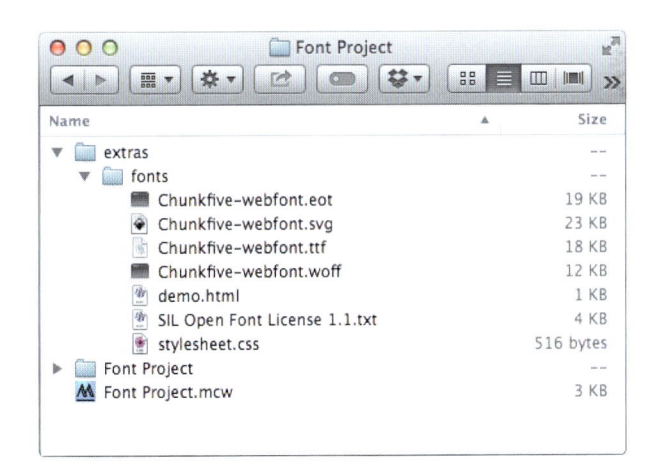

**NOTE** This setup is not compatible with Macaw's Remote Preview server. If you want to load fonts, or anything else, from a folder next to your published Macaw folder, you must disable Remote Preview in your project's Publish Settings and open your pages directly in your browser (the URLs will start with file instead of http).

## Adding the custom CSS

The webfont generator provides the CSS in a file called stylesheet.css, which looks like this:

```
@font-face {
    font-family: 'ChunkFiveRegular';
    src: url('Chunkfive-webfont.eot');
    src: url('Chunkfive-webfont.eot?#iefix')
  → format('embedded-opentype'),
        url('Chunkfive-webfont.woff') format('woff'),
        url('Chunkfive-webfont.ttf') format('truetype'),
        url('Chunkfive-webfont.svg#ChunkFiveRegular')
  → format('svg');
    font-weight: normal;
    font-style: normal;
}
```

If you've bought your fonts from a reputable provider, you should have something similar. If you were to paste this CSS into a `<style>` tag in the Head & Tail in File > Publish Settings (⌘-Shift-P/Ctrl-Shift-P), it wouldn't work yet.

To make this work correctly, you need to modify the URLs for the font files and the font-family line so that they match what Macaw has inserted in the CSS. Preview your project, click the CSS button in the Preview window (labeled { }) and look for the font definition of your custom font. With Chunk, it shows up in the generated CSS font tags

Appendix D: Custom Integrations

as ChunkFive-Roman (in the Macaw UI, it's ChunkFive, but we don't have to worry about that). Here is the CSS, modified to match the file layout from Figure D.3. The updates are highlighted in bold.

```
@font-face {
    font-family: 'ChunkFive-Roman';
    src: url('../extras/fonts/Chunkfive-webfont.eot');
    src: url('../extras/fonts/Chunkfive-webfont.eot?#iefix')
    → format('embedded-opentype'),
        url('../extras/fonts/Chunkfive-webfont.woff')
        → format('woff'),
        url('../extras/fonts/Chunkfive-webfont.ttf')
        → format('truetype'),
        url('../extras/fonts/Chunkfive-webfont.
        → svg#ChunkFiveRegular') format('svg');
    font-weight: normal;
    font-style: normal;
}
```

You can add this code directly to the Head & Tail in a `<style>` tag, as shown in **Figure D.6**.

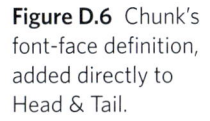

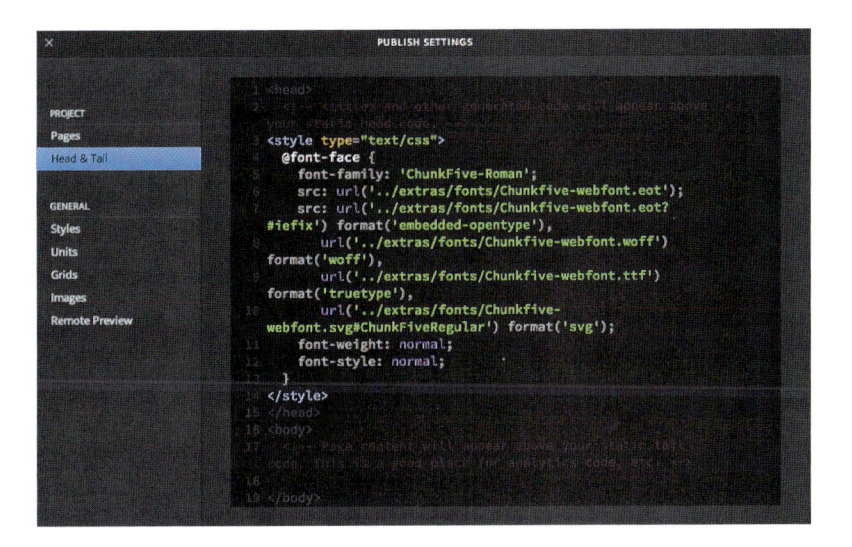

**Figure D.6** Chunk's font-face definition, added directly to Head & Tail.

You could also set this up using a style sheet in your extras folder. Be sure to adjust the paths as needed to point to the font files, and add a `<link>` tag to the Head & Tail settings. If you prefer to edit your CSS in Macaw using Head & Tail, though, this is the way to go.

### Changes before uploading

When uploading your files, make sure that the paths will resolve correctly. If you upload your Macaw project folder and the extras folder together just as they are on your computer, everything will continue to work.

If you want to be able to upload both the extras folder and all your Macaw files in a single directory on the server (you can't do this safely with Macaw because it wipes out its project folder every time it publishes), you'll need to update the custom CSS—for example, removing `../` from the `url()` paths. The specifics of your hosting setup, and how you want your site's URLs to look, will dictate what changes you need to make, but it is something you'll need to keep an eye on.

### Loading fonts from the Internet

If you want to avoid the folder hassles, you could also upload your web font files to your web server and use those online URLs in your Head & Tail instead. Just update the CSS so that all the URL lines look something like this (the change is shown in bold):

```
src: url('http://example.com/path-to-my-fonts/
→ Chunkfive-webfont.eot');
```

## Custom JavaScript

Adding custom JavaScript code in Macaw is pretty easy using View > Show Scripts. Any variable names you've set on elements in the Inspector will be shown in the sidebar (see **Figures D.7** and **D.8**). When published, those names are turned into jQuery objects, via the copy of jQuery (the most popular JavaScript library) that Macaw has built in. The variable names are shown in the Script panels, as are any color swatches you've defined (in case you want to refer to those colors in

**Appendix D:** Custom Integrations   255

your JavaScript). You can also write custom JavaScript that does not touch jQuery at all in this panel, but once anything is written here, Macaw will include jQuery in the published version, followed by your custom JavaScript. JavaScript is not executed on the Macaw canvas, but in the preview window it will be (for the most part—and in a real browser, everything will execute).

**Figure D.7** Here, `div.slides` is assigned to the jQuery variable `$slides`.

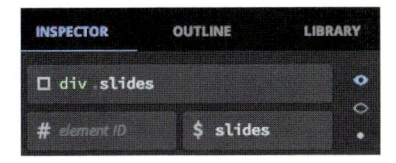

**Figure D.8** The Scripts panel. Any defined variable names and swatches appear on the left side.

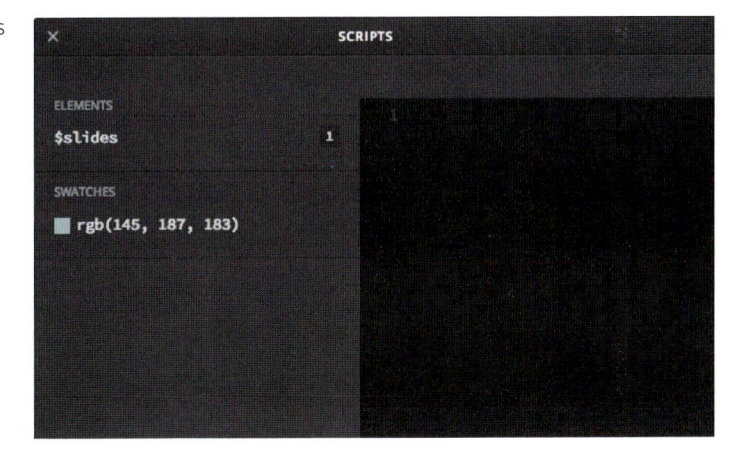

## Loading the plugin

Integrating a JavaScript plugin (most depend on jQuery) involves some more work. The process can be similar to web fonts (using an extras folder and loading scripts from it) if you want to use local copies, but given the wide availability of plugins hosted online, we'll use that method here. It means less messing around with paths (and it's compatible with Macaw's Remote Preview).

Let's use an example of a project like the one shown in **Figure D.9**. There are three `<div>` tags in a container, stacked on top of one another, and we want to use the very popular jQuery Cycle plugin to make a slideshow of them.

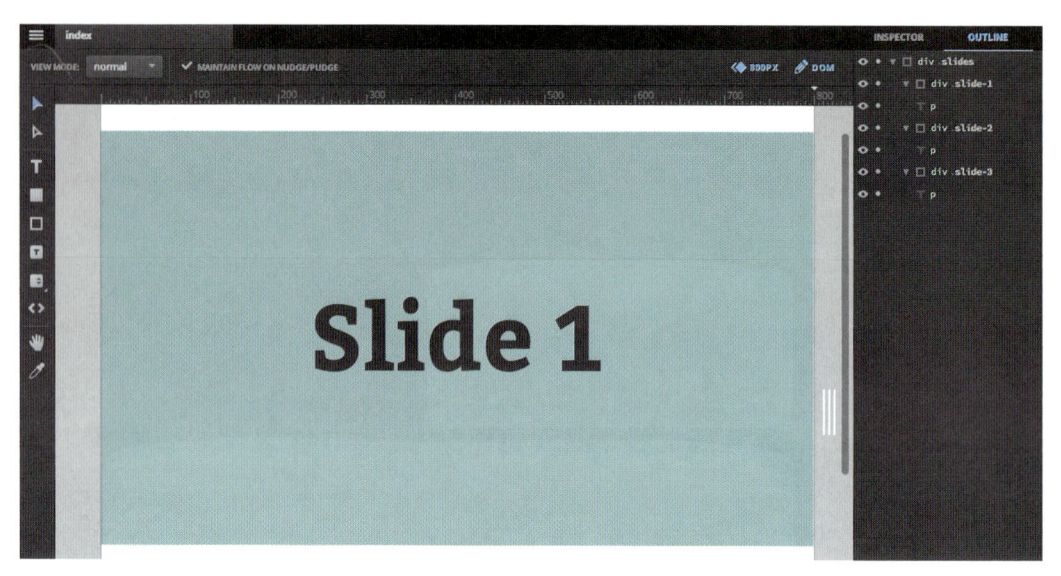

**Figure D.9** The sample Macaw project. Only the first slide is visible because they're stacked up, but there are three of them there.

To add the JavaScript plugin, first we need a copy of it somewhere on the Internet. jQuery Cycle is available on jsDelivr, and to make it available in the Macaw project you need to add it in the Publish Settings under Head & Tail. It's preferable to load JavaScript as late in the page as possible, to prevent them from blocking other resources from downloading. So add the script tag to the tail (before the closing `</body>` tag), as shown in **Figure D.10**.

**Figure D.10** jQuery Cycle (the Lite version) has been added to the tail of every page in the project.

```
1 <head>
2   <!-- <title> and other generated code will appear above
     your static head code. -->
3
4 </head>
5 <body>
6   <!-- Page content will appear above your static tail
     code. This is a good place for analytics code, etc. -->
7   <script
     src="//cdn.jsdelivr.net/cycle/3.0.2/jquery.cycle.lite.js">
     </script>
8 </body>
```

Adding the plugin here will load it on every page in the project. If this is not appropriate, you can add the plugin inline to a page's Scripts panel (see Option 2 in the next section).

## Activating the plugin

You have successfully added jQuery Cycle to the page, but it doesn't actually do anything yet—the plugin needs to be instantiated (in other words, pointed at whatever it's supposed to act on and told to do it). Every plugin has a different method for doing this, so you'll need to refer to its documentation. In the case of jQuery Cycle, we need to call the `cycle()` method on the element containing all the slides—`div.slides` in this example. So somewhere, we'll need code like this:

```
$(document).ready(function(){
    $('.slides').cycle();
});
```

This code says, "As soon as the document has finished loading, grab the `.slides` div, send it to jQuery, and call the `cycle()` method on it." The question is: Where does this code go?

We've seen the Scripts panel, but if we put this code in there now, it won't work. If there is code present in the Scripts panel, it triggers Macaw to include, in this order:

1. jQuery itself (using a copy built into Macaw—open jquery-min.js in the published project folder to see which version)

2. Any JavaScript from your page's Scripts panel

3. Anything from the Tail section of Head & Tail

jQuery Cycle is loaded in step 3, but the code that depends on it loads in step 2, so that won't work.

There are at least three ways to work around this problem:

1. Keep the Scripts panel empty, and keep all code that depends on jQuery in the Head & Tail settings. With this setup, you'll need to load your own copy of jQuery as well (from code.jquery.com or any other popular CDN), before any plugins it depends on, and then add any further JavaScript afterward. For this example, the result is shown in **Figure D.11**.

**Figure D.11** All the scripts added to Head & Tail, in the tail section.

```
5  <body>
6     <!-- Page content will appear above your static tail
       code. This is a good place for analytics code, etc. -->
7  <script src="//code.jquery.com/jquery-1.11.0.min.js">
   </script>
8  <script
   src="//cdn.jsdelivr.net/cycle/3.0.2/jquery.cycle.lite.js">
   </script>
9  <script>
10    $(document).ready(function(){
11       $('.slides').cycle();
12    });
13 </script>
14 </body>
```

> **NOTE** The URLs here leave off the http://, which makes sure that the plugins will load over http or https, depending on what the page calling them is using. The URLs are a little shorter, and you never see a warning about a page mixing secure and insecure content. This is called a network-path reference, often referred to as a "protocol-relative URL." You have to be using Macaw's Remote Preview for these to work. If you have that feature turned off in Publish Settings, you'll need to add the HTTP protocol back in for the scripts to load.

2. Keeping the Scripts panel empty prevents Macaw from loading its copy of jQuery (the Scripts panel has to be completely empty for jQuery not to load—no comments, no nothing!). Having two copies is inefficient (jQuery is big for a JavaScript file, and should be loaded at most once) and could also cause confusion in your code. Make sure jQuery loads only once.

3. Load everything that depends on jQuery in the Scripts panel, including the plugin. You can't load external JavaScript in the Scripts panel, so you need to open the plugin file, copy the entire thing, and paste it in there. This makes for a very crowded Scripts panel, as shown in **Figure D.12**, but it does work. This is also your only option if a plugin should only load on a single page.

**Figure D.12**
In California, they call this sort of thing "gnarly."

```
tion(){return i(u,a,a.rev?1:-1)}),a.timeout&&
(this.cycleTimeout=setTimeout(function(){r(u,a,0,!a.rev)},a.timeout+
(a.delay||0)))})},e.fn.cycle.custom=function(t,n,r,i){var
s=e(t),o=e(n);o.css(r.cssBefore);var u=function()
{o.animate(r.animIn,r.speedIn,r.easeIn,i)};s.animate(r.animOut,r.speedO
ut,r.easeOut,function()
{s.css(r.cssAfter),r.sync||u()}),r.sync&&u()},e.fn.cycle.transitions=
{fade:function(e,t,n){t.not(":eq(0)").hide(),n.cssBefore=
{opacity:0,display:"block"},n.cssAfter={display:"none"},n.animOut=
{opacity:0},n.animIn={opacity:1}},fadeout:function(t,n,r)
{r.before.push(function(t,n,r,i){e(t).css("zIndex",r.slideCount+
(i===!0?1:0)),e(n).css("zIndex",r.slideCount+(i===!0?
0:1))}),n.not(":eq(0)").hide(),r.cssBefore=
{opacity:1,display:"block",zIndex:1},r.cssAfter=
{display:"none",zIndex:0},r.animOut={opacity:0},r.animIn=
{opacity:1}}},e.fn.cycle.ver=function(){return t},e.fn.cycle.defaults=
{animIn:{},animOut:{},fx:"fade",after:null,before:null,cssBefore:
{},cssAfter:
{},delay:0,fit:0,height:"auto",metaAttr:"cycle",next:null,pause:!1,prev
:null,speed:1e3,slideExpr:null,sync:!0,timeout:4e3}})(jQuery);

$(document).ready(function(){
    $('.slides').cycle();
});
```

Whichever method you choose, make sure you view the page in a real web browser to confirm that it's working. Be sure to check the JavaScript console for errors.

## Recommendation

These techniques work, but we can't really call them elegant. If they work for you, that's excellent, but we still generally recommend adding JavaScript plugins after publishing.

# Index

## A

absolute positioning, 67, 72–73, 184
accessibility resources, 239
Advanced palette, setting for images, 173
Align palette, using in navigation, 113
Alt key. *See* keyboard shortcuts
Anchor palette, using with footer, 158
arithmetic in fields, tip for, 231
arrow keys, using, 231

## B

background gradient, creating for Macawfrence, 92–93
background images. *See also* images
   adding quote marks as, 149
   adding to header, 99–100
   creating for Macawfrence, 90–92
   making room for, 128
   PNG file, 128
   SVG file, 128
   using, 126
Backgrounds palette, accessing, 52
"Big Button" global style, 21
big text area, creating for Contact form, 200–203
"Big Text" global style, 21–22
black box. *See also* containers
   adding company name, 75
   Border palette, 74
   changing text color, 76
   Outline, 77
   selecting company name, 77
   selecting logo circle, 77
   as site header, 73
   Typography palette, 76
   WidgetCo header, 77
   width and height, 73
blue outlines, checking, 137
Border palette, using with black box, 74
breakpoint information
   locating, 28
   reading, 30
breakpoints
   adding, 16
   best practices, 16
   changing, 15
   copying settings to, 231
   creating, 14, 17–18
   creating with resize handles, 18
   default, 14–15, 144
   extra large, 15
   finding in Inspector, 13
   versus frames, 15
   identifying in user interface, 12
   interaction with grids, 56
   jumping between, 34
   large, 15

breakpoints (*continued*)
  managing, 16
  medium, 15
  palette, 14
  resizing, 69
  setting, 41–42, 89–90, 103–107
  setting first, 15–16
  setting for prototype, 48–51
  showing, 15
  small, 15
  switching, 69
  using grids with, 51
  using media queries with, 13
  using popovers with, 90
Breakpoints palette, accessing, 50
browser
  designing in, 4–5
  opening pages in, 123
Button tool, 32
button type, indicating, 203

## C

canvas
  breakpoints, 34
  described, 33
  grid, 33–34
  identifying, 28
  locating, 33
  maximizing space for, 12
  resize handle, 34–35
  response to width changes, 18
  result of resizing, 80–81
  ruler, 34
Center Canvas command, using, 51
centered origin, using, 71
centering identity group, 84

check boxes
  creating, 197
  selecting, 14
Chrome developer tools, 238
Chromium, 10
circle, turning square into, 74
classes, best practices, 42
clicking on options, 14
closing projects, 245
CodeMirror, 10
color of text, changing, 76
Color Picker
  making swatch for Macawfrence, 96
  using, 53
company name, adding, 75
components
  creating from elements, 23
  delete button, 24
  features of, 23
  naming, 23
  placing on canvas, 24
  templates, 23
  using, 45
Contact form. *See also* form elements
  adding inner shadow, 195
  big text area, 200–203
  building, 191
  editing inner shadow, 200
  field types, 194
  First Name field, 192–195
  form field global style, 195
  form label global style, 195
  Gradient Editor, 194
  gradient settings, 201
  input.form-text tag, 193
  input options, 193

 medium breakpoint, 204–205
 placeholder text, 192
 positioning cleanup, 204
 radio buttons, 197–198
 select box, 198–200
 small breakpoint, 206–207
 submit button, 200–203
 text fields, 196–197
Contact form fields
 company name, 196
 email, 197
 first name, 196
 last name, 196
 phone, 197
 website, 196
Contact page
 creating title for, 190
 updating navigation menu, 191
containers. *See also* black box; prototyping process
 converting elements to, 133
 editing contents of, 79
 Expand command, 83
 Fit To command, 83
 fixing spacing in, 134
 using, 43
 workflow for, 80
Container tool, using, 31, 90–91
content, workflow for, 80
content area. *See also* main content; secondary content
 Agenda image, 184
 big text box, 170–171
 container for stacked group, 174–176
 establishing images as links, 174
 fixing negative margins, 172
 image grids, 171–176

 medium breakpoint, 181–182
 reviewing for mock-up, 89
 small breakpoint, 182–183
context menus, displaying for pages, 163
Copy All command, using, 134
copying
 folders, 217
 settings to breakpoints, 231
 visual properties, 229
Copy Visual Properties command, using, 170
cropping, in-app, 176–177
CSS (Cascading Style Sheets)
 introduction of, 3
 negative margins in, 77–78
 reset style sheet, 99
CSS3, support for, 52
CSS custom integration, 248–249
CSS files, running through optimizer, 217
CSS positioning, 63
CSS transforms and filters, 177–178, 239
Ctrl key. *See* keyboard shortcuts
custom integrations
 CSS (Cascading Style Sheets), 248–249
 JavaScript, 254–259
 web fonts, 250–254

# D

date and location header, placing, 165
deployment, automating, 217
designing in browser, 4–5
Details page. *See also* pages
 changing title of, 163
 copying, 162
 creating, 162
 duplicating, 190
 medium breakpoint, 165–166

Details page (*continued*)
  medium-small breakpoint, 166
  renaming, 162
  revising header for, 163–165
  small breakpoint, 166–167
details text box, 171
developers block, resetting, 155–156
Direct Selection tool, using, 30, 100, 138
DOM (Document Object Model), 15, 68, 147
DOM information
  locating, 28
  reading, 30
Down arrow key, using, 231
drop shadows, adding to images, 181
Duplicate command, using, 51–52
duplicating
  elements, 109–110, 196, 229
  pages, 190

## E

element positioning, 78
  absolute, 67, 72–73
  fixed position and origins, 66–67
  Maintain Flow on Nudge/Pudge, 63–65
  Origin settings, 70–71
  position and breakpoints, 65–66
  static positioning and flow, 61–63
elements
  changing stacking order of, 68
  moving at breakpoints, 65–66
  placing in containers, 180
  resizing at breakpoints, 65–66
Element tool, using, 31, 48–49, 187–188
email field, including in Contact form, 197
embedded maps, 185–188, 240–241
Embed tool, using, 32, 186–187
Eyedropper tool, using, 32, 53, 96

## F

Facebook icon
  background settings for, 110
  positioning, 123
feedback
  locating links for, 28
  sending, 245
Feedback tool, 33
files, converting into templates, 217
Firefox developer tools, 238
First Name field, building and styling, 192–196
fixed position and origins, 66–67
folders, copying, 217
font panel, using, 76–77. *See also* web fonts
footer
  Anchor palette, 158
  building, 157–160
  creating for Macawfrence, 95–96
  fixing for breakpoints, 159–160
  reviewing for mock-up, 87
  states button group, 159
  states for links, 159
  underline versus bottom border, 158
form elements. *See also* Contact form
  accessing, 192
  styling, 194
forums, posting in, 245
front-end toolkits, hosted, 241
front-end web developer tools, 238
full screen, accessing, 12
future of Macaw. *See also* Macaw
  background images at breakpoints, 225
  component editing, 222
  custom fonts, 222
  custom library folders, 224
  custom states for elements, 223
  enhanced SVG styling, 223

enhanced swatches, 225
export components, 223
frameworks, 221
global style options, 224
global styles, 223
icons, 222
import components, 223
linked image assets, 221
mobile-first workflow, 220
multiple open projects, 224
preset components libraries, 221
share components, 223
swapping images from library, 224
template files, 222
workspace customization, 225

## G

General settings
   Grids, 216
   Images, 216
   Remove Preview, 216–217
   Styles, 214–215
   Units, 215–216
global styles
   benefit of, 132
   "Big Button," 21
   "Big Text," 21–22
   defining, 132
   features of, 20–21
   granularity of, 199
   identifying in user interface, 12
   locating links for, 28
   managing, 22
   mapping to CSS classes, 21
   naming, 22
   for navigation items, 131–133
   overriding, 133, 139

   properties, 22
   using, 44–45
   using Stamp icon with, 22
Global Styles tool, 33
Gradient Editor, using with Contact form, 194
gradients, generating, 93
gradient settings, using with Contact form, 201
grid lines, snapping to, 19
grids
   changing units, 17
   creating for prototype, 51–57
   default settings, 17
   extending, 54
   fixed-width, 55
   "fluid," 16–20
   identifying in user interface, 12
   interaction with breakpoints, 56
   resize handles, 18
   setting to pixels, 17
   setting up for Macawfrence project, 89–90
   snapping, 54–55
   using, 44
   using with breakpoints, 51
   visibility settings, 19
   working statically, 17
grid settings, changing at breakpoints, 20
Grids publish setting, 216
grid systems, changing, 17
grouping elements, 43, 73, 77–78, 113

## H

Hand tool, 32
Head & Tail settings, 213
header content
   background image, 99–100
   box for logo, 98–99
   explained, 98

header content (*continued*)
  hiding text, 101
  image replacement technique, 102
  indentation setting, 101–102
  positioning heading, 100
headers
  converting to containers, 98
  date and location, 165
  resizing for Details page, 163–164
  reviewing for mock-up, 87
  revising for Details page, 163–165
  setting maximum width on, 101
hiding
  palettes in Macawfrence, 98
  text in headers, 101
  tools in Macawfrence, 98
HiDPI images, support for, 26
highlight blocks
  medium breakpoint, 136, 138
  placing, 131
  resetting container width, 135
  warnings in, 133
highlights. *See also* Macawfrence project
  background image, 128
  header settings, 127
  image size, 138
  medium-small breakpoint, 139, 141–142
  padding text box, 128
  point text for header, 127
  small breakpoint, 139–141
  speakers background image, 128–129
  speaker text and header, 130
  text block below header, 128
  three-column setup, 126
  type size, 138
horizontal origin settings, 71

hosted front-end toolkits, 241
:hover, clicking, 167
HTML tags, best practices, 42–43
hyperlinks. *See* links

I

icons in text fields, using, 231
identity group, centering, 84
identity header, appearance of, 82–83
IDs, setting, 43
image grids, creating, 171–176
image optimizer, using, 217
Image palette, displaying, 172
images. *See also* background images; responsive images
  device-specific, 178–179
  downloading for mock-ups, 89
  establishing as links, 174
  extracting from mock-ups, 88
  importing, 36, 171
  replacing in headers, 102
  responsive, 240
  retina-safe, 240
  setting Advanced palette for, 173
  swapping, 178–179
images folder, contents of, 211
image shadow global style, creating, 181
Images publish setting, 216
importing images, 36, 171
in-app cropping, 176–177
indentation setting, invoking, 101–102
Input palette, resize setting for, 200–201
Input tools
  changing to text area, 200
  using, 32
  using with Contact form, 192

Index **267**

Inspector
  explained, 35
  locating, 29
  switching to, 112
interface. *See also* UI (user interface)
  canvas, 28, 33–35
  documentation, 37
  left side, 28, 30–33
  menu bar, 37
  right side, 35–36
  top area, 28–30
Internet Explorer developer tools, 238

## J

JavaScript custom integration, 254–259
Jekyll, using with static sites, 217

## K

keyboard shortcuts
  Button tool, 32
  Center Canvas command, 51
  Container tool, 31
  Copy All command, 134
  copying settings to breakpoints, 231
  copying visual properties, 229
  Copy Visual Properties, 170
  default breakpoint, 144
  Direct Select tool, 30
  Duplicate command, 51
  duplicating items, 109–110, 229
  Element tool, 31
  Embed tool, 32
  expanding elements, 229
  Eyedropper tool, 32
  Feedback tool, 33
  grids, 33
  grouping items, 229

  Hand tool, 32
  Input tools, 32
  Inspector, 112
  keyboard focus on class name, 229
  large breakpoint, 170
  for Mac users, 230
  medium breakpoint, 165, 181
  navigating Outline, 230
  New Project, 89
  nudging pixels, 229
  nudging to grid, 229
  Outline, 96, 230–231
  Paste Visual Properties, 170
  pasting visual properties, 229
  publish and preview page, 230
  Publish command, 120
  Publish Settings, 177–178, 212
  Pudge, 229–230
  Select All, 112
  Select tool, 30
  sending feedback to developers, 230
  Swatches palette, 33
  switching breakpoints, 69
  switching to Outline, 57
  Text tool, 31
  Tight Group command, 77, 97, 113
  Toggle Snap, 48
  tools, 228
  ungrouping elements, 229
  view, 228–229
  viewing publish settings, 230
  for Windows users, 231

## L

large breakpoint, switching to, 170
layers, thinking about, 86–87
layout surprises, dealing with, 137

Library pane
  explained, 36
  locating, 29
link field, contents of, 169
links, adding for navigation, 168-169
locking elements, 137
logo, creating box for, 98-99
"lorem ipsum" text, 129

## M

Macaw. *See also* future of Macaw
  default interface, 8
  as design solution, 9
  as development solution, 9
  downloading, 10
  explained, 8
  as prototyping tool, 9
  resources, 234
  trends in usage, 9
  UI (user interface), 12
  uses of, 8-9
  using features of, 46
  web-based foundation, 10
  workflows, 9
Macawfrence folder, files in, 210-211
Macawfrence project. *See also* highlights; mock-ups; navigation; projects; testimonials area
  accessing, 85
  in-app cropping, 176-177
  background gradient, 92-93
  background image, 90-92
  building content area, 169-176
  checking stacking order, 96
  creating pages, 162-167
  CSS transforms and filters, 177-178
  device-specific images, 178-179
  embedded map, 185-188

footer, 95-96, 157-160
header content, 98
hiding palettes, 98
hiding tools, 98
main content, 94
medium breakpoint, 103
"Meet the Developers" section, 152-156
menu bar, 92-93
outline order, 97
page background, 95-96
page header, 90-92
preview site, 121
referring to comps for, 89
reviewing, 96-98
reviewing mock-up for, 86
revising navigation, 167-169
secondary content, 94-95, 152-156, 185-188
setting up breakpoints, 89-90
setting up grid, 89-90
small breakpoint, 104-107
swatch in Color Picker, 96
Typography settings, 104
main content. *See also* content area
  creating for Macawfrence, 94
  reviewing for mock-up, 87
Maintain Flow on Nudge/Pudge, 63-64
maps, embedding, 185-188, 240-241
math in fields, tip for, 231
media queries, using with breakpoints, 13
medium breakpoint
  Contact form, 204-205
  content area, 181-182
  Details page, 165-166
  highlight blocks, 136, 138
  Macawfrence project, 103
  navigation, 114-117
  testimonials area, 150

medium-small breakpoint
  Details page, 166
  highlights, 139, 141–142
menu bar
  creating for Macawfrence, 92–93
  explained, 37
  identifying, 28
mobile, considering first, 40–41
mock-ups. *See also* Macawfrence project
  content area, 89
  downloading images for, 89
  extracting images from, 88
  footer, 87
  header, 87
  main, 87
  navigation, 87
  resources, 236–237
  reviewing, 162, 190
  reviewing for Macawfrence, 86
  secondary, 87
movement, thinking about, 86–87

# N

navigation. *See also* Macawfrence project
  adding letter spacing, 108
  adding links, 168–169
  adding text box, 107
  adjusting background, 108–109
  adjusting items, 115
  Align palette, 113
  clicking :hover, 167
  converting to container, 107
  duplicating items, 109
  Global Style Properties, 109
  grouping items, 113
  hiding background image, 109
  hover behavior for links, 108

image replacement CSS settings, 110
medium breakpoint, 114–117
placement of items, 111–112
point text box, 110
p.text and warnings, 111
reviewing for mock-up, 87–88
setting fixed width for, 114
small breakpoint, 117–119
social icons, 109–110
navigation items, using global styles with, 131–133
navigation menu, updating for Contact page, 191
nodes
  creating in text blocks, 170
  explained, 147
normalize.css project, 211

# O

operating system menu bar, locating, 29
options bar
  described, 30
  locating, 28
Opt key. *See* keyboard shortcuts
Origin settings, centering, 70–71
OS X, stationery files on, 241
Outline
  alert icon, 60
  checking for Macawfrence, 96
  class of element, 58–59
  display control, 58
  explained, 36
  including warnings in, 77
  locating, 29
  lock control, 58–59
  semantics, 60
  switching to, 57
  type indicator, 58–59
  type of element, 58–59

Outline (*continued*)
  using, 60–61
  using with black box, 77
  visibility controls, 58
Outline shortcuts, 230–231
Outline tab
  features of, 25
  identifying in user interface, 12

## P

page background, creating for Macawfrence, 95–96
page header, creating for Macawfrence, 90–92
Page Manager
  locating, 28
  tabs, 29–30
pages. *See also* Details page
  creating, 29
  displaying context menus for, 163
  features of, 25
  identifying in user interface, 12
  naming, 163
Pages publish settings, 212–213
palettes, hiding in Macawfrence project, 98
Parties image, examining, 184
Paste Visual Properties command, 170
photography website, linking to, 158
<picture> element, 26
pixels
  setting grids to, 17, 55
  setting type in, 105
polyfill, explained, 46
popovers
  displaying, 66
  using, 68
  using to copy widths, 81
  using with breakpoints, 90

position and breakpoints, 65–66
positioning guides, using, 196
posting in forums, 245
preview window
  opening, 49
  publishing to, 120–123
  shrinking, 122
project folder, automatic overwriting of, 211
projects. *See also* Macawfrence project
  closing, 245
  starting, 89
project settings
  Head & Tail, 213
  Pages, 212–213
prototyping process. *See also* containers
  absolute positioning, 72–73
  Element tool, 48–49
  fixed position and origins, 66–69
  flow, 61–64
  origins, 70–71
  position and breakpoints, 65–66
  setting breakpoints, 48–51
  setting up grid, 51–57
  static positioning, 61–64
  using Outline, 57–61
prototyping tool, Macaw as, 9
publishing to web, 211
Publish Settings command, using, 177–178, 212

## Q

quitting Macaw, 244

## R

radio buttons, adding to Contact form, 197–198
redo and undo, support for, 244
"Remote Preview," 122

Remote Preview publish setting, 216–217
reset style sheet, 211
resize handles
   appearance of, 176
   creating breakpoints with, 18
   using, 34
   using with grids, 18
resizing
   breakpoints, 69
   canvas, 80–81
   remembering, 42
   windows, 70
responsive images, 26, 240. *See also* images
responsive web design, 4, 235. *See also* Web Standards Project
restarting Macaw, 244
Retina images, support for, 26
retina-safe images, 240
reusables
   components, 20–24
   global styles, 20–24
   overview, 44–45
ruler, locating, 34

## S

Safari developer tools, 238
Save, Quit, Restart, 244
saving work, 107
secondary content. *See also* content area
   adding shadow, 153
   embedded map, 185–188
   "Meet the Developers" section, 152–156
   reviewing for mock-up, 87
   setting up, 94–95
Select All, using with container items, 112
select box, adding to Contact form, 198–200
Select tool, 30

semantics
   keeping track of, 42–43
   using with Outline, 60
Send To Front command, using, 68–69
Set Current, changing to Set All, 97
settings. *See* project settings
shadow, adding to secondary content, 153
Shift key. *See* keyboard shortcuts
shortcuts
   Button tool, 32
   Center Canvas command, 51
   Container tool, 31
   Copy All command, 134
   copying settings to breakpoints, 231
   copying visual properties, 229
   Copy Visual Properties, 170
   default breakpoint, 144
   Direct Select tool, 30
   Duplicate command, 51
   duplicating items, 109–110, 229
   Element tool, 31
   Embed tool, 32
   expanding elements, 229
   Eyedropper tool, 32
   Feedback tool, 33
   grids, 33
   grouping items, 229
   Hand tool, 32
   Input tools, 32
   Inspector, 112
   keyboard focus on class name, 229
   large breakpoint, 170
   for Mac users, 230
   medium breakpoint, 165, 181
   navigating Outline, 230
   New Project, 89
   nudging pixels, 229

shortcuts (*continued*)
  nudging to grid, 229
  Outline, 96, 230–231
  Paste Visual Properties, 170
  pasting visual properties, 229
  publish and preview page, 230
  Publish command, 120
  Publish Settings, 177–178, 212
  Pudge, 229–230
  Select All, 112
  Select tool, 30
  sending feedback to developers, 230
  Swatches palette, 33
  switching breakpoints, 69
  switching to Outline, 57
  Text tool, 31
  Tight Group command, 77, 97, 113
  Toggle Snap, 48
  tools, 228
  ungrouping elements, 229
  view, 228–229
  viewing publish settings, 230
  for Windows users, 231
sites, publishing to web, 211
site header, elements of, 73
sketches, making, 40
small breakpoint
  Contact form, 206–207
  content area, 182–183
  Details page, 166–167
  highlights, 139–141
  testimonials area, 150-151
social icons, adding, 109–110
speakers image, placing, 173

sprites
  availability of, 149
  maintainability of, 126
  performance of, 126
square, turning into circle, 74
stacking order
  changing, 68
  checking for Macawfrence, 96
Stamp icon, using with global styles, 22
static positioning
  versus absolute positioning, 184
  and flow, 61–63
  and vertical centering, 84
static site, maintaining, 217
sticky settings, applying, 71
styles, sharing between text blocks, 170
Styles publish settings
  Add Browser Prefixes, 215
  Advanced Selectors, 215
  Consolidate Styles, 214
  Shorthand Properties, 214
  Tag Selectors, 215
  Trim Whitespace, 215
subheader, applying Typography settings to, 104
submit button, creating for Contact form, 200–203
SVI images, support for, 26
swatches
  locating links for, 28
  making in Color Picker, 96
Swatches tool, 33

# Index

## T

Tag Selectors setting, enabling, 215
templates, converting files into, 217
testimonials area. *See also* Macawfrence project
   adding background images, 149
   div.pager positioning origin, 148
   div.testimonial container, 147
   div.testimonial positioning origin, 148
   interactivity, 142–143
   medium breakpoint, 150
   mocking up the look, 144–150
   overlapping behavior, 148
   pager bullets, 145–146
   quote marks, 149
   removing negative margin warnings, 147
   resizing canvas, 148
   small breakpoint, 150–151
   styling nodes, 146–147
   text block for attribution, 144–145
   text block for quote, 144
text
   adding to canvas, 75
   hiding in headers, 101
text blocks, sharing styles between, 170
text box, creating for details, 171
text color, changing, 76
text fields
   creating, 196–197
   using icons in, 231
Text tool
   selecting, 75
   using, 31
   using to create logos, 98–99
thinking
   about layers, 86–87
   about movement, 86–87
Tight Group command, using, 77, 97, 113
Toggle Snap, enabling, 48
toolbar, locating, 28
toolkits, hosted front-end, 241
tools
   Button, 32
   Container, 31, 90–91
   Direct Select, 30, 100
   Direct Selection, 138
   Element, 31, 187–188
   Embed, 32, 186–187
   Eyedropper, 32, 53, 96
   Feedback, 33
   Global Styles, 33
   Hand, 32
   hiding in Macawfrence project, 98
   Input, 32, 192
   Select, 30
   shortcuts, 228
   Swatches, 33
   Text, 31, 75, 98–99
troubleshooting, 244–245
Twitter icon, positioning, 123
Twitter link, creating, 110
type, setting in pixels, 105
Typography palette, settings in, 76
Typography settings, applying to subheader, 104

## U

UI (user interface). *See also* interface
   appearance of, 12
   custom check boxes in, 14
undo and redo, support for, 244
Units publish settings
   Font Size, 216
   Geometry, 216

Unsplash.com link, 158
Up arrow key, using, 231

## V

values, setting, 175
View modes
  features of, 25–26
  identifying in user interface, 12
  toggle in options bar, 30
viewport, explained, 48
view shortcuts, 228–229
visual properties, copying, 229

## W

warnings
  dealing with, 97
  including in Outline, 77
  removing, 147
web fonts, custom integration, 250–254. *See also* font panel
website field, including in Contact form, 196
websites, publishing, 211
Web Standards Project, 3. *See also* responsive web design
whitespace, adjusting, 179
WidgetCo header, clicking, 77
windows, resizing, 70
wireframing process. *See* prototyping process
workflows
  considering mobile first, 40–41
  for containers and content, 80
  grouping items, 43
  making sketches, 40
  resizing, 42
  reusing elements, 44
  semantics, 42–43
  setting breakpoints, 41–42
  using containers, 43
workshops image, 175